CiTY·SMaRT™
GUIDEBOOK

Cincinnati

by Billie Felix Jeyes

John Muir Publications
Santa Fe, New Mexico

John Muir Publications, P.O. Box 613, Santa Fe, New Mexico 87504

Printed in the United States of America.
First edition. First printing May 1998

ISBN 1-56261-402-9
ISSN 1097-6094

Editors: Sarah Baldwin, Nancy Gillan
Graphics Editor: Heather Pool
Production: Marie J. T. Vigil, Nikki Rooker
Design: Janine Lehmann
Cover Design: Suzanne Rush
Typesetter: Melissa Tandysh
Map Production: Julie Felton
Printer: Publishers Press
Front Cover Photo: © J. Miles Wolf
Back Cover Photo: © J. Miles Wolf

Distributed to the book trade by
Publishers Group West
Berkeley, California

CONTENTS

How to Use This Book   v

1 Welcome to Cincinnati   1
A Brief History of Cincinnati 2 • Getting to Know the Cincinnati Metro Area 5 •
The People of Cincinnati 8 • Business and Economy 11 • Housing 11 •
Schools 12 • Taxes 12 • Cost of Living 14 • When to Visit 14 • Calendar of
Events 15 • Cincinnati's Weather 18 • Dressing in Cincinnati 18

2 Getting Around Cincinnati   19
City Layout 19 • Public Transportation 24 • Driving in Cincinnati 27 • Biking
in Cincinnati 28 • Cincinnati–Northern Kentucky International Airport 28 •
Other Airports 30 • Train Service 30 • Interstate and Regional Bus Service 31

3 Where to Stay   32
Downtown Cincinnati 33 • Uptown Cincinnati 36 • East Cincinnati 39 • West
Cincinnati 44 • South of the River 46

4 Where to Eat   52
Downtown Cincinnati 54 • Uptown Cincinnati 63 • East Cincinnati 65 • West
Cincinnati 68 • South of the River 69

5 Sights and Attractions   74
City Tours 74 • Downtown Cincinnati 75 • Uptown Cincinnati 84 • East
Cincinnati 86 • West Cincinnati 88 • South of the River 90

6 Kids' Stuff   93
Animals and the Great Outdoors 93 • Fun and Educational 94 • Museums and
Libraries 95 • Performing Arts 98 • Stores Kids Love 99 • Theme Parks 100 •
Places to Play 102

7 Museums, Galleries, and Public Art   103
Art Museums 104 • Science and History Museums 104 • Other Museums 106 •
Galleries 108 • Public Art 111

8 Parks, Gardens, and Recreation Areas   115

9 Shopping   124
Shopping Areas 124 • Other Notable Stores 134 • Major Department Stores
136 • Shopping Malls 138 • Outlet Centers 139

10 Sports and Recreation   140
Professional Sports 140 • Recreational Activities 144

11 Performing Arts   156
Theater 156 • Classical Music and Opera 160 • Dance 162 • Concert Venues
164 • Buying Tickets 165

12 Nightlife   166
Live Music 166 • Dance Clubs 171 • Pubs and Bars 173 • Coffee Houses
178 • Comedy Clubs 179 • Dinner Theater 179 • Movie Houses of Note 179

13 Day Trips from Cincinnati   181
Lebanon 181 • Waynesville 183 • Dayton 184 • Louisville, Kentucky 185 •
Lexington, Kentucky 186

Appendix: City•Smart Basics   189

Index   193

MAP CONTENTS

Greater Cincinnati Zones   vi

2 Getting Around
Transit Map   23
CNKI   29

3 Where to Stay
Downtown Cincinnati   34
Greater Cincinnati   40

4 Where to Eat
Downtown Cincinnati   55
Greater Cincinnati   60

5 Sights and Attractions
Downtown Cincinnati   76
Greater Cincinnati   82

9 Shopping
Shopping near the Skywalk   125

10 Sports and Recreation
Golf Courses in
Greater Cincinnati   150

13 Day Trips
Cincinnati Region   182

HOW TO USE THIS BOOK

Whether you're a visitor, a new resident, or a Cincinnati native, you'll find *City•Smart Guidebook: Cincinnati* indispensable. Author Billie Felix Jeyes brings you an insider's view of the best Cincinnati has to offer.

City•Smart Guidebook: Cincinnati presents the Cincinnati metropolitan area in five geographic zones. The zone divisions are listed below and are shown on the map on the following pages. Look for a zone designation in parentheses at the end of each listing. You'll also find maps of downtown Cincinnati and the greater Cincinnati area in Chapters 3, 4, and 5 to help you locate the accommodations, restaurants, and sights covered in those chapters.

Cincinnati Zones

Downtown Cincinnati
Bounded on the north by Central Parkway, on the east by Eggleston Avenue, on the south by the Ohio River, and on the west by I-75.
This area covers Cincinnati's downtown business district.

Uptown Cincinnati
Bounded on the north by the Norwood Lateral, on the east by I-71, on the south by Central Parkway, and on the west by I-75.
This area covers the rest of the downtown basin (Over-the-Rhine, West End, and Queensgate), as well as the University of Cincinnati, Mt. Auburn, Clifton Heights, Corryville, Fairview, Clifton, Avondale and Paddock Hills, and parts of St. Bernard and Norwood.

East Cincinnati
Bounded on the west by I-71, the Norwood Lateral, and I-75; on the north and east by I-275; and on the south by I-275 and the Ohio River.
This area covers Mt. Adams, Eden Park, Walnut Hills, Hyde Park, Oakley, Mt. Lookout, Mt. Washington, Columbia Tusculum, the East End, California, and other neighborhoods and townships.

West Cincinnati
Bounded on the north and west by I-275, on the east by I-75, and on the south by the Ohio River.
This area covers Price Hill, Sedamsville, Riverside, Sayler Park, Westwood, Northside, College Hill, Mt. Airy, Winton Hills, Winton Place, Carthage, Hartwell, part of St. Bernard, and other neighborhoods and townships.

South of the River
Bounded on the west, north, and east by the Ohio River, and on the south by I-275.
This area covers the Kentucky cities of Covington, Newport, Ft. Thomas, Southgate, Ft. Mitchell, Ft. Wright, Park Hills, Bellevue, Ludlow, Bromley, Villa Hills, and Wilder.

GREATER CINCINNATI ZONES

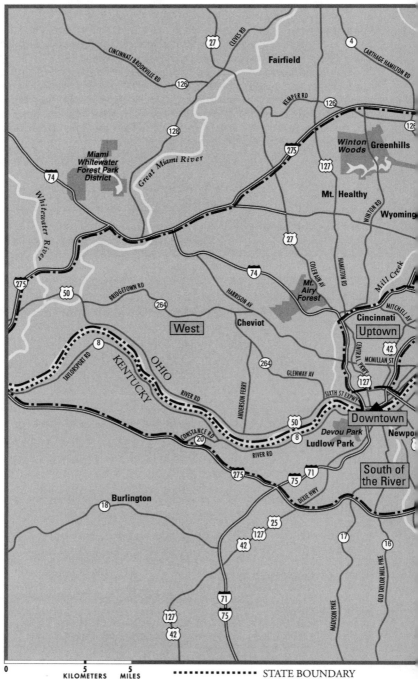

0   5   5
   KILOMETERS MILES   ·············· STATE BOUNDARY

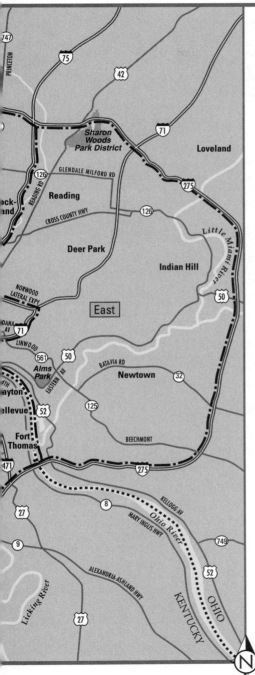

CINCINNATI ZONES

Downtown Cincinnati
Bounded on the north by Central Parkway, on the east by Eggleston Avenue, on the south by the Ohio River, and on the west by I-75.

Uptown Cincinnati
Bounded on the north by the Norwood Lateral, on the east by I-71, on the south by Central Parkway, and on the west by I-75.

East Cincinnati
Bounded on the west by I-71, the Norwood Lateral, and I-75; on the north and east by I-275; and on the south by I-275 and the Ohio River.

West Cincinnati
Bounded on the north and west by I-275, on the east by I-75, and on the south by the Ohio River.

South of the River
Bounded on the west, north, and east by the Ohio River, and on the south by I-275

1

WELCOME TO CINCINNATI

In a basin alongside the Ohio River lies the city of Cincinnati. Hills carved out by Ice Age glaciers and prehistoric rivers rise to the north, east, and west. Looking down at the city from the observation deck of Carew Tower, Cincinnati's tallest building, you can see the confluence of the Ohio and Licking Rivers and the hills of Kentucky to the south. Looking north, you see Vine Street winding its way through downtown into the old German neighborhood of Over-the-Rhine and up the hill to Clifton Heights. Face east and you see Mt. Adams and Eden Park. If you turn around, you'll see Union Terminal, the largest half-dome structure in the Western Hemisphere, set against the hills.

As this view suggests, rich history and physical beauty mingle and thrive in Cincinnati. In 1994, *Places Rated Almanac* named Cincinnati the country's Most Livable City, much to the delight of its residents. The city is home to the nation's oldest song festival, the second-oldest opera company, and the fifth-oldest symphony orchestra, in addition to many other important cultural institutions. Downtown's nightlife has been revitalized by the Aronoff Center for the Arts, whose three theaters and art gallery straddle half a downtown block, and also by Over-the-Rhine's emerging Main Street Entertainment District. Cincinnati's downtown also extends southward, with six bridges connecting to the Northern Kentucky cities of Covington and Newport; this triumvirate brings exceptional variety and vitality to the city. Yet for all its big-city attractions, Cincinnati manages to retain a small-town feel. When you walk down the street, don't be surprised if people actually smile at you—you might even find yourself smiling back.

A Brief History of Cincinnati

The Indians

Very little is known about the Ohio Valley's first settlers, the Adena Indians, but they did leave a lasting impression on the land: the Serpent Mound, a 210-meter-long effigy mound built on a terrace above Brush Creek in Adams County, Ohio. The Adenas' successors, the Hopewell Indians, left marks of their own on the terrain—Fort Ancient, a 100-acre metropolis just north of Cincinnati. The city itself was built on a series of mounds, referred to as "the Ancient Works" by the first European settlers. By the eighteenth century, the Ohio Valley had become part of a vast hunting ground claimed by several tribes, including the Shawnee, who had a large settlement in Chillicothe, about 100 miles north.

The Arrival of the Europeans

Benjamin Stites, who stumbled across the area while pursuing some Indians, was so impressed with the land between the two Miami Rivers that he went to New York with the express purpose of persuading others to organize a land company. He found an ally in John Cleves Symmes, who, along with 23 others, arranged for the purchase of the area, then part of the Northwest Territory.

The first European settlement was at Columbia, the site of the present-day Lunken Airport. Benjamin Stites and his party of 26 set ashore near the mouth of the Little Miami River on November 18, 1788. Six weeks later John Patterson established a second village a few

---

Cincinnati, U.S.A.

The place Winston Churchill once called "the most beautiful inland city in the United States" has been given several nicknames over the course of time. In the nineteenth century, when it was the largest pork-packer in the nation, it was known as Porkopolis. A more flattering sobriquet, the Queen City, was bestowed by Henry Wadsworth Longfellow. The City of Seven Hills is bit of a misnomer since no one can agree on which of Cincinnati's many hills make up the seven. The Blue Chip City, a more recent moniker, is a favorite of the Chamber of Commerce. And, just in case you forget what country you're in, the expressway signs are marked "Cincinnati, U.S.A."

Two Harrisons in the Oval Office

Virginia native William Henry Harrison moved to North Bend, Ohio, when he married the daughter of Cincinnati founder John Cleves Symmes. After winning the presidency with the unforgettable slogan "Tippecanoe and Tyler too," the nation's ninth president rode to his inauguration without a coat or hat and went on to deliver the longest inaugural address on record, speaking for 45 minutes. He caught pneumonia and died a month later, on April 4, 1841.

William Henry Harrison's grandchild, Benjamin Harrison, became this nation's twenty-third president in 1888. These two Harrisons represent the only grandfather-grandchild presidents in United States history.

miles to the west. The new settlement was named Losantiville, meaning "town opposite the mouth" of the Licking River, by John Filson (who later disappeared into the wilderness). A month later, John Cleves Symmes founded North Bend to the west of Losantiville, on the mouth of the Great Miami River. To protect the area from Indian raids, a fort was established at Losantiville. When Arthur St. Clair, Governor of the Northwest Territory, visited Fort Washington shortly thereafter, he pooh-poohed the name and immediately changed it to Cincinnati, after the Society of Cincinnatus, an organization of Revolutionary War officers founded by George Washington.

In 1784, after losing the Battle of Fallen Timbers, a group of subjugated Indians surrendered their claims to most of Ohio and parts of Indiana. The Treaty of Greenville brought an end to frontier hostilities and Europeans also began settling on the southern banks of the Ohio River. In 1815 the city of Covington, west of the Licking River, was platted by John Gano, Richard Gano, and Thomas Carneal. On the east side of the Licking River lay the village of Newport, incorporated as a city in 1834.

River City

Cincinnati soon became a thriving river town and a midway port for traffic between Pittsburgh and New Orleans. Fueled by the advent of the steamboat and the construction of the Miami & Erie Canal that connected Cincinnati to the Great Lakes, the city began to prosper. By the 1840s, it had become the sixth-largest city in the United States and the nation's leading pork-packer. The rise of the railroads saw the fall of river traffic, and Cincinnati was soon surpassed in size by Chicago.

Its proximity to Kentucky made Cincinnati a gateway to the South, but this trade was halted by the Civil War. Commerce picked up, though, as Cincinnati converted its peacetime foundries into munitions factories and supplied the war effort with new boats and other essential provisions. Plans for the first bridge to span the Ohio River were also delayed by the Civil War. By 1867, however, the project was finally completed, and a suspension bridge—named after its architect, John A. Roebling—finally linked Covington to Cincinnati.

The Twentieth Century

The city, like the Ohio River, has had its fair share of ups and downs in the twentieth century. Before World War I, Cincinnati was a lively city—known as the Paris of America—filled with beer gardens, concert halls, opera houses, theaters, and shooting galleries. Vine Street alone had so many saloons (113) that when Carry Nation visited the city in 1901 with her hatchet, she didn't break even a single window, declaring, "I would have dropped dead from exhaustion before I had gone one block." By World War I, Cincinnati had become home to a lively German community.

The Great War, however, put an end to this flowering of culture. Street names were anglicized, German was no longer taught in the schools, and the German-language newspapers closed down. By the time Prohibition had shut down Cincinnati's breweries and beer gardens, Cincinnati had lost much of what made it so vibrant.

The rise of the automobile changed the city, too. As African Americans and Appalachians moved into the core of the city, Whites fled further up the hills into the newly formed suburbs. "White flight" extended so far north that Cincinnati's northernmost suburbs are shared with Dayton, Ohio. In 1967, the same year Paul Brown founded the Cincinnati Bengals, Cincinnati experienced a full week of race riots.

The 1970s saw the rise of baseball's Big Red Machine (the Cincinnati Reds), the destruction of downtown's theater district, and the ouster of its strip joints, while the 1980s were marked by the savings-and-loan crisis and a decline in downtown's retail establishments. The 1990s, however, have seen a resurgence in downtown business and nightlife, and the gentrification of the Main Street Historic District—all of which has made Cincinnati more robust than ever.

TRIVIA

Cincinnati-born George Hunt Pendleton sponsored the 1883 Pendleton Act, creating the U.S. civil service system.

Recommended Reading

The Bicentennial Guide to Greater Cincinnati, *Geoffrey J. Giglieramo (Cincinnati Historical Society, 1988)*

Cincinnati: City of Charm, *Nick Clooney (Towery, 1991)*

Cincinnati: The Queen City, *Daniel Hurley (Cincinnati Historical Society, 1982)*

Cincinnati Then and Now, *Iola Hessler Silberstein (League of Women Voters of Cincinnati, 1982)*

Domestic Manners of the Americans, *Frances Milton Trollope (Whittaker, Treacher, 1832)*

Extenuating Circumstances, *Jonathan Valin (Dell, 1990)*

The Frontiersman, *Allan W. Eckert (Bantam, 1984)*

Jim Borgman's Cincinnati, *Jim Borgman (Colloquial Books, 1992)*

The River Book: Cincinnati and the Ohio River, *edited by Joyce V. B. Cauffield and Carolyn E. Bonfield (Program for Cincinnati)*

Trouble Making Toys, *Albert Pyle (Walker & Co., 1985)*

Vas You Ever in Zinzinnati?, *Dick Perry (Doubleday, 1969)*

Getting to Know the Cincinnati Metro Area

Visitors have always complimented Cincinnati on its downtown area. Clean, compact, and filled with a wide variety of stores and restaurants, downtown survived the recession of the '80s and has begun to reinvent itself. Several swanky new restaurants have opened recently, and a new downtown mall has given shoppers a place to go after 6 p.m.

The riverfront area, cut off from downtown by Fort Washington Way, is not as accessible as it should be but is worth the trip nonetheless. On the east are two riverfront parks. Walkways take you to the riverfront stadiums—the Crown (home of the Cincinnati Cyclones hockey team) and Cinergy Field (shared, for the time being, by the Cincinnati Reds and the Cincinnati Bengals). Plans for a new riverfront football stadium are in the works, and there has been heated discussion about the placement of a new baseball stadium, with Reds owner Marge Schott insisting on a riverfront site and other factions arguing for a site

CINCINNATI TIME LINE

1000 B.C.– **A.D. 200**	The Adena Indians build a series of mounds on the site of Cincinnati.
300–700	The Hopewell Indians add more mounds to the Cincinnati site.
800–1794	The Ohio Valley is a vast hunting ground for various Indian tribes.
1786	Benjamin Stites goes to New York and persuades John Cleves Symmes to organize a land company, resulting in the Miami Purchase.
1788	Three settlements are founded on the banks of the Ohio River: Columbia, Losantiville, and North Bend.
1789	To ward off Indian attacks, Fort Washington is established at Losantiville.
1790	The city of Covington is platted.
1794	The Indians cede most of Ohio and parts of Indiana to the Americans, bringing an influx of settlers.
1795	The village of Newport is incorporated.
1802	Cincinnati is incorporated as a town.
1803	Fort Washington moves across the river to Newport.
1811	The *New Orleans* becomes the first steamboat to navigate the Ohio River, heralding a new era.
1840	Cincinnati becomes the sixth-largest city in the United States.
1845	The Miami & Erie Canal links the Ohio River to Lake Erie.
1851	Harriet Beecher Stowe's *Uncle Tom's Cabin* is published.
1867	The Cincinnati Red Stockings become the first professional baseball team, and the John A. Roebling Bridge becomes the first bridge to span the Ohio River.
1903	The Ingalls Building becomes the first skyscraper to be built using steel-reinforced concrete.
1920	The Miami & Erie Canal is drained.
1933	Union Terminal, a magnificent art deco half-dome, is built.
1935	After taunting the pitcher, nightclub entertainer Kitty Burke becomes the only woman to bat in a major league baseball game.
1937	The Ohio River passes flood stage (52 feet) and crests at 79.9 feet.

Ezzard Mack Charles defeats "Jersey Joe" Walcott to become World Heavyweight Champion. The next year "the Cincinnati Cobra" defends his title successfully, beating former champ Joe Lewis.	1949
The Cincinnati Gardens opens.	1949
Dorothy Dolbey becomes Cincinnati's first woman mayor.	1954
WCET becomes the first TV station in the nation funded by private subscribers.	1954
Dr. Albert Sabin's oral polio vaccine is licensed by the U.S. Public Health Service.	1961
Coney Island, which had been "Whites Only" since its inception, finally allows African Americans to use its facilities.	1961
300,000-year-old mastodon bone is found in Norwood.	1966
Paul Brown moves to Cincinnati and founds a new football franchise, the Cincinnati Bengals.	1968
The first section of the downtown skywalk system opens.	1971
Theodore M. Berry becomes Cincinnati's first African American mayor.	1972
The Cincinnati Reds, a.k.a. the Big Red Machine, win the World Series two years in a row.	1975-76
Hustler magazine publisher Larry Flynt is charged with conspiring to pander obscenity. Although he loses the case, he eventually wins on appeal.	1976
Riverfront Stadium opens.	1976
Eleven die at Riverfront Coliseum (The Crown) during a Who concert.	1979
The first Taste of Cincinnati is held.	1980
Marge Schott purchases the Cincinnati Reds, becoming the first woman to buy a major league sports team.	1984
Nurse's aide Donald Harvey admits to killing 24 people at Drake Hospital. The final tally is much higher.	1987
The Reds sweep Oakland in the World Series, 4 games to 0.	1990
The Contemporary Arts Center and its director, Dennis Barrie, are charged with obscenity for exhibiting "The Perfect Moment," a series of photographs by the late Robert Mapplethorpe. The defendants are acquitted.	1990
The Ohio River floods, cresting at 64.5 feet.	1997

closer to downtown's eastern edge. The outcome, at this point, is anybody's guess.

Just north of downtown lies Over-the-Rhine (OTR), an old German neighborhood now populated mostly by Appalachians and African Americans. In OTR you'll find Elm Street's Music Hall, which houses the Cincinnati Symphony Orchestra, the Cincinnati Opera, and the Cincinnati Ballet. Ensemble Theater of Cincinnati has made its home on Vine Street, and in the last couple of years the Main Street area has undergone extensive gentrification, becoming one of the city's hottest nightspots.

Mt. Adams lies just east of downtown and is one of the most charming neighborhoods in the city. Nestled next to Eden Park, home of the Cincinnati Art Museum and the Krohn Conservatory, it's reminiscent of a European village, with higgledy-piggledy streets, cozy bars and restaurants, and nineteenth-century houses. Cincinnati's oldest professional theater, Playhouse in the Park, is also located here.

The University of Cincinnati dominates the hills just north of downtown, also known as Pill Hill because of its many hospitals. The hilltop area draws a somewhat younger crowd and boasts some of the best music venues in the city. And, as with any college town, it has a large number of bars and affordable restaurants.

The People of Cincinnati

Mark Twain once said that if the world were to end, he wanted to be in Cincinnati because things happen there ten years later than anywhere

Bicentennial Commons at Sawyer Point, one of two riverfront parks near downtown

Stephanni Cohen/©Cincinnati Recreation Commission

Cincinnati Inventions

Reaper, 1853, Obed Hussey

Floating soap, 1879, Procter & Gamble

Clay pigeon target, 1880, George Ligowsky

California bungalow, 1902, Charles and Harry Greene

Formica, 1913, Herbert Faber and Daniel O'Connor

Refrigerated box car, 1940, Frederick McKinley Jones

Preparation H, 1950s, Dr. George Sperti

Disposable diapers, 1962, Procter & Gamble

else. His words still ring true. Bordered on the north, east, and west by hills, and on the south by the Ohio River, Cincinnati changes slowly, and you get the feeling that many of its inhabitants like it that way.

Partly as a result of this mentality, Cincinnati has gained a reputation as a conservative city. Though there is truth in this preconception, it is somewhat undeserved. The city's prosecution of the Contemporary Arts Center for displaying the works of Robert Mapplethorpe was well-chronicled in the national media, but the ensuing "not guilty" verdict delivered by 12 of its citizens was barely mentioned. Though the city has its share of reactionaries, many residents come from the opposite political extreme (and most are somewhere in between).

Culturally, Cincinnati has a strong German flavor. If a Cincinnatian looks at you questioningly and says, "Please?" it's not meant to be a polite request. What they really mean to say is, "Could you repeat that?" or "What did you just say?" This peculiar phrase is a direct translation of the German *bitte* and is as good an indication as any of the city's German heritage.

Although Cincinnati's earliest residents were of Anglo-Saxon descent—mostly Presbyterians, Baptists, and Methodists—the influx of Germans in the nineteenth century transformed the city's ethnic makeup. The Irish also came in great numbers, fleeing the potato famines. Though the majority of Germans and Irish were Catholic, the two nationalities didn't mix much, even building separate churches. The Irish tended to live closer to the river, while the Germans found a home in Over-the-Rhine, so called because it was to the north of the Miami & Erie Canal.

After the failed 1848 revolution in Germany a second wave of German

Cincinnati Firsts

1823: Nation's first teaching hospital, founded by Dr. Daniel Drake

1835: World's first airmail, transported by hot air balloon

1849: First U.S. city to hold a song festival, Saengerfest

1850: Nation's first greeting card company—Gibson; nation's first Jewish hospital

1869: World's first professional baseball team; first U.S. city to found a weather bureau

1870: World's first industrial expo

1875: Nation's first Jewish theological college, Hebrew Union College

1880: First and only U.S. city to build and own a major railroad

1897: Nation's first municipal tuberculosis sanitarium

1902: World's first concrete skyscraper, the Ingalls Building

1905: World's first outdoor telephone booth

1935: Major League Baseball's first night game, at Crosley Field

1952: World's first heart-lung machine, at Children's Hospital

1954: Nation's first licensed Public TV Station, WCET-TV

1961: World's first oral polio vaccine, developed by Dr. Albert Sabin

1963: World's first medical laser laboratory, at Children's Hospital

immigrants arrived, as did a large number of German Jews. Before this time, Cincinnati's Jews were of British descent. Once again, despite a shared religion, the two nationalities didn't mix well, resulting in the creation of Reformed Judaism.

After World War II, Appalachians and African Americans migrated to Cincinnati and settled near the center of the city while the original residents moved further up the hills. More recently, Italians, Greeks, Lebanese, Asians, and Hispanics have modified Cincinnati's racial makeup. But despite the two World Wars and the influx of different cultures, the city retains much of its German character, evidenced by its Oktoberfests, beer consumption, and love of music.

Business and Economy

Situated between Pittsburgh, Pennsylvania, and Cairo, Illinois, Cincinnati was a perfect midway port for goods traveling down the Ohio River. With the advent of the steamboat in 1811 Cincinnati grew at a phenomenal rate, and by the 1840s it led the nation in the production of pork, beer, and liquor. It was also a leading manufacturer of steamboats, furniture, shoes, and ready-made clothes. With the advent of the railroad Cincinnati's river trade waned, but the city adapted and is now a leading manufacturer of robotics, machine tools, playing cards, jet engines, soaps, and detergents. And despite the decline in river trading, more freight passes through the city of Cincinnati than through the Panama Canal.

Procter & Gamble, founded in 1837, made its fortune by manufacturing soap and candles from the byproducts of the pork packers. Now the nation's leading producer of household goods, P&G is headquartered downtown, its two glimmering towers a dominant part of the Cincinnati skyline. P&G is one of several Fortune 500 companies headquartered here, including Chiquita Brands International, Cinergy Corp., Federated Department Stores, the Kroger Company, Mercantile Stores Co., Eagle-Picher, Cincinnati Milacron, E.W. Scripps, Nine West, American Financial, and Ohio Casualty. No wonder Cincinnati is sometimes called "the Blue Chip City."

Other major Cincinnati employers include GE Aircraft Engines, AK Steel, Ford Motor Company, Cincinnati Bell Telephone, and Delta Airlines, which has a hub at the Cincinnati–Northern Kentucky International Airport. All in all, Cincinnati's workforce is almost 1 million strong, with an unemployment rate of only 4.2 percent.

Housing

The median price of an existing Cincinnati house is about 12 percent below the national average and well below averages for other U.S. cities: A $100,000 house in Greater Cincinnati would cost $179,000 in Boston, $171,000 in San Diego, and $159,000 in Seattle. An acre of land in Cincinnati costs $65,340, as compared to $87,120 in Louisville,

TRIVIA

The University of Cincinnati, founded in 1870, was the nation's first municipal university.

Kentucky; and $124,146 in Dallas, Texas. The average apartment rental in Cincinnati is $556 per month. You can, of course, spend big bucks on housing in Cincinnati if you want to. The Village of Indian Hill, a city in its own right, is the most expensive address in town, with mansions going for up to $3 million. Other high-ticket neighborhoods include Glendale, Amberley Village, Hyde Park, and Northern Kentucky's Fort Thomas.

Schools

The Cincinnati Public School System serves about a quarter of a million students. The quality of education varies widely, usually depending on the relative wealth of the neighborhood it serves. To combat this disparity, CPS has developed a magnet program that gives students the opportunity to attend the school of their choice. Elementary schools offer Montessori and Paideia Critical Thinking programs. Walnut Hills High is probably the most well-regarded public school in the city. Another notable public high school is the School for Creative and Performing Arts.

Cincinnati's large Catholic population is served by the Cincinnati Archdiocese Schools. Covington Latin School, run by the Diocese of Covington, offers the area's sole accelerated college-prep program.

Area colleges include the University of Cincinnati, Xavier University, Mt. St. Joseph's, Miami University, Northern Kentucky University, and Thomas More College.

Taxes

State income tax rates in Ohio and Kentucky are levied on a graduated basis on modified federal adjusted gross income. In Ohio, the tax rates range from .743 percent to 7.5 percent. In Kentucky, they range from 2 to 6 percent. Both Ohio and Kentucky tax wages at rates of up to 2.5 percent. Property taxes, which are levied at the county level, are based on assessed values, ranging from average net effective tax rates of $1.02 per $100 in Kentucky to $1.66 per 100 in Ohio. Sales tax in Cincinnati is 6 percent; Kentucky sales tax is 5.5 percent.

The Contemporary Arts Center, site of the battle over Robert Mapplethorpe's work

The Contemporary Arts Center

The Myth of the Seven-Hilled City

by William Schottelkotte, music editor of Everybody's News— *Cincinnati's weekly newspaper—and founder of the rock group* Love America

The people of Cincinnati have historically had what could be called a "Rome fixation." After all, they named the burgeoning metropolis after a prominent Roman soldier and statesman. For centuries Cincinnatians have endeavored to draw countless comparisons to the ancient city, from the architecture to the climate to the Western Hills Viaduct. The most notable comparison, however, is the common and widely accepted misconception that Cincinnati, like Rome, is a city with seven hills looming high above the plain. Latin teachers especially have been guilty of perpetrating such a notion in their efforts to aid students in learning the seven hills of Rome.

While the city's sprawling landscape does indeed dip and rise with smooth grace, those "hills," as they are so belovedly known, reach no majestic peak to boast of. In fact, the highest point in Hamilton County is barely 500 feet above the Ohio River pool, which sits at about 450 feet above sea level. Cincinnati's geographical makeup is marked not so much by hills as by the valleys and basins formed by the numerous creeks and rivers that have cut through the earth for thousands of years, creating a tame, serene, undaunting landscape.

Moreover, throughout the city's history, Latin and geography scholars alike have had great trouble in deciding which of the city's numerous hills actually constitute the magic seven. In 1873 the West American Review *cited Mt. Adams, Walnut Hills, Mt. Auburn, Vine Street Hill, Fairmount, Harrison (Westwood), and College Hill, while another attempt 11 years later in the* History of Cincinnati *cited not seven hills, but ten. In 1958 the* Times-Star *offered an equivalent but different list. So what's the real answer? In all honesty, no one really knows—although some insist they do. Check out a map, take a stroll around town, and make a guess. Yours is as good as any.*

Cost of Living

Although Cincinnati's cost of housing is lower than the national average, goods and services are on par with the rest of the country. Below is a list of some typical goods and services and what you can expect to pay for them.

5-mile taxi ride: $8
Average dinner for two: $30
Daily newspaper: 50 cents
Average hotel double room: $75
Movie admission: $7.50
Gallon of gas: $1.19
Gallon of milk: $1.29

When to Visit

When you choose to visit Cincinnati depends at least in part on your interests. Cincinnatians love their outdoor festivals, and during the summer you can find something going on almost every weekend. If you like drinking beer, eating *brats* and *metts* (different types of German sausage), and doing the Chicken Dance, a spate of Oktoberfests begins in August, the largest of which is held downtown in September. Labor Day is marked by Riverfest and its dazzling display of fireworks.

If you're a sports fan, think about coming to the city during your favorite professional season to catch some live action: the Bengals begin their preseason football games in early August and end late in December; the Reds' baseball season begins in early April and ends late in September; the Cyclones' hockey season runs from October through April; and thoroughbred horse racing seasons are divided between Kentucky's Turfway Park (September through October and December through April) and Cincinnati's River Downs (April through September).

The theater season usually begins in September and runs through

---

TRIVIA

Cincinnati native Salmon P. Chase's Abolitionist stance may have cost him the presidential nomination, but it didn't stop him from becoming Governor of Ohio and serving two terms in the senate. In 1861 Lincoln appointed him Secretary of the Treasury, putting him in charge of organizing the nation's new banking system. Chase also served as Chief Justice of the Supreme Court.

Oktoberfest—Zinzinnati, one of the many festivals that take place throughout the year

June, though you can see touring shows throughout the year. For other special interests, consult the Calendar of Events below.

Calendar of Events

JANUARY
Cincinnati Travel, Sports & Boat Show, Cincinnati Convention Center
Kahn's African Culture Fest, Museum Center
Pre-Spring Show, Krohn Conservatory

FEBRUARY
Cincinnati International Wine Fest, Cincinnati Convention Center
Fine Arts Fund Sampler Weekend, Downtown
Great American Train Show, Cincinnati Convention Center
Home & Garden Show, Cincinnati Convention Center
Mainstrasse Mardi Gras, Covington, KY

MARCH
American Negro Spiritual Festival, Music Hall
Cincinnati Heart Mini Marathon, Downtown
Spring Show, Krohn Conservatory
St. Patrick Parade, Downtown
Jim Beam Stakes, Turfway Park
New Car Show, Cincinnati Convention Center

APRIL
Cincinnati Zoo Spring Floral Celebration
Cincinnati Flower Show, Ault Park

Newport Arts and Music Festival,
    Newport, KY
Opening Day of Baseball Season

MAY
Appalachian Festival, Coney Island
Cincinnati May Festival, Downtown
Delta Queen Homecoming,
    Downtown
Greater Cincinnati Jewish Folk
    Festival
Jammin' on Main, Downtown
Jewish Folk Festival, Burnet Woods
Maifest, Covington, KY
Taste of Cincinnati, Downtown
Wright Memorial Glider Meet,
    Caesar Creek

Mt. Adams, a neighborhood in Cincinnati

JUNE
BBQ & Blues Festival,
    Yeatman's Cove Park
Cincinnati Juneteenth Celebration, Eden Park
A Day in Eden, Eden Park
Italian Festival, Newport, KY
Kids' Fest, Riverfront
Midwest Beerfest, Riverbend Music Center
Panegyri Greek Festival, Holy Trinity St. Nicholas
    Greek Orthodox Church
Summerfair, Coney Island

JULY
Christmas in July, Covington, KY
Coors Light Rhythm & Blues Festival, Cinergy Field, Downtown
Hamilton County Fair, Hamilton County Fairgrounds, Cincinnati
Kids' Expo, Cincinnati Convention Center
Queen City Blues Fest, Bicentennial Commons, Downtown
Queen City's Taste of Ebony Multicultural Culinary Block Party,
    Downtown
St. Rita Fest, St. Rita School for the Deaf, Cincinnati

AUGUST
ATP Tennis Tournament
Black Family Reunion, Sawyer Point, Downtown
The Cincinnati Original Oktoberfest, Germania Park, Cincinnati
Great Inland Seafood Festival, Sawyer Point, Downtown
Kentucky State Championship Chili Cookoff and Car Show, Newport, KY
Midwest Region Black Family Reunion Celebration, Sawyer Point

SEPTEMBER
Cincinnati Celtic Music and Cultural Festival, Ault Park
Head of the Licking Regatta
Kentucky Cup Day of Champions, Turfway Park
Kitchen & Bath Show, Cincinnati Convention Center
Klosterman Family Oktoberfest, Covington, KY
Light Up Cincinnati, Downtown
Oktoberfest-Zinzinnati, Downtown
Riverfest, Riverfront

OCTOBER
Cincinnati Antiques Festival, Sharonville Convention Center
Cincinnati Gold Star ChiliFest, Downtown
Cincinnati Kitchen, Bath Show, Cincinnati Convention Center
Scarefest, Sawyer Point, Downtown
Schwaben Oktoberfest, Donaushwaben Park, Cincinnati
Taste of Findlay Market, Downtown

NOVEMBER
Candlelight Walk, Covington, KY
Cincinnati Crafts Affair, Cincinnati Convention Center

Climate Chart

Average monthly high/low temperatures in degrees
Fahrenheit. Average monthly precipitation in inches.

	High	Low	Precipitation
January	37.3	20.4	3.13
February	41.2	23.0	2.73
March	51.5	32.0	3.95
April	64.5	42.4	3.58
May	74.2	51.7	3.84
June	82.3	60.5	4.09
July	85.8	64.9	4.28
August	84.8	63.3	2.97
September	78.7	56.3	2.91
October	66.7	43.9	2.54
November	52.6	34.1	3.12
December	41.9	25.7	3.00

Source: The Weather Almanac, Gale Research Inc.

Festival of Lights, Cincinnati Zoo
Holiday Show, Krohn Conservatory
Light Up the Square, Downtown
Toys for Adults, Cincinnati Convention Center

DECEMBER
Boar's Head & Yule Log Festival, Christ Church, Downtown
Festival of Lights, Cincinnati Zoo
Festival of Lights, Fountain Square
Holiday in Lights, Sharon Woods
Victorian Christmas Tour, Newport, KY

Cincinnati's Weather

Cincinnati has a continental climate with wide-ranging temperatures from winter to summer. Winters are quite cold; spring brings mild temperatures and frequent showers, and it never seems to last long enough; summers are hot and humid; and fall is fairly chilly but beautiful nonetheless.

Some local wag once commented that if you don't like the weather in Cincinnati, just wait an hour and it will change. As with many clichés, this comment has some truth to it, manifested particularly in the sudden appearance and disappearance of rain showers in spring and summer. In short: bring an umbrella.

Dressing in Cincinnati

Cincinnatians are happiest when they're casually attired. Downtown workers don the traditional office garb, but people rarely dress up except for the theater, ballet, opera, or other special occasions. If you're going out for dinner, dress casually unless the place is fancy—call ahead to be sure. If your dinner destination is a Cincinnati chili parlor, however, I advise you to dress way down. Despite the fact that many parlors provide diners with bibs, chili will inevitably spatter on your favorite article of clothing.

Cincinnati/Northern Kentucky International Airport

2

GETTING AROUND CINCINNATI

Cincinnati lies on the northern side of the Ohio River with the Northern Kentucky cities of Covington and Newport on the southern side. Hills surround the downtown basin to the east, west, and north. The City of Cincinnati is 77.2 square miles; the downtown area, however, is only 11 by nine blocks wide, so it's easy to walk around. An extensive downtown skywalk system connects the Cincinnati Convention Center to most of the major hotels and shops.

If you want to explore Greater Cincinnati, your best bet is to rent a car or to take a taxi. There are taxi stands in front of the major downtown hotels. The most reliable method for getting a cab, however, is to call a local company. If you decide to use the bus system, remember that it shuts down after midnight.

City Layout

Cincinnati Streets

Downtown Cincinnati is designed on a grid. Streets running east and west, parallel to the Ohio River, are numbered—except for 2nd Street, renamed Pete Rose Way; Court Street (10th Street); and Central Parkway (11th Street), which divides downtown from Over-the-Rhine neighborhood and takes a northerly turn at the west side of downtown. A portion of 8th Street, between Vine and Elm Streets, is named Garfield. From east to west, the downtown cross streets are Broadway, Sycamore, Main, Walnut, Vine, Race, Elm, Plum, and Central Avenue

At the turn of the century, Cincinnati was the world's biggest manufacturer of carriages, and when Henry Ford and J. W. Packard came to the Queen City with the express purpose of raising capital to found a new industry, they were rebuffed. The future automobile manufacturers went to Detroit instead.

(not to be confused with Central Parkway). Vine Street divides east from west Cincinnati.

Cincinnati also has one of the nation's two downtown skywalk systems (Minneapolis has the other). The first section of the second-level walkway, completed in 1971, connects the Dr. Albert B. Sabin Convention Center to Fountain Square. The second-level walkway now spans from 4th to 7th Streets, from Elm to Main Streets, and links downtown to both Cinergy Field and The Crown.

Downtown Covington and Newport

On the south side of the river are Covington and Newport, both designed on a grid with the numerical streets counting up from the Ohio River. Downtown Covington's east-to-west cross streets are Garrard, Greenup, Scott, Madison, Russell, Johnson, Main, Bakewell, and Philadelphia. Downtown Newport's cross streets are, from east to west, Overton, Washington, Saratoga, Monmouth, York, Columbia, Central, and Isabella. The Veterans Memorial Bridge links Covington's 4th Street to Newport. The 12th Street Bridge also serves as a connector between the two cities.

Major Arteries

Cincinnati's neighborhoods, separated by hills and valleys, are very much self-contained, and the 1948 Metropolitan Master Plan, responsible for the routing of the Queen City's expressways today, kept this in mind. The Millcreek Expressway, now part of I-75, cuts through the western edge of downtown Cincinnati and heads in a northerly direction to Dayton, Ohio. The Northeast Expressway, now part of I-71, cuts through the eastern edge of downtown Cincinnati and heads toward Columbus, Ohio.

These days, I-75 runs from Miami, Florida, to Detroit, Michigan, and I-71 from Louisville, Kentucky, to Cleveland, Ohio. The two roads merge just north of Walton, Kentucky, then separate after they cross the Ohio River at the Brent Spence Bridge. To stay on I-75, stay on the left-hand side of the road. To reach I-71, get in the right-hand lane and bear east onto Fort Washington Way, a very busy roadway that runs parallel to 3rd Street, dividing downtown's business district from the riverfront. Both I-71 and I-75 eventually run into I-70 about 55 miles north of the city.

Movies Filmed in the Greater Cincinnati Area

Airborne—*A 1993 rollerblading movie starring Shane McDermott and Chris Conrad.*

City of Hope—*John Sayles directed this 1991 movie about life in the inner city. It starred Vincent Spano, Angela Bassett, and Gina Gershon.*

Eight Men Out—*Another Sayles movie, from 1988, about the "Black Sox" scandal. It starred John Cusack, Christopher Lloyd, Charlie Sheen, and John Mahoney.*

Fresh Horses—Hoosiers *director David Anspaugh helmed this 1988 love story starring Molly Ringwald and Andrew McCarthy.*

An Innocent Man—*Peter Yates directed this 1989 frame-up movie starring Tom Selleck and F. Murray Abraham.*

Little Man Tate—*Jodie Foster's 1991 directorial debut about a child prodigy starred Foster, Dianne Wiest, and Harry Connick Jr.*

Lost in Yonkers—*This 1993 adaptation of Neil Simon's Pulitzer Prize–winning play starred Richard Dreyfuss and Mercedes Ruehl.*

Milk Money—*Richard Benjamin directed this 1994 hooker-with-a-heart-of-gold movie starring Melanie Griffith, Ed Harris, Anne Heche, and Malcolm McDowell.*

The Public Eye—*This 1992 film, inspired by the life of New York photographer Weegee, starred Joe Pesci, Barbara Hershey, Stanley Tucci, and Jerry Adler.*

A Rage in Harlem—*This 1991 adaptation of the Chester Himes novel starred Forest Whittaker, Gregory Hines, Robin Givens, and Danny Glover.*

Rain Man—*This 1988 film, directed by Barry Levinson and starring Dustin Hoffman, won three Oscars: Best Picture, Best Actor, and Best Screenplay. It also starred Tom Cruise and Valeria Golino.*

Tango and Cash—*Sylvester Stallone, Kurt Russell, Jack Palance, and Teri Hatcher starred in this 1989 caper movie.*

Fort Washington Way also serves as a link to Columbia Parkway, which runs eastward along the Ohio River, and to I-471, a 5-mile expressway that crosses the Daniel Beard Bridge into Northern Kentucky. I-471 connects to I-275 and ends when it meets U.S. 27, near the campus of Northern Kentucky University. Fort Washington Way is a treacherous stretch of roadway with exits on both sides that confuse even local drivers. Plans are in the works for this road to be reconfigured, so don't be surprised to see orange barrels there for the next few years.

Other major arteries include the AA Highway, which begins in Alexandria, Kentucky, and ends in Ashland, Kentucky, connecting to I-64; the Circle Freeway (I-275), surrounding the metropolitan area and passing through Southwestern Ohio, Northern Kentucky, and Southeastern Indiana; and the Norwood Lateral (S.R. 562), which links I-71 to I-75, as does the more northerly Ronald Reagan Cross County Highway. The Cross County Highway runs further west to I-74, which begins north of downtown Cincinnati at I-75 and runs westward through Indianapolis, intersecting with I-80 and I-70 before ending at Quad Cities, Iowa.

The Bridges

Six bridges span the Ohio River from downtown Cincinnati. Starting from the west, they are the Brent Spence Bridge, which carries I-75/I-71 traffic from Covington; the Clay Wade Bailey Bridge, linking Covington's Main Street to Cincinnati's 3rd Street; the John A. Roebling Suspension Bridge, connecting Covington's 3rd Street to Cincinnati's Main Street, Pete Rose Way, I-71, and I-75; the Taylor-Southgate Bridge, joining Newport's 2nd Street to Cincinnati's Pete Rose Way; the L&N Bridge, linking Newport's Saratoga Street to Cincinnati's East 3rd Street; and the Daniel Beard Bridge, which carries I-471 traffic to Cincinnati's Columbia Parkway, I-75, and I-71. The Circle Freeway (I-275) crosses the Ohio River twice. The Combs-Hehl Bridge connects Northern Kentucky to Ohio on the east and the I-275 Bridge West links Northern Kentucky with Southeastern Indiana.

TRIVIA

Cincinnati spent $6.1 million on a subway system that was never used. In 1914 voters approved the bond issue, and the Miami and Erie Canal was drained in 1919 with the idea that portions of it were to provide tunnels for the rapid transit system. By 1927 there were 2.2 miles of subway tunnels and 7.7 miles of open-cut construction, but funds had run out, and the extra $10.6 million needed to complete the project never materialized.

TRANSIT MAP

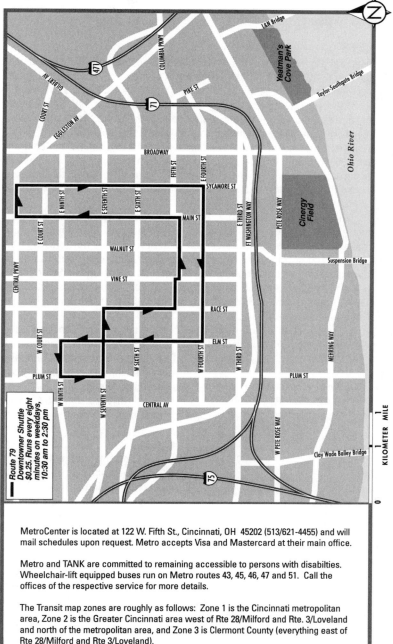

Route 79
Downtowner Shuttle
$0.25. Runs every eight
minutes on weekdays,
10:30 am to 2:30 pm

MetroCenter is located at 122 W. Fifth St., Cincinnati, OH 45202 (513/621-4455) and will mail schedules upon request. Metro accepts Visa and Mastercard at their main office.

Metro and TANK are committed to remaining accessible to persons with disabilties. Wheelchair-lift equipped buses run on Metro routes 43, 45, 46, 47 and 51. Call the offices of the respective service for more details.

The Transit map zones are roughly as follows: Zone 1 is the Cincinnati metropolitan area, Zone 2 is the Greater Cincinnati area west of Rte 28/Milford and Rte. 3/Loveland and north of the metropolitan area, and Zone 3 is Clermont County (everything east of Rte 28/Milford and Rte 3/Loveland).

Public Transportation

Bus Systems

Metro

Metro is a nonprofit service of Southwest Ohio Regional Transit Authority serving the Greater Cincinnati area north of the river. It has 44 bus routes running through three zones seven days a week. Bus stops are usually located every two blocks along the route and are marked, either by an orange stripe on a utility light, a sign pole, or a "Metro Stop" sign.

Fares are 65 cents during non-rush hour times and 80 cents during rush hour (weekdays from 6 to 9 a.m. and from 3 to 6 p.m.). Zone changes cost 30 cents and transfers cost 10 cents. On weekends and holidays, no zones apply, transfers are free, and the fare is reduced to 50 cents. Transfers from Metro buses to Northern Kentucky's TANK buses cost 40 cents with a transfer slip.

The Downtowner shuttle, Route 79, costs only 25 cents and runs every eight minutes from 10:30 a.m. to 2:30 p.m. on weekdays. The bus makes a circle starting at Government Square: it goes north (away from the river) on Main Street, turns right on Central Parkway, goes south on Sycamore Street, turns right on 4th Street, goes north on Elm Street, turns left on 9th Street, goes 2 blocks south on Plum Street, turns left on 7th Street, goes south on Race Street, then turns left on 5th Street back to Government Square.

Access, Metro's curb-to-curb service for people with disabilities, operates within the I-275 beltway and requires riders to pre-register and schedule their trips in advance. Metro also has wheelchair lift–equipped buses on selected routes.

CNKI Airport's terminals make generous use of glass to help orient travellers.

Cincinnati/Northern Kentucky International Airport

Bus drivers demand exact change and allow passengers to board and disembark only at designated stops. Also, no eating, drinking, or smoking is allowed. A word of warning: If the service name is printed in burgundy ink on the bus schedule, it's an express bus; make sure you want to go the final destination or you'll find yourself hurtling down the expressway with no way to get off.

The Metro Sales Center is located across the street from Government Square, its main downtown terminus (120 E. 4th St.). For more information, call 513/621-4455

Cincinnati's Inclines

Cincinnati used to be connected by a series of inclines (trolley cars). The first one to be built ran from Main Street to Mt. Auburn. Other inclines followed: the Price Hill, Mt. Adams, Fairview, and Bellevue. The inclines, however, were not entirely accident-free.

The Mt. Auburn Incline's clutch failed one day, sending all but one of the platform's occupants to their deaths. Another time, the cable broke on the Price Hill Incline, sending a team of horses, a man, and a wagonload of manure to the bottom. Although the horses were killed on impact, the man survived by jumping into the steaming manure. A nearby saloon celebrated the incredible escape by giving the rather smelly man drinks on the house. The Price Hill Incline was built by William Price, a teetotaler whose anti-liquor injunction earned Price Hill the moniker "Buttermilk Mountain." Drinks could be had at the foot of the hill in bars with names like First Chance, Next Chance, and Last Chance. One by one the inclines shut down; the last holdout was the Mt. Adams Incline, which closed in 1948.

(Metro TDD) or 513/632-7590 (Access). Customer Service reports: 513/632-7575. Lost and Found: 513/632-9450.

TANK

TANK (Transit Authority of Northern Kentucky) operates 365 days a year and provides service throughout Northern Kentucky, as far south as Walton and Grant's Lick. All the bus routes begin and end in downtown Cincinnati, with stops at 4th and Main Streets, 6th and Walnut Streets, 5th and Race Streets, and 3rd and Walnut Streets.

Fares are 75 cents for anywhere within TANK's service area, 35 cents for seniors ages 65 and over, and disabled people. To obtain the Senior Citizen and Disabled card ($1), you must show proof of age, Medicare, or SSI assistance. Transfers from one TANK bus to another are free, but a transfer to a Metro bus costs 40 cents plus zone charges. Don't forget to ask your driver for a transfer slip, though, or you'll have to pay full fare.

RAMP (Regional Area Mobility Program) serves disabled people by providing door-to-door service for those who can't use TANK's regular service. However, 70 percent of TANK's regular buses are lift-equipped to accommodate people in wheelchairs. TANK's main terminus is at 3375 Madison Pike in Fort Wright, Kentucky. For more information, call 606/331-TANK. Lost and Found: 606/341-TANK, ext. 21.

Taxis

Don't expect to flag down a taxi on the street, even if you're downtown. Your best bets are to stand in front of a hotel where the taxis line up for fares, to walk to the taxi stand at 6th and Vine Streets, or to call one of the local companies.

Cab companies usually confine their fares to their home states except going to or from Cincinnati–Northern Kentucky International Airport. If you're coming from the airport to downtown, call Newport Yellow Cab (606/261-4400); if you're going from downtown to the airport, call Cincinnati Yellow Cab (513/241-2100). A one-way fare is usually $22. To get in a cab costs approximately $2 right off the bat, then about $1.20 each mile. You should tip 10 to 15 percent.

Jetport Express

If you don't feel like coughing up $22 for a cab ride to Cincinnati/Northern Kentucky International Airport, Jetport Express (606/767-3702) is a convenient and affordable way to go, costing $10 for a one-way trip and $15 for a round-trip. Shuttles leave every half-hour from the Westin Hotel, the Crowne Plaza, the Cincinnatian, the Regal Hotel, the Hyatt Regency, and the Omni Netherland Plaza. Less-frequent shuttles operate from Covington's Embassy Suites, Hampton Inn and Holiday Inn Riverfront, downtown's Garfield House, and the Holiday Inn Queensgate. If you're coming from the airport, you can purchase tickets in the baggage claim areas of Terminals 1, 2, and 3. If you're coming from a hotel, contact your concierge or bell captain.

A Metro stop in Cincinnati (with a traveller who has waited longer than you)

Metro

The I-75 stretch through Cincinnati was one of the first expressways in the United States and has many exits on the left-hand side of the road. If you're not sure which side the exit is on, stay in the middle lane so when the sign comes up you don't have to cross too many lanes.

Driving in Cincinnati

Cincinnati drivers tend to be very courteous, albeit somewhat cautious—especially during winter snowstorms, when traffic can slow to a deathly crawl. Despite Cincinnati's "City of Seven Hills" moniker, there are many more hills than seven and some of them are extremely steep. Drivers should be extra-careful on the bends, as some of them tend to wind around for longer than expected and can be treacherous.

It's best to stay off the expressways during rush hour. I-75 gets extremely congested, and I-71 is in the midst of a seemingly endless renovation project—it narrows to one lane along certain strips, and the speed limit drops to 45 miles per hour. Fines in these constructions zones are doubled, and the police are very strict about enforcing the speed limit. The expressway's speed limit is usually 55 miles per hour; some stretches of I-275 allow drivers to go 65 miles per hour.

There are many viaducts connecting downtown to certain suburbs, and although they might look and feel like expressways, the speed limit is usually 35 miles per hour. Try not to speed on overhead passes, either, since these too may be speed traps. Certain communities are heavily policed, and the mere fact that you have an out-of-state license plate is enough for the local constabulary to pull you over even if you're going only a fraction over the speed limit. In residential areas, make sure you stay under the limit or you will surely be stopped. According to locals, police in Fort Thomas, Kentucky, are notorious for this practice.

Right-hand turns are permitted on red lights in Ohio and Kentucky after a complete stop, unless a sign forbids it. Children ages 4 and under or weighing less than 40 pounds are required by law to ride in safety restraints. In Ohio, drivers and passengers in the front seat can be fined for not wearing seat belts only if they are pulled over for another violation. In Kentucky, there is no penalty for not wearing a seat belt.

Parking Tips
The closer you get to the middle of downtown, the more expensive the parking meter. If you're just running an errand, though, you can park at any downtown meter, turn the handle, and get ten free minutes. Just

make sure you don't overstay your welcome. Downtown parking meters do not require money after 5 p.m.

Downtown Cincinnati has quite a few garages and parking lots. Unless you're prepared to pay a hefty fee, it's best to avoid having to use these lots. However, several parking garages downtown have extremely reasonable rates—some as low as $1 for three hours. These garages include one beneath Fountain Square, with an entrance on Vine Street; one next to the Regal Hotel on 5th Street; one on the corner of 7th and Elm Streets; and another on 9th Street between Vine and Race Streets.

Biking in Cincinnati

Although there are quite a few bike trails in Cincinnati—the most spectacular being the 22-mile Little Miami Scenic River Bikeway running from Milford to Morrow—there are practically no roadside berms. Bicyclists, therefore, have to contend with traffic, which can sometimes be a problem since some drivers seem to have no idea of the cyclists' presence and others seem to resent the fact that they have to share the road with such a slow method of transportation. Remember to stay within three feet of the curb or, where there are parked cars, three feet to the left of them.

A Metro bus on the move

Metro

Cincinnati/Northern Kentucky International Airport

Cincinnati/Northern Kentucky International Airport (CNKI) was opened in 1947 in Boone City, Kentucky, as a temporary stopgap until a bond issue could be passed to expand the airport in Blue Ash, Ohio. By 1955 voters had turned down three bond issues and the decision was made to go ahead and improve the Northern Kentucky airport. Now the world's fastest-growing airport, it offers more than 500 daily nonstop departures to 106 cities, including London, Paris, Frankfurt, Montreal, Toronto, Vancouver, and Zurich. It's also Delta's second-largest hub—second only to Atlanta—and the airline invested $375 million in an expansion that was completed in 1994.

Getting to CNKI

Approximately 12 miles, or 15 minutes, from downtown Cincinnati, the airport is located off I-275, Exit 4. If you're coming from I-75, take Exit 185, the Junction I-275/Airport Exit.

Short-term parking is located just across the street from the three terminals and costs $1 for every 30 minutes, to a maximum of $7 a day. Long-term parking is off Donaldson Road, costs $1 for every four hours or $3 a day, and offers free shuttle service to the terminals. Car-rental agencies are located just across the street from the long-term parking facility and include Avis, Hertz, Budget, and National.

Getting Around CNKI

Terminal 1 is home to Airtran, Northwest, USAir, and Skyway; Terminal 2 houses American Eagle, Continental Express, TWA, and United; and Delta and Comair share Terminal 3, the newest and ritziest terminal, complete with three concourses. Concourses A and B, both of which serve Delta, are connected by an underground train. Concourse C, for Comair, is connected to Concourse B by shuttle. For airport information, call 606/767-3144.

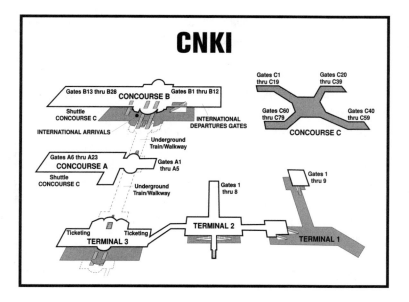

Other Airports

Lunken Airport (262 Wilmer Ave., 513/321-4132), located on a huge flood-plain next to the Ohio River, was formerly a polo field used by World War I pilots to land their planes. A runway was built in 1925, and five years later Lunken Municipal Airport was dedicated, soon becoming home base for American Airlines. Its geographical location prevented it from becoming Cincinnati's major airport since periodic floods earned it the nickname "Sunken Lunken." It's now used primarily for corporate, charter, and private planes. Flying lessons are also offered.

Train Service

The only Amtrak train that passes through Cincinnati travels between Chicago, Illinois, and Washington, D.C. The Chicago-bound train runs

The Hollow Earth Theory

John Cleves Symmes II, nephew and namesake of one of Cincin-nati's founding fathers, was convinced that the Earth was hollow and that it contained "warm and rich land, stocked with thrifty vegetables and animals, if not men." He also believed that the way to get to it was through the two poles. He spent years trying to get Congress to finance expeditions, but his efforts were in vain.

Symmes' followers wanted to call the inside of the Earth Symmzonia, and one of them, J. N. Reynolds, managed to raise funds from the private sector to finance a trip to the South Pole. The expedition was stalled early on because of the unnavigable ice. Worse still, his crew mutinied and dumped the luckless ex-plorer somewhere on the coast of South America. An American warship happened upon him some time later and brought him back to the United States. When Symmes died, he was buried in Hamilton; his grave is marked by a monument displaying a hol-low sphere.

on Monday, Thursday, and Saturday, leaving Cincinnati at 1:40 a.m. and arriving in Chicago at 9:45 a.m. Chicago time. The Washington-bound train runs on Sunday, Wednesday, and Friday, leaving Cincinnati at 5:44 a.m. and arriving in Washington at 8:10 p.m. Trains depart from Union Terminal, 1301 Western Avenue, Queensgate. For more information, call 800/872-7245.

Interstate and Regional Bus Service

Greyhound is the major bus company serving the Queen City and providing access to the contiguous United States and Canada. It's located at 1005 Gilbert Avenue just east of downtown, on the west side of I-71. For more information, call 513/352-6020 or 800/231-2222.

Hyatt Regency Cincinnati

3

WHERE TO STAY

Greater Cincinnati has more than 18,500 rooms of hotel space. Only seven of the major hotels are located downtown, however, and they are considerably more expensive than the outlying ones. If you plan to stay at one of the downtown hotels, be sure to book your room well in advance, since they sell out quickly—especially when there is a convention in town. If you're a corporate traveler and you find yourself shut out of downtown, you might want to look for a hotel near the Sharonville Convention Center. These hotels do not fill up as quickly as their downtown counterparts, they tend to be more reasonably priced, and they are only a 20-minute drive from the city center. The most notable hotel outside the downtown area is the Vernon Manor, a luxurious hostelry located close to the University of Cincinnati, often used to house visiting professors and lecturers.

If you want to be close to the city without the accompanying hustle and bustle, the riverside hotels in Northern Kentucky are a mere bridge trip away from downtown and boast the best views of the celebrated Cincinnati skyline. Also on the south side of the river are a number of bed-and-breakfasts, most of which are gorgeous historic homes loaded with charm and character. For travelers on a budget, cheap motels are plentiful, especially on Central Parkway and in Northern Kentucky. Wheelchair accessibility is indicated by the & symbol.

Price rating symbols:
$ **Under $50**
$$ **$50 to $75**
$$$ **$75 to 125**
$$$$ **$125 and up**

Note: Prices reflect a general range and may fluctuate depending on season and availability.

DOWNTOWN CINCINNATI

Hotels/Motels

THE CINCINNATIAN HOTEL
601 Vine St.
Cincinnati, OH 45202
513/381-3000 or 800/942-9000
$$$$

Designed by Samuel Hannaford in the French Second Empire style, The Cincinnatian opened in 1882 as The Palace. By 1983, however, this grand old hotel had become a dilapidated shell of its former self and was almost set for demolition. A group of local investors came to its rescue and closed it down in the mid-1980s for a $23-million restoration. It reopened in 1987 with 147 rooms, eight suites, and a workout facility with a sauna, a fine dining restaurant with an Old World atmosphere, and a comfortable bar surrounded by low tables and overstuffed chairs. ᕕ (Downtown Cincinnati)

THE CROWNE PLAZA HOTEL
15 W. 6th St.
Cincinnati, OH 45202
513/381-4000
$$$

This hotel has undergone a succession of owners. Built in 1948 in the International style, it was originally adorned with works by Miro, Calder, and Steinberg. When it was sold to the Hilton chain in 1956, the works were donated to the Cincinnati Art Museum, where they can be viewed today. Now owned by Holiday Inn, it features 336 rooms, 38 suites, a fitness center with a sauna, the Queen City Café, and an eighth-floor Lobby Bar. Check-in is a mite confusing since the lobby is situated on the eighth floor. The eighteenth-floor Gourmet Room, once one of the finest dining establishments in the city, is now used for private functions. ᕕ (Downtown Cincinnati)

GARFIELD SUITES HOTEL
2 Garfield Pl.
Cincinnati, OH 45202
513/421-3355
$$$$

Built in 1982 in the International style, the 140-suite hotel sits on the corner of Garfield Park opposite the recently expanded Cincinnati Public Library. A fitness center, the Garfield Deli, and the Garfield Bar are located within the building, as is Le Boxx Café. Room service is provided by Le Boxx and by the Longhorn Steakhouse, located half a block south on Vine Street. ᕕ (Downtown Cincinnati)

HYATT REGENCY CINCINNATI
151 W. 5th St.
Cincinnati, OH 45202
513/579-1234
$$$$

Connected to the skywalk system and sharing quarters with Saks Fifth Avenue, the 22-story, International-style building opened in March 1984, with 487 rooms, 13 suites, Findlay's (a casual restaurant which serves lunch and breakfast), Champs Italian Chophouse (a fine-dining establishment that serves lunch and dinner), Champ's Lounge, a heated indoor swimming pool, and a fitness center. ᕕ (Downtown Cincinnati)

OMNI NETHERLAND PLAZA
35 W. 5th St.
Cincinnati, OH 45202
513/421-9100 or 800/843-6664
$$$$

Housed within the Carew Tower, Cincinnati's tallest building, the Omni Netherland was built in 1930 in the American Modern style with art deco motifs. Former guests include

DOWNTOWN CINCINNATI

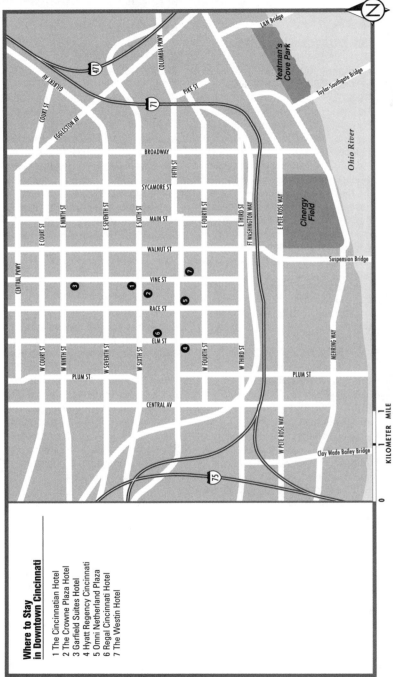

**Where to Stay
in Downtown Cincinnati**

1 The Cincinnatian Hotel
2 The Crowne Plaza Hotel
3 Garfield Suites Hotel
4 Hyatt Regency Cincinnati
5 Omni Netherland Plaza
6 Regal Cincinnati Hotel
7 The Westin Hotel

Eleanor Roosevelt, presidents Truman and Eisenhower, Bing Crosby, and Winston Churchill. When the Hilton chain took over in 1956 it made some needed improvements but also some misguided decorating choices, namely covering the beautiful terra-cotta walls with vinyl wallpaper and carpeting over the terrazzo floors. By 1981 the Omni's reputation had suffered and management was turned over to Dufey Hotels, who closed the facility down and spent $28 million on a two-year restoration.

In 1983 the Omni reopened with 621 guest rooms and 13 suites. The Omni's two restaurants—Orchids at the Palm Court and the more casual Café at the Palm Court—share the same room, as does its cocktail bar, the Lounge at the Palm Court. The Orchids' Sunday brunch is not to be missed, but be sure to make advance reservations to ensure a table. Guests also have access to the Carew Tower Fitness Center in the basement, which features an indoor swimming pool. ♿ (Downtown Cincinnati)

REGAL CINCINNATI HOTEL
150 W. 5th St.
Cincinnati, OH 45202
513/352-2100 or 800/876-2100
$$$
The International-style hotel was built in 1970 and known as The Clarion until October 1995, when new management took over. Since then it has been renovated and now sports a new name, 887 rooms, 32 suites, two restaurants—the revolving Seafood 32 and the more casual Elm Street Grill—and High Spirits, a cocktail lounge with an excellent view of the city. Connected to the Dr. Albert B. Sabin Convention Center by the skywalk, the Regal also offers an outdoor swimming pool; guests have access to Moore's Nautilus, located on the skywalk above 5th and Race Streets. ♿ (Downtown Cincinnati)

THE WESTIN HOTEL
At Fountain Square
Cincinnati, OH 45202
513/621-7700
$$$$
This International-style hotel, built in 1981, sits on the site of the Albee Theater directly south of Fountain Square. The 448-room, 18-suite hotel's restaurant and cocktail lounge both overlook the Square: the Albee Restaurant is on the second level and the 5th and Vine Street Bar is on the street level with outdoor seating. The Westin is connected to the skywalk system on the second floor and features a workout room. There is also a swimming pool on the seventeenth floor. Check-in is on the second floor. ♿ (Downtown Cincinnati)

TRIVIA

When Winston Churchill stayed at the Omni Netherland Plaza in 1932, he requested blueprints of the yellow-tiled bathroom in his room so that he could build one of his own when he got back to England.

The Westin Hotel, Birthplace of *The Jerry Springer Show*

British-born talk-show host Jerry Springer moved to the Queen City soon after he graduated from Northwestern Law School. He was elected to the city council in 1971, and while in office he engaged the services of a prostitute. Unfortunately for him, he made the mistake of paying her with a check, and the scandal soon hit the local newspapers, causing Springer to confess to his misdeed at a 1974 news conference. Undeterred by their councilman's lack of good sense, the voters elected him mayor of Cincinnati by a huge landslide three years later.

In 1981 he resigned his position to become news anchorman for the local NBC affiliate, WLWT-TV. In 1991 Springer jumped on the talk-show bandwagon and began taping The Jerry Springer Show at Cincinnati's Westin Hotel. The show became a big success and was hastily moved to a bigger market, Chicago, a year later.

UPTOWN CINCINNATI

Hotels/Motels

BUDGET HOST TOWN CENTER MOTEL
3356 Central Pkwy.
Cincinnati, OH 45225
513/559-1600
$

This 56-room motel is a five-minute drive from downtown and features the recently opened Pit Stop cocktail lounge and an outdoor swimming pool. க் (Uptown Cincinnati)

CENTRAL HOTEL AND SUITES
4747 Montgomery Rd.
Cincinnati, OH 45212
513/351-6000 or 800/292-2079
$$$

This 146-room hotel—owned by Frisch's Big Boy—is in the city of Norwood, about 7 miles north of downtown. There's a Frisch's restaurant next door, but for more upscale dining a Dockside VI Seafood Restaurant is inside the building. The hotel also features an outdoor pool, and banquet facilities for up to 400 people. Guests who want access to a fitness facility can obtain passes to the local YMCA, which is within walking distance. க் (Uptown Cincinnati)

CINCINNATI TRAVELODGE
3244 Central Pkwy.
Cincinnati, OH 45225
513/559-1800 or 800/578-7878
$$

Situated just outside downtown, this no-frills motel has 71 rooms and an outdoor swimming pool. Although there are no dining facilities within the complex, a Frisch's Big Boy restaurant can be found next door. (Uptown Cincinnati)

DAYS INN CINCINNATI
2880 Central Pkwy.
Cincinnati, OH 45225
513/559-0400 or 800/325-2525
$$

Located just north of downtown, this 103-room motel, complete with outdoor swimming pool, is geared toward those who aren't concerned with luxury but who want to be close to the city without paying downtown prices. (Uptown Cincinnati)

INTERSTATE MOTEL
3035 W. McMicken Ave.
Cincinnati, OH 45215
513/559-0600
$

A small motel with a mere 34 rooms, this accommodation is for the bare-bones traveler. Ten minutes from downtown, the motel's main attractions are its affordability and satellite TV. ♿ (Uptown Cincinnati)

VERNON MANOR HOTEL
400 Oak St.
Cincinnati, OH 45219
513/281-3300
$$$$

Opened in 1924, this luxurious hotel was reputedly modeled after the Hatfield House, a stately home in England. After a multimillion-dollar makeover in the 1980s, the 173-room, 58-suite hotel has regained its former reputation for excellence and is often used by the nearby University of Cincinnati to house visiting professors. The Forum Restaurant has one of

the city's best Sunday brunches, but be sure to make reservations in advance. For libations, visit the Beagle Lounge, which provides guests with complimentary hors d'oeuvres.

There is a veiled reference to the Vernon Manor in the movie *Rain Man* when Dustin Hoffman's character refers to Kmart's location as being 400 Oak Street, an inside joke for the cast and crew who were housed there during the filming. Although the hotel has no fitness facilities, it provides access and transportation to downtown's Carew Tower Health Club, which features an indoor swimming pool. ♿ (Uptown Cincinnati)

Bed and Breakfasts

ARLENE'S STONE PORCH BED AND BREAKFAST
1934 Hopkins Ave.
Cincinnati, OH 45212
513/531-4204
$$

The Cincinnatian Hotel, p. 33

The Cincinnatian Hotel

Empty Nest Bed and Breakfast

Built in 1889, this Norwood home first belonged to Judge Aaron McNeil and is now run as a bed-and-breakfast by Helen and Dennis Wagner. A complimentary full country breakfast is provided each morning and served in the dining room or east-facing breakfast room. A screened-in patio with comfortable seating and a hot tub is also available for guests. No smoking or pets. (Uptown Cincinnati)

EMPTY NEST BED
AND BREAKFAST
2707 Ida Ave.
Cincinnati, OH 45212
513/631-3494
$$
This turn-of-the-century Victorian bed-and-breakfast has two guest areas: the North Suite, with two adjoining bedrooms, and the South Room, with a sitting area, desk, and king-size brass bed. Both suites have private bathrooms. Owners Maryann and Hank Burwinkel bring coffee, herbal tea, or hot chocolate to your bedroom door in the morning and serve a home-cooked breakfast in the dining room between 7 and 9:30 a.m. Guests have access to a refrigerator, TV, and telephone. No smoking or pets. (Uptown Cincinnati)

PARKER HOUSE
2323 Ohio Ave.
Cincinnati, OH 45219
513/579-8236
$$
Located two blocks south of the University of Cincinnati campus and 1 mile north of downtown, this Queen Anne–style home was built for Charles Hoefinghoff, a molder from Gleiwitz-Schleisen, Germany, who immigrated to Cincinnati in 1854 and established a foundry. Decorated with period furniture, the Parker has 12-foot-high ceilings and murals by Francis Pedretti (1828–1891). Owners Mark and Patricia Parker provide complimentary breakfasts, and some rooms have private bathrooms. Free parking is also available. (Uptown Cincinnati)

PROSPECT HILL
BED AND BREAKFAST
408 Boal St.
Cincinnati, OH 45210
513/421-4408
$$$

This restored 1867 Italianate townhouse is situated in the Prospect Hill National Historic District, mere minutes away from the heart of downtown. Its four rooms are decorated with period antiques, and the decks have a spectacular view of the city. Upon arrival, fresh fruit and cookies are provided, and each morning a full breakfast buffet is served. Other amenities include TVs, fax machines, wood-burning fireplaces, a garden, and a hot tub. (Uptown Cincinnati)

EAST CINCINNATI

Hotels/Motels

AJ'S ROADHOUSE
6735 Kellogg Ave.
Cincinnati, OH 45230
513/231-2447
$

Built in the 1920s, this motel has recently been remodeled and now has 11 singles, two doubles, and one small efficiency. It's best known for its restaurant, also called AJ's Roadhouse, a popular surf-and-turf hangout that serves breakfast on the weekends and lunch and dinner daily, with karaoke on Wednesday and Friday nights. (East Cincinnati)

AMERISUITES CINCINNATI
BLUE ASH
11435 Reed Hartman Hwy.
Blue Ash, OH 45241
513/489-3666
$$$

All 128 suites are equipped with phones, TVs, refrigerators, microwaves, wet bars, and coffeemakers with coffee. Other amenities include an outdoor pool and laundry facilities. Guests receive a complimentary continental breakfast and have access to a local health spa. Meeting facilities are also available. The "Taking Care of Business Suites" have dual speaker phone lines, snacks, office supplies, and executive desks and chairs. ♿ (East Cincinnati)

BEST WESTERN
MARIEMONT INN
6880 Wooster Pike
Cincinnati, OH 45241
513/271-2100
$$

This Tudor-style 58-room hotel is located in Mariemont, an English-style village originally built for working-class people but now an upscale community in the eastern part of town. Within the building is the National Exemplar Restaurant—run by Cincinnati's Comisar family, who also own the Maisonette, La Normandie, and the nearby Bistro Gigi—and Southerby's Pub, a lounge with overstuffed sofas and a fireplace. Set at the corner of a square, this inn is within walking distance of a movie theater, an ice-cream parlor, and other village shops. (East Cincinnati)

BLUE ASH HOTEL AND
CONFERENCE CENTER
5901 Pfeiffer Rd.
Cincinnati, OH 45242
513/793-4500
$$

Located near Paramount's King's Island, this hotel has 217 rooms, an indoor pool, Café 71 restaurant, and the Oasis lounge. All rooms have on-demand movies and in-room Nintendo. ♿ (East Cincinnati)

GREATER CINCINNATI

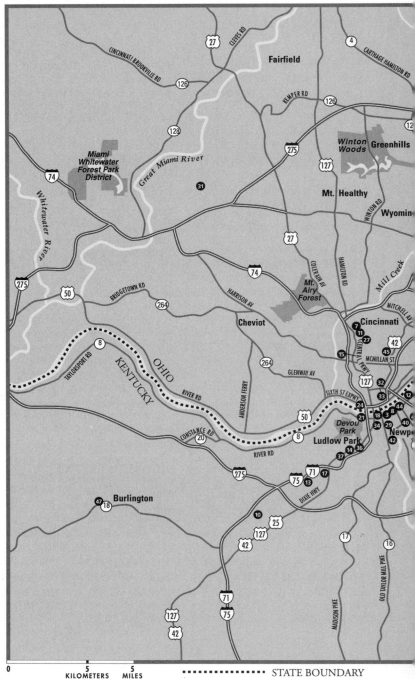

0   5   5
KILOMETERS MILES   •••••••••••••••• STATE BOUNDARY

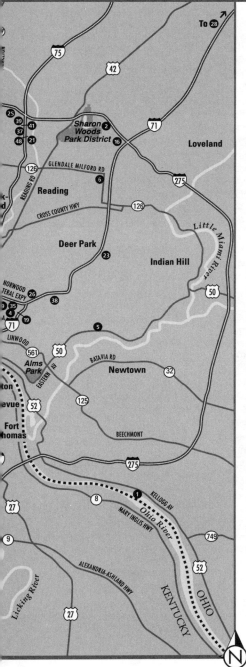

Where to Stay in Greater Cincinnati

1 AJ's Roadhouse
2 Amerisuites Cincinnati Blue Ash
3 Amos Shinkle Townhouse
4 Arlene's Stone Porch Bed and Breakfast
5 Best Western Mariemont Inn
6 Blue Ash Hotel and Conference Center
7 Budget Host Town Center Hotel
8 Carneal House Inn
9 Central Hotel and Suites
10 Chandler Inn
11 Cincinnati Travelodge
12 Comfort Suites
13 Cross Country Inn
14 Days Inn
15 Days Inn Cincinnati
16 Doubletree Guest Suites
17 The Drawbridge Inn and Convention Center
18 Embassy Suites Hotel
19 Empty Nest Bed and Breakfast
20 Gateway Bed and Breakfast
21 Hampton Inn Cincinnati
22 The Hannaford
23 Harley Hotel of Cincinnati
24 Holiday Inn
25 Homewood Suites
26 Howard Johnson Inn East
27 Interstate Motel
28 Kings Manor Inn
29 Licking Riverside Bed and Breakfast
30 Mary's Belle View Inn
31 Paradise Gardens
32 Parker House
33 Prospect Hill Bed and Breakfast
34 Quality Hotel Riverview
35 Quality Hotel Central
36 Ramada Inn
37 Red Roof
38 Red Roof Inn
39 Residence Inn by Marriott
40 Sandford House Bed and Breakfast
41 Signature Inn
42 Summer House
43 Taylor Spinks House
44 Travelodge Cincinnati Riverfront
45 Vernon Manor Hotel
46 Weller Haus Bed and Breakfast
47 Willis Graves Bed and Breakfast
48 Woodfield Inn and Suites

DOUBLETREE GUEST SUITES
6300 Kemper Rd.
Cincinnati, OH 45241
513/489-3636
$$$

Located near Paramount's King's Island, the Doubletree has 151 suites, all of which have two color TVs, coffee- and tea-makers, and refrigerators with snacks and beverages. Guests also receive freshly baked chocolate-chip cookies on arrival. For business travelers, there are two meeting rooms that can seat up to 85 people and six suites designed for 15 people. Other amenities include an indoor/outdoor heated pool, a fully equipped health club with a Jacuzzi, and the Bistro Bar and Grill. ᶼ (East Cincinnati)

HAMPTON INN
10900 Crowne Point Dr.
Cincinnati, OH 45241
513/771-6888
$$$

With 130 rooms, two of which are specially designed for handicapped people, the Hampton is near Sharon Woods. All rooms come with clock-radios, cable TV, and well-lit desk areas. Recreational facilities include an outdoor pool, a Moore's Fitness Center, and a golf course. Guests receive a complimentary continental breakfast, a *USA Today*, and the *Wall Street Journal* each morning. The inn also has a dry-cleaning service. ᶼ (East Cincinnati)

HARLEY HOTEL OF CINCINNATI
820 Montgomery Rd.
Cincinnati, OH 45236
513/793-4300
$$

Next to Kenwood Towne Centre, this 152-room hotel has both indoor and outdoor heated swimming pools, a whirlpool, saunas, lighted tennis courts, and Sigee's Restaurant and Lounge. Guests receive a complimentary morning paper Monday through Friday. Some rooms are non-smoking. ᶼ (East Cincinnati)

HOMEWOOD SUITES
2670 N. Kemper Rd.
Cincinnati, OH 45241
513/772-8737
$$$

All 111 suites offer microwave ovens, refrigerators, dishwashers, coffee-makers, utensils, place settings, two TVs, VCRs, dining areas, full-size sleeper sofas, plus irons and ironing boards. Guests receive a free pantry breakfast and *USA Today* each morning. Evenings include a social hour with complimentary hors d'oeuvres and beverages. Amenities include an exercise room, sports court and swimming pool, an on-site convenience store, guest laundry, and complimentary grocery-shopping service. There are three types of suites: the Homewood Suite (with a king-size bed or two double beds), the Master Suite (with a fireplace, expanded living area, king-size bed or two double beds), and the Guest suite (expanded living area, king-size bed or two double beds, no fireplace). ᶼ (East Cincinnati)

HOWARD JOHNSON INN EAST
5410 Ridge Ave.
Cincinnati, OH 45213
513/631-8500 or 800/IGO-HOJO
$$

This 120-room hotel has one suite equipped with a Jacuzzi. A Hooligan's Pub is on the premises and a Denny's 24-hour restaurant within walking distance. Other amenities include an outdoor swimming pool; free HBO, ESPN, TNT, TBS, and CNN; guest laundry; and a complimentary *USA Today*. 🕭 (East Cincinnati)

QUALITY HOTEL CENTRAL
4747 Montgomery Rd.
Norwood, OH 45212
513/351-6000
$$
This 146-room hotel offers one suite, a lounge, an outdoor swimming pool, and Dockside VI Seafood Restaurant, a quality surf-and-turf establishment that was voted "Best" by *Cincinnati Magazine* twice in one year. A YMCA within walking distance accepts visitors' room keys as passes. 🕭 (East Cincinnati)

RED ROOF INN
5300 Kennedy Ave.
Cincinnati, OH 45213
513/531-6589 or 800/THE-ROOF
$$
This 80-room hotel has both smoking and nonsmoking rooms, all with free ESPN, Showtime, and CNN. Guests receive complimentary coffee and a copy of *USA Today* in the lobby each morning. Cribs are provided free of charge. Pets are welcome, but they must be under 25 pounds and caged if left in the room. 🕭 (East Cincinnati)

WOODFIELD INN AND SUITES
11029 Dowlin Dr.
Cincinnati, OH 45241
513/771-0300
$$$
Located near the Sharonville Convention Center, all of Woodfield's 151 suites have TVs, irons and ironing boards, a phone, hair dryers, microwaves, minifridges, and coffeemakers. Guests receive a complimentary continental breakfast and evening cocktails. Other amenities include a fitness facility on the premises with an indoor pool and a whirlpool. Small children can play in the indoor Kids' Town USA and adults can enjoy the Billiard Room. Services include guest laundry and valet dry-cleaning. Non-smoking suites and conference facilities are also available. 🕭 (East Cincinnati)

Tip of de Timz

In 1848 the five Longley brothers began publishing a new magazine called Tip of de Timz *in an effort to sway the American public to abandon traditional spelling in favor of phonetic spelling. The brothers also founded the short-lived American Phonetic Society, which, before its dissolution in 1862, produced phonetic translations of several classics, including Pope's* Essay on Man *and Oliver Goldsmith's* The Vicar of Wakefield. *Perhaps the catalyst for the Cincinnati brothers' intense dislike of traditional spelling was the rather bizarre names that their parents gave them: Servetus, Septimus, Elias, Cyrenius, and Alcander.*

Parker House, p. 38

Bed and Breakfasts

KINGS MANOR INN
1826 Church St.
Kings Mills, OH 45034
513/459-9959
$$$
This turn-of-the-century manor house was built by Colonel George C. King and is registered as one of Ohio's historic structures. Four rooms are available: the Evangeline Room, with rose walls, lace curtains, a stained-glass window, an oriental rug, period antiques, and an adjoining bath; the Audrenia Room, a two-room suite with period antiques and a hand-carved mantle; the Colonel George King Room, decorated in jewel-green and burgundy with an adjoining bath; and the Scarlett Room, with both a queen-size and a day bed, private bath, pink marble shower, and whirlpool tub. Guests can relax in the Sun Room with TV, refreshments, and board games. Kings Mill is north of the I-275 belt and close to Lebanon, Waynesville,

and Paramount's King's Island. Senior citizen discounts. (East Cincinnati)

VICTORIA INN
3567 Shaw Ave.
Cincinnati, OH 45208
513/321-3567
$$$
This bed-and-breakfast, run by Tom Possert and Debra Moore, has three rooms and one suite; all have private phones, cable TV, and private baths. The Victoria Room has hand-carved 1880s furniture, an adjoining whirlpool bath, and a TV. The Country Manor Room has a private screened-in porch that overlooks the pool. The English Garden Room offers turn-of-the-century furnishings, a vanity desk, an overstuffed chair, and a clawfoot tub. The Wedgewood Room has dark mahogany furnishings and a featherbed. Guests have access to a fax machine, copier, and refrigerator. Breakfast is brought to rooms or served in the dining room. There's an outdoor pool located on the premises and a workout facility nearby—the Cincinnati Sports Club. If you like to jog, you can join the owners for a run in Hyde Park. (East Cincinnati)

WEST CINCINNATI

Hotels/Motels

HOLIDAY INN CINCINNATI
800 W. 8th St.
Cincinnati, OH 45203
513/241-8660
$$$
Located just west of downtown, this 244-room hotel has two suites and eight executive guest rooms. All

rooms have TVs and free HBO movies. Other amenities include Corporate Corner Restaurant, banquet facilities, free parking, a lounge, and an outdoor swimming pool. ♿ (West Cincinnati)

MOTEL 6
2000 E. Kemper Rd.
Cincinnati, OH 45241
513/772-5944 or 800/466-8356
$

Just half a mile from the Sharonville Convention Center and 15 minutes from Paramount's King's Island, this no-frills motel has 126 units. Amenities include an outdoor pool and a coin-operated laundry. ♿ (West Cincinnati)

RED ROOF
11345 Chester Rd.
Cincinnati, OH 45241
513/771-5141
$$

Located 15 minutes from downtown, this 108-room hotel is adjacent to the Queen City Racket Club, for which guests can obtain $6 day passes. All rooms have free ESPN, Showtime, and CNN. Guests receive free coffee and a complimentary *USA Today* in the lobby each morning. Pets are welcome, but they must be under 25 pounds and caged if left in the room. Both smoking and nonsmoking rooms are available. ♿ (West Cincinnati)

RESIDENCE INN BY MARRIOTT
11689 Chester Rd.
Cincinnati, OH 45246
513/771-2525
$$

Located near the Sharonville Convention Center, all 144 suites come with fully equipped kitchens and voice mail; some have living areas with a wood-burning fireplaces. Guests can obtain complimentary passes to the nearby Queen City Racket Club, which has an outdoor pool, a whirlpool, and sports courts. In the morning, guests receive a complimentary continental breakfast and a free newspaper. Also available are complimentary grocery-shopping service, daily housekeeping, and same-day valet service. ♿ (West Cincinnati)

SIGNATURE INN
11385 Chester Rd.
Cincinnati, OH 45246
513/772-7877 or 800/822-5252
$$

On a site next to the Sharonville Convention Center, the Signature Inn's 130 rooms all include cable TV and phones. Recreational facilities include an outdoor swimming pool and access to the nearby Queen City Racket Club ($3 with a room key). Guests receive a complimentary continental breakfast and a free *USA Today* and *Wall Street Journal.* Nonsmoking rooms are available and the hotel provides guests with an airport shuttle service. ♿ (West Cincinnati)

Campgrounds

PARADISE GARDENS
6100 Blue Rock Rd.
Cincinnati, OH 45247
513/385-4189
$

This is a nudist resort set on 35 acres of wooded land with camping facilities, whirlpool, sauna, and pool. The lake is not intended for swimming; paddle boats are available for use. Dogs and cats are allowed. Exit 31 off I-275; the Blue Rock Road, Ronald Reagan Cross Country Highway Exit. (just outside West Cincinnati zone)

SOUTH OF THE RIVER

Hotels/Motels

COMFORT SUITES
420 Riverboat Row
Newport, KY 41071
606/291-6700
$$$
One of the newest additions to the Newport riverfront, this motel has 124 rooms, nine of which have Jacuzzis. Some rooms have river views. Other amenities include an exercise facility and guest laundry facilities. ♿ (South of the River)

CROSS COUNTRY INN
2350 Royal Dr.
Ft. Mitchell, KY 41017
606/341-2090
$
This inn has a drive-through check-in/out, and all of their 106 rooms come equipped with cable TV, ESPN, and Showtime. There's also a heated outdoor pool. Nonsmoking rooms are available. (South of the River)

DAYS INN
1945 Dixie Hwy.
Ft. Wright, KY 41011
606/341-8801
$
This no-frills motel offers 115 rooms, some nonsmoking, and an outdoor pool. Small pets allowed. ♿ (South of the River)

THE DRAWBRIDGE INN AND CONVENTION CENTER
I-75 at Buttermilk Pike
Ft. Mitchell, KY 41017
606/341-2800 or 800/354-9793
$$$
One of the finest hotels in Northern Kentucky, the 500-room Drawbridge Estate is located next to the Oldenberg Brewery Complex and has three quality on-site restaurants and a lounge: Josh's, the Gatehouse Taverne, the 24-hour Chaucers, and the Crossbow Tavern. Other amenities include pools (two outdoor, one indoor); tennis, basketball, and volleyball courts; whirlpool; sauna; game room; and full-service fitness center. All rooms have cable TV with Showtime and HBO, and room service is available. Several conventions meet here and use the London Hall Ballroom, which can accommodate up to 1,500 people. ♿ (South of the River)

EMBASSY SUITES HOTEL
10 E. RiverCenter Blvd.
Covington, KY 41011
606/261-8400
$
Next to the Ohio River, just west of the John A. Roebling Suspension Bridge, this recently built hotel has 226 suites, all of which have microwaves, wet bars, coffeemakers, refrigerators, two TVs with cable and in-room movies, and two-line telephones with a computer data port. Amenities include an

---

TRIVIA

Susie, the world's first trained gorilla, arrived in Cincinnati on the Graf Zeppelin in 1931 and took up residence in a four-room apartment, where she was taught to use a knife and fork. Susie died in 1947.

Hyatt Regency Cincinnati, p. 33

indoor pool, sun deck, sauna, and fitness center. The E Room Restaurant and Lounge is on the lobby level with a view of the river. The Behle St. Café, a Cajun restaurant, is not part of the hotel but is just west of the lobby. Guests receive a complimentary cooked-to-order breakfast and a free newspaper each morning. Valet and room service are provided. ⅃ (South of the River)

HAMPTON INN
200 Crescent Ave.
Covington, KY 41011
606/581-7800
$$$

One of the most recent additions to Covington's hotel scene, this Hampton Inn has 151 rooms, an indoor pool, and a fitness room. Guests are provided with a complimentary continental breakfast and a free copy of *USA Today* each morning. ⅃ (South of the River)

THE HANNAFORD
803 E. 6th St.

Newport, KY 41071
606/491-9600
$$

Located in the Mansion Hill Historic District on a 3-acre private estate mere minutes away from the Daniel Beard Bridge, this familiar landmark has been newly renovated into 60 corporate suites and apartments. Amenities include a clubhouse with a large swimming pool, basketball and volleyball courts, a playground, permanent outdoor cooking grills, and free private parking. (South of the River)

HOLIDAY INN
600 W. 3rd St.
Covington, KY 41011
606/291-4300
$$$

On the west side of Covington, close to the Brent Spence Bridge, this hotel has 153 rooms and three two-room suites. All rooms have irons and ironing boards, TVs, two phones with data ports, and stocked coffeemakers. Guests receive a free continental breakfast each morning. Other amenities include an new outdoor pool, exercise facilities, a sun deck, the Greenery Restaurant, free parking, and room service. ⅃ (South of the River)

HOLIDAY INN
2100 Dixie Hwy.
Ft. Mitchell, KY 41011
606/331-1500
$$$

This 214-room hotel is distinguished by its Holidome Indoor Recreation Center, which includes an indoor pool, whirlpool, arcade, shuffleboard, and Ping-Pong tables. All rooms have HBO, Disney, CNN, ESPN, and On-Command Video. Other amenities include J.T. Ashley's Restaurant and

Lounge and complimentary airport transportation. ♿ (South of the River)

QUALITY HOTEL RIVERVIEW
666 W. 5th St.
Covington, KY 41011
606/491-1200
$$$

This riverside hotel is distinguished by its eighteenth-floor revolving restaurant, which provides patrons with a bird's-eye view of the Ohio River Valley. The lounge, Kelley's Landing, looks onto the outdoor pool. All of the 236 rooms come with Showtime and HBO, and there is also an indoor pool. Nonsmoking rooms are available. ♿ (South of the River)

RAMADA INN
1939 Dixie Hwy.
Ft. Wright, KY 41011
606/331-1400
$

This 90-room motel allows pets but charges an extra $15 per night for the privilege. Amenities include an outdoor pool and Jacuzzi. (South of the River)

TRAVELODGE CINCINNATI RIVERFRONT
222 York St.
Newport, KY 41071
606/291-4434
$$

Located in Newport, close to the new Central Bridge, some of this motel's 104 rooms have a skyline view and all come with refrigerators and coffeemakers. The motel has an outdoor pool. (South of the River)

Bed and Breakfasts

AMOS SHINKLE TOWNHOUSE
215 Garrard St.

Covington, KY 41011
606/431-2118
$$$

Located in the Historic Riverside District, this Greco-Italianate home was built in 1854 by Amos Shinkle, a banker, philanthropist, developer, industrialist, and promoter of the John A. Roebling Suspension Bridge. It has seven opulent rooms. The Main House consists of the Amos Shinkle Room (with a whirlpool tub and crystal chandelier), the Sarah Shinkle Room, and the Bradford Shinkle Room. The Carriage House has four rooms: the Stable Room, the Carriage Room, the Tack Room, and the Hay Loft Room. All rooms are decorated with antique furniture and have private baths. Each morning your hosts, Bernie and Don, prepare their signature Covington dish: *goetta* and eggs. No pets. ♿ (South of the River)

CARNEAL HOUSE INN
405 E. 2nd St.
Covington, KY 41011
606/431-6130
$$$

Built in 1820–21 for Aaron G. Gano, this Federal-style house was sold to William W. Southgate, a lawyer, politician, and slave-owner. The house is rumored to have been a "station" on the underground railway, but modern historians say this is unlikely considering that it belonged to a pro-slavery family. Situated across the river from downtown Cincinnati in the Historic Licking Riverside District, it's now a bed-and-breakfast with four rooms (smoking and nonsmoking) and a lounge. Pets allowed. (South of the River)

CHANDLER INN
467 Erlanger Rd.
Erlanger, KY 41018

Crowne Plaza Cincinnati, p. 33

606/727-4777
$$$
Unlike most bed-and-breakfasts, Chandler Inn is not a converted house but was built expressly to be a bed-and-breakfast. The inn is owned by flight attendant Martha Ramsey, who recognized the need for a home away from home. There are 11 rooms and two suites, which are slightly larger with fireplaces and king-size beds. Guests receive a complimentary continental breakfast in the morning and homemade soup in the evening. All rooms have phones and private baths. Corporate and airline rates are available. ♿ (outside South of the River zone)

GATEWAY BED AND BREAKFAST
326 E. 6th St.
Newport, KY 41076
606/581-6447
$$$
This 1878 Italianate townhouse, recently restored by Ken and Sandy Clift, was the winner of the Great American Homes Award for bed-and-breakfast restoration from the National Trust for Historic Preservation. Its three rooms are on the second floor. Each room has a telephone, private bath, and TV with Showtime and HBO. Included in the price is a full breakfast. There is off-street parking, and access to a fax machine and a computer. No smoking or pets. (South of the River)

LICKING RIVERSIDE BED AND BREAKFAST
516 Garrard St.
Covington, KY 41011
606/291-0191 or 800/483-7822
$$$
Located on the east side of Covington, this bed-and-breakfast has two rooms and a suite, two of which come with a Jacuzzi. All three have private baths and TVs. (South of the River)

MARY'S BELLE VIEW INN
444 Van Voast St.
Bellevue, KY 41071

606/581-8337 or 800/483-7822
$$
All three rooms have private baths, private entrances, TVs, and VCRs. Guests can use the kitchen (equipped with a microwave, refrigerator, and table) and have access to a large deck with a Cincinnati skyline view. (South of the River)

SANDFORD HOUSE BED AND BREAKFAST
1026 Russell St.
Covington, KY 41011
606/291-9133
$$
This bed-and-breakfast, run by Dan and Linda Carter, is located in the Old Seminary Square District and is composed of a main building and its carriage house—both of which are listed on the National Register. The house was originally built on the Federal style in the early 1820s but was changed to a Victorian style with a mansard roof after an upper-story fire in the 1880s. Its original owner, Thomas Sandford, came to Kentucky

Prospect Hill Bed and Breakfast, p. 39

Prospect Hill Bed and Breakfast

from Virginia around 1790, acquired 300 acres of land in the Northern Kentucky area, attended the Second Constitutional Convention in 1779, and became the first Northern Kentuckian elected to the U.S. Congress. The main house has three rooms: a double room, a garden suite with a whirlpool bath, and a furnished apartment with a washer, dryer, and view of the Cincinnati skyline. The carriage house has two bedrooms, two baths, living/dining room, and kitchen. All rooms have private entrances, baths, and cable TV. No smoking. ♿ (South of the River)

SUMMER HOUSE
610 Sanford St.
Covington, KY 41011
606/431-3121
$$$
Located in the Historic Riverside District of Covington, this bed-and-breakfast has four suites. The Gardenside Suite has a private porch and Jacuzzi whirlpool bath, the Sandpiper Suite has a skylight, king-size bed, and sitting area; the Peachtree Suite features a private porch; and the Plantation Room has a private bath with a skylight and Jacuzzi whirlpool bath. A complimentary continental or full breakfast is served between 7 and 9 a.m. weekdays (8 to 10 a.m. weekends), and you can eat it in your room, the kitchen, the porch, or the dining room. Guests have access to cable TV and a library, and therapeutic massage is available by appointment. Checks not accepted. (South of the River)

TAYLOR SPINKS HOUSE
702 Overton St.
Newport, KY 41071
606/291-0092 or 888/675-0092
$$$

Two suites are housed in this 1878 Italianate mansion in Newport's East Row Historic District. Both suites have private baths; one has a Jacuzzi. The Back Suite, composed of two rooms, can hold up to four people and is ideal for a family or two couples. Guests receive a full or continental breakfast each morning. No pets. (South of the River)

WELLER HAUS
BED AND BREAKFAST
319 Poplar St.
Bellevue, KY 41073
606/431-6829
$$$

This family-operated B&B has five suites, a garden, and a lounge spread over two adjoining Victorian Gothic houses. Run by Mary and Vernon Weller, all rooms have private baths and guests have access to a phone, a fax machine, and kitchen facilities. Nancy's Garden Room has a Steamboat Gothic brass bed; the Rooftop

Suite has a private entrance to the second floor; the Church Steeple Suite accommodates up to four guests, with two rooms, art deco furnishings, and a private entrance; and the Dream Suite has a queen-size bed, a hidden water closet, and Jacuzzi bath for two. No smoking or pets. (South of the River)

WILLIS GRAVES
BED AND BREAKFAST
5825 N. Jefferson St.
Burlington, KY 41005
606/689-5096
$$$

A restored 160-year-old farmhouse set on 2 acres, this family-operated bed-and-breakfast has one suite and two bedrooms, all with private baths. Hostess Jean Brames cooks up a large breakfast each morning. The house is within walking distance of downtown Burlington, which is home to a variety of antique and craft shops. Take Exit 181 off I-75, the Florence/Burlington Exit. (South of the River)

4

WHERE TO EAT

Food is a passion for many Cincinnatians, and a wealth of restaurants caters to the grand diversity of tastes in the Queen City. The most famous of the city's fine restaurants is downtown's Maisonette, which consistently receives the Mobil Guide's most prestigious rating, the Five Star Award. Many other local restaurants rate three or four stars from Mobil, thanks in large part to the dedicated chefs who develop name recognition and gain loyal followings. If a celebrated chef changes establishments, Cincinnatians will follow—and the replacement at the original place will be scrutinized carefully.

Though you can find everything from French and Italian to Sri Lankan cuisine in the city, Cincinnati is probably best known for its chili, developed in 1922 by Macedonian immigrant Athanas Kiradjieff. Texans may argue, but Cincinnati is indeed the chili capital of the world, with more chili parlors per square mile than anywhere else.

This chapter begins with a list of restaurants organized by the type of food each offers. Each restaurant name is followed by an abbreviated zone designation in parentheses. Abbreviations are as follows: Downtown Cincinnati is DC; Uptown Cincinnati is UC; East Cincinnati is EC; West Cincinnati is WC; and South of the River is SR. The page numbers in the listings refer to the next section, where each restaurant is described in detail. In that section, restaurants are organized alphabetically by geographical zone. The price rating for each restaurant indicates how much you can expect to spend for a typical entrée. Wheelchair accessibility is indicated by the ♿ symbol.

Price rating symbols:
$	Under $10
$$	$10 to $20
$$$	$20 and up

Barbecue/Ribs
Montgomery Inn Boathouse (EC), p. 67

Breakfast
First Watch (DC, EC), p. 54
Hathaway's (DC), p. 56
Inn the Wood (UC), p. 63
Tucker's Restaurant (UC), p. 65

Burgers and more
Anchor Grill (SR), p. 69
Carol's Corner Café (DC), p. 54
The Diner (UC), p. 63
Rookwood Pottery (EC), p. 68

Cajun
Behle St. Café (SR), p. 69
Dee Felice Café (SR), p. 70

Chinese
China Gourmet (EC), p. 66
Pacific Moon Café (EC), p. 67
Wah Mee Chinese Restaurant (DC), p. 62

Contemporary
Boca Restaurant and Bar (WC), p. 68
Chateau Pomije (EC), p. 66
Coach and Four Restaurant (SR), p. 69
Coco's (SR), p. 69
DiJohn Restaurant and Bar (SR), p. 70
Petersen's Restaurant (DC, EC), p. 58
Pigall's Café (DC), p. 59
Plaza 600 (DC), p. 59
Washington Platform Saloon and Restaurant (DC), p. 62
The Waterfront (SR), p. 72
York Street International Café (SR), p. 73

Delis
Izzy's: The Original I (DC), p. 56
Mediterranean Foods (UC), p. 65
Scalea's (SR), p. 72

Fine Dining
Celestial Restaurant and Incline Lounge (EC), p. 66

Maisonette (DC), p. 57
Orchids at Palm Court (DC), p. 58
The Palace (DC), p. 58
Primavista (WC), p. 69

French
Bistro Gigi (EC), p. 65
La Normandie Taverne and Chop House (DC), p. 57
La Petite France (EC), p. 66
Maisonette (DC), p. 57

German
Café Vienna (EC), p. 66
Mecklenburg Gardens (UC), p. 65

Indian
Ambar India Restaurant (UC), p. 63
Anand Indian Restaurant (EC), p. 65
Mayura Indian Restaurant (UC), p. 64

Italian
Ciao Baby Cucina (DC), p. 54
Nicola's Ristorante Italiano (UC), p. 65
Pompilio's (SR), p. 71
Primavista (WC), p. 69
Spazzi (SR), p. 72

Japanese
Ko-Sho Japanese Restaurant (DC), p. 56
Samurai Japanese Steak and Seafood (DC), p. 59

Mediterranean
Corinthian Restaurant and Lounge (UC), p. 63
Mediterranean Foods (UC), p. 65

Mexican/Tex-Mex
Cactus Pear (UC), p. 63
Silvia's Mexican Restaurant (SR), p. 72

Pizza
La Rosa's Pizzerias (WC), p. 68
No Anchovies (UC), p. 65

Seafood
J's Fresh Seafood Restaurant (EC), p. 66

Seafood 32 (DC), p. 62

Spanish
Mallorca (DC), p. 57

Sri Lankan
Aralia (DC), p. 54

Steaks
Dante's Restaurant (WC), p. 68
Gatehouse Tavern (SR), p. 70
La Normandie Taverne and Chop
     House (DC), p. 57
The Precinct (EC), p. 67

Thai
Teak Thai Cuisine and Bar (EC), p. 68

Vegetarian-Friendly
Carol's Corner Café (DC), p. 54
Mullane's Parkside Café (DC), p. 58

DOWNTOWN CINCINNATI

ARALIA RESTAURANT
815 Elm St., Cincinnati
513/723-1217
$
Triset DeFonseka, Aralia's chef, came
to prominence in the Queen City with
the publication of her cookbook, *Easy
Cooking With Herbs and Spices*, and
her book signings were always popular events, partly because of her delicious food samples. Now people can
enjoy DeFonseka's Sri Lankan cuisine
within the comfort of a restaurant. The
entrées come with chutney and bas-
mati rice, and they go especially well
with ginger beer. Lunch Monday
through Friday; dinner Monday
through Saturday; brunch Saturday;
afternoon tea Tuesday through Saturday. (Downtown Cincinnati)

CAROL'S CORNER CAFÉ
825 Main St., Cincinnati

513/651-2667
$
This downtown hot-spot is constantly
packed. The menu is a cut above your
usual pub grub, with oversized vegetarian sandwiches and burgers. It's a
lively joint with an eclectic mix of
people. The cabaret club upstairs
showcases the talents of Carol her-
self singing torch songs and also offers improv comedy one or two
weekends a month. Carol's serves
food until 1 a.m.—later than most
downtown eateries. Lunch Monday
through Friday; brunch Sundays; dinner daily. Reservations not accepted.
& (Downtown Cincinnati)

CIAO BABY CUCINA
700 Walnut St., Cincinnati
513/929-0700
$$
This is one of the most popular new
eateries downtown, partly because of
its incredible layout. The kitchen is in
full view of the dining room, which is
spacious, loft-like, and very comfort-
able. The Italian American cuisine,
coupled with the European atmos-
phere, make for a very pleasant
evening. Try the *farfelle* with chicken
and gorgonzola—and if you're feeling
adventurous, the tuna Tartar is aw-
fully good, too. Reservations recom-
mended; lunch and dinner daily;
brunch on weekends. & (Downtown
Cincinnati)

FIRST WATCH
700 Walnut St., Cincinnati
513/721-4744
$
This clean, bright place has a friendly
atmosphere and some of the comforts
of home, including large pitchers of
iced water on the tables and coffee
served in huge flasks. Primarily a
breakfast spot, First Watch also serves

DOWNTOWN CINCINNATI

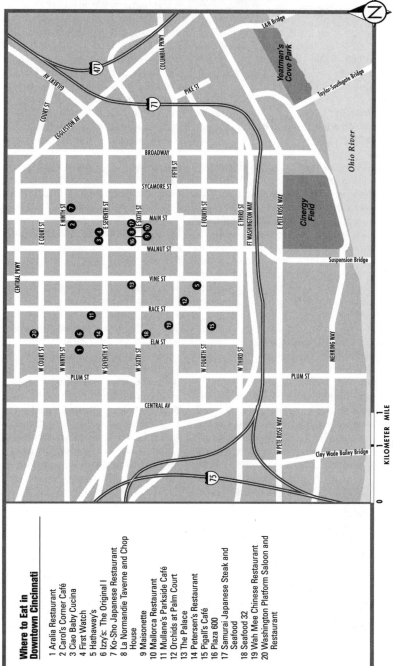

Where to Eat in Downtown Cincinnati

1 Aralia Restaurant
2 Carol's Corner Café
3 Ciao Baby Cucina
4 First Watch
5 Hathaway's
6 Izzy's: The Original I
7 Ko-Sho Japanese Restaurant
8 La Normandie Taverne and Chop House
9 Maisonette
10 Mallorca Restaurant
11 Mullane's Parkside Café
12 Orchids at Palm Court
13 The Palace
14 Petersen's Restaurant
15 Pigall's Café
16 Plaza 600
17 Samurai Japanese Steak and Seafood
18 Seafood 32
19 Wah Mee Chinese Restaurant
20 Washington Platform Saloon and Restaurant

sandwiches; the crepe dishes are excellent, and there are egg substitutes for the health-conscious. A second location is in the Rookwood Pavilion (2692 Madison Road, Norwood, 513/531-7430). Breakfast and lunch daily. Reservations not accepted. & (Downtown Cincinnati)

HATHAWAY'S
441 Vine St., Cincinnati
513/621-1332
$
Located in the Carew Tower Arcade, Hathaway's harkens back to the days of the old-style diners. The servers have worked there for years and are a show unto themselves. Be sure to sit at the counter or you'll miss the entertainment. The food is your standard diner fare: sandwiches, breakfast items, and soups. Breakfast and lunch daily. Reservations not accepted. & (Downtown Cincinnati)

IZZY'S: THE ORIGINAL I
800 Elm St., Cincinnati
513/721-4241
$
Izzy Kadetz was a legend in his lifetime and remains so even after his death. He and his wife, Rose, ran the business and would argue incessantly, much to the amusement of the customers. Also, prices weren't listed

on the menu or anywhere in the restaurant; Izzy would just charge you what he thought you could afford. The atmosphere is still boisterous. The potato pancakes are good and greasy, and the soups (especially Saturday's pea soup) are homemade and scrumptious. Pickles and sauerkraut are available free of charge on each table and the kosher-style sandwiches are at least 3 inches thick. Great meatloaf sandwiches and Reubens. The second location, also downtown, is at 612 Main Street, 513/241-6246. Lunch daily. Reservations not accepted. & (Downtown Cincinnati)

KO-SHO JAPANESE RESTAURANT
215 E. 9th St., Cincinnati
513/665-4950
$$
The sparse decor, inherited mostly from its Mexican predecessor, belies the quality of the dining experience. This is the place to come for sushi and sashimi. Best bets include the miso soup and the California roll (crab, avocado, and salmon roe). Although Ko-Sho's wine list is extensive, you'll want to try the sake—but beware: the prices are unlisted and a bottle of the good stuff can run you up to $25. Lunch Monday through Friday; dinner daily; reservations recommended. (Downtown Cincinnati)

TRIVIA

When Austrian Charles Fleischmann visited Cincinnati in 1865, he was disgusted to find that breadmakers leavened their product with fermented potato skins or stale beer. He moved to the Queen City with his brother, Maximillian, soon afterward and showed his Viennese yeast samples to distiller James Gaff. The three of them went into business together, and the rest is history: Fleischmann's Yeast.

Seafood 32 in the Regal Cincinnati Hotel, p. 62

LA NORMANDIE TAVERNE AND CHOP HOUSE
118 E. 6th St., Cincinnati
513/721-2761
$$

Owned by the Comisar family of Maisonette fame and located beneath that five-star restaurant, La Normandie shares a kitchen and a great many items with its acclaimed upstairs neighbor—but prices are more friendly for the casual diner. The London broil is especially good and the daily fish special is always outstanding. The bar has an Olde English atmosphere, and you can throw your peanut shells on the floor. Lunch Tuesday through Friday; dinner Monday through Saturday; closed Sundays; reservations recommended. (Downtown Cincinnati)

MAISONETTE
114 E. 6th St., Cincinnati
513/721-2260
$$$

Ask any Cincinnatian to name the best restaurant in town and you'll get the same answer—Maisonette, the place where Cincinnati's power brokers meet, greet, and eat. A national treasure, Maisonette is one of only 15 restaurants in North America to have earned Mobil's Five Star Award for 33 consecutive years. The service is impeccable and discreet. Literally every item on chef Jean Robert de Cavel's menu is delicious and beautifully presented. The rack of lamb is a local favorite. The service is impeccable. Lunch and dinner Monday through Saturday; closed Sunday; reservations required. &. (Downtown Cincinnati)

MALLORCA RESTAURANT
124 E. 6th St., Cincinnati
513/723-9506
$$

At this popular Spanish restaurant with an authentic Iberian atmosphere, the serving staff speak either Spanish, Portuguese, or both. The wine list is excellent and they even stock Vinho Verde, a young Portuguese white wine almost impossible to find in the United States. To its credit, the portions are enormous and the fish specials are fresh and well-prepared. Lunch and dinner daily; reservations recommended. ♿ (Downtown Cincinnati)

MULLANE'S PARKSIDE CAFÉ
723 Race St., Cincinnati
513/381-1331
$

This charming, laid-back restaurant, on the corner of Race and Garfield, is like a European café for American expatriates, with ever-changing art on the walls and tables that could be mistaken for art. The food is prepared from scratch and the soups are always good. The Greek salad, with its sesame-seed vinaigrette, is a perfect starter. Although this is not a strictly vegetarian restaurant, all meals can be tailored for vegans. The red beans and rice is also a good bet, as is the spinach sauté. There are many excellent seafood features in the evening, and requests for half portions are happily accepted. Best of all, the owner is often on hand to make sure that your dining experience is a pleasant one. Lunch Monday through Friday; dinner Monday through Saturday; closed Sunday. No credit cards; reservations not accepted. (Downtown Cincinnati)

ORCHIDS AT PALM COURT
Omni Netherland Plaza
35 W. 5th St., Cincinnati
513/421-9100
$$$

One of the most beautiful dining rooms in town, Orchids has high ceilings, art deco motifs, and huge two-story windows. If you're in town on a Sunday, be sure to come here for brunch. Omelets are made on request; pork tenderloin and rare roast beef are sliced by the attending chef. And if that's not to your taste, there are plenty of other options, including a vast array of seafood. For dinner, try the châteaubriand for two or the potato-encrusted halibut. If you're feeling really adventurous, get the fire-roasted antelope, which is served with tomato pecan waffles and a fresh blackberry peppercorn sauce. Lunch Monday through Saturday; brunch Sundays; dinner Tuesday through Saturday; reservations recommended. ♿ (Downtown Cincinnati)

THE PALACE
Cincinnatian Hotel
601 Vine St., Cincinnati
513/381-3000
$$$

The Palace is no ordinary hotel restaurant. It has a decidedly Old World feel, with gracious service and ornate surroundings, and offers American cuisine at its best. The tenderloin medallions over saffron potatoes with portabello mushrooms and braised leeks are a menu highlight, as is the grilled swordfish. Lunch Monday through Saturday; breakfast and dinner daily; reservations recommended. ♿ (Downtown Cincinnati)

PETERSEN'S RESTAURANT
700 Elm St., Cincinnati
513/723-1113
$$

This unpretentious eatery has an eclectic menu that borrows from many culinary traditions; it's best known for its black-bean burrito and its assortment of sumptuous desserts. The daily fish specials are always fresh and exquisitely prepared. Petersen's tends to get pretty busy on the weekends, but you can bide your time at the small but charming bar. There's also a Petersen's in Mt. Adams (1111 St. Gregory, Mt. Adams, 513/651-4777). Lunch Monday through Friday; dinner daily;

Top Ten Power Lunches in Cincinnati
by Tyrone K. Yates, Cincinnati Council member

1. **Orchids** at the Omni Netherland Plaza Hotel, 5th and Race Streets, Cincinnati, 513/421-9100.
2. **Maisonette**, 114 E. 6th St., Cincinnati, 513/721-2260.
3. **Celestial Restaurant and Incline Lounge**, 1071 Celestial St., Mt. Adams, 513/241-4455.
4. **Banker's Club**, Dubois Tower, Cincinnati, 513/651-3660.
5. **Rookwood Pottery**, 1077 Celestial St., Mt. Adams, 513/721-5456.
6. **Queen City Club**, 331 E. 4th St., Cincinnati, 513/621-2708.
7. **Petersen's**, 641 Walnut St., Cincinnati, 513/723-1113.
8. **Montgomery Inn Boathouse**, 925 Eastern Ave., Cincinnati, 513/721-7427.
9. **First Watch**, 2692 Madison Rd., Norwood, 513/531-7430.
10. **Busken Bakery**, 324 W. 9th St., Cincinnati, 513/651-5222.

closed Sunday; reservations recommended. ও (Downtown Cincinnati)

PIGALL'S CAFÉ
127 W. 4th St., Cincinnati
513/651-CAFE (651-2233)
$$
From the outside Pigall's looks like a quaint bistro, and the mural of Paris on the inside back wall reinforces its French feel. The cuisine, on the other hand, is American. The best item on the menu is the blackened salmon over pasta. Lunch Monday through Friday; dinner Monday through Saturday; reservations recommended. (Downtown Cincinnati)

PLAZA 600
600 Walnut St., Cincinnati
513/721-8600
$$

This is one of downtown's most exciting new restaurants—haute cuisine with a casual flair. Floor-to-ceiling glass windows look onto 6th and Walnut Streets, providing an airy atmosphere and a view of passers-by. The kitchen is a show of its own, with ringside seats for those who enjoy watching good food being made (with lots of fire and élan). The small bar, located in the front, is staffed by friendly and knowledgeable bartenders. The mussels in white wine make for a great appetizer, the daily risotto special is cooked to perfection, and be sure to leave room for the crème brûlée. Lunch Monday through Friday; dinner Monday through Saturday; closed Sunday. ও (Downtown Cincinnati)

SAMURAI JAPANESE
STEAK AND SEAFOOD

GREATER CINCINNATI

0   5   5
KILOMETERS   MILES
•••••••••••••••••• STATE BOUNDARY

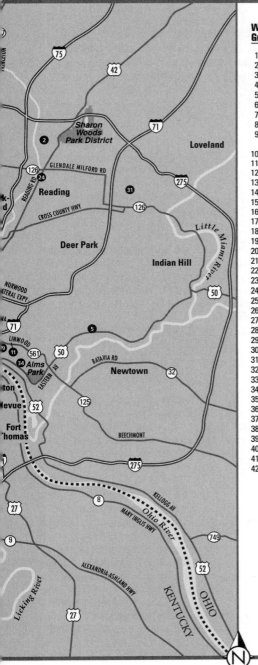

Where to Eat in Greater Cincinnati

1 Ambar India Restaurant
2 Anand Indian Restaurant
3 Anchor Grill
4 Behle St. Café
5 Bistro Gigi
6 Boca Restaurant and Bar
7 Cactus Pear
8 Café Vienna
9 Celestial Restaurant and Incline Lounge
10 Chateau Pomije
11 China Gourmet
12 Coach and Four Restaurant
13 Coco's
14 Corinthian Restaurant and Lounge
15 Dante's Restaurant
16 Dee Felice Café
17 DiJohn Restaurant and Bar
18 The Diner
19 First Watch
20 Gatehouse Tavern
21 Inn the Wood
22 J's Fresh Seafood Restaurant
23 La Rosa's Pizzerias
24 Le Petite France
25 Mayura Indian Restaurant
26 Mecklenburg Gardens
27 Mediterranean Foods
28 Montgomery Inn Boathouse
29 Nicola's Ristorante Italiano
30 No Anchovies
31 Pacific Moon Café
32 Petersen's Restaurant
33 Pompilio's
34 The Precinct
35 Primavista
36 Rookwood Pottery
37 Scalea's
38 Silvia's Mexican Restaurant
39 Teak Thai Cuisine and Bar
40 Tucker's Restaurant
41 Window on the Water
42 York Street International Café

TRIVIA

After years of unsuccessful experimentation with European grapes, Cincinnatian Nicholas Longworth finally struck gold with the native Catawba grape in 1825 and produced the nation's first champagne. Unfortunately, black rot destroyed his many acres of vines in the 1840s, bringing this flourishing industry to a sober halt.

126 E. 6th St., Cincinnati
513/421-1688
$$
When you walk into this dark, windowless restaurant, you feel like you're entering another world—and you are. The food is the show here, and you'll get to watch the chefs prepare your repast in front of your eyes. The hand-eye coordination of these culinary prestidigitators alone is worth the visit. Lunch Monday through Friday; dinner daily; reservations required. (Downtown Cincinnati)

SEAFOOD 32
Regal Cincinnati Hotel
150 W. 5th St., Cincinnati
513/352-2160
$$$
Fresh seafood with a view. Situated on the thirty-second floor of the Regal Hotel, this is Cincinnati's only revolving restaurant (Northern Kentucky has the Quality Hotel in Covington). The Maryland blue-crab cakes, although only appetizers, are not to be missed. Dinner Tuesday through Saturday; closed Sunday and Monday; reservations required. ♿ (Downtown Cincinnati)

WAH MEE CHINESE RESTAURANT
120 W. 5th St., Cincinnati
513/579-0544
$$

Situated at the bottom of a huge flight of stairs, Wah Mee is a cavernous underground world unto itself. Although the menu is extensive, the food preparation never seems to take too long. The bar is usually filled with servers from other restaurants after work—a true sign of a good bartender and good food. Lunch and dinner daily; reservations recommended for parties of six or more. (Downtown Cincinnati)

WASHINGTON PLATFORM
SALOON AND RESTAURANT
1000 Elm St., Cincinnati
513/421-0110
$$
Washington Platform has become such a popular joint that several years ago it expanded into the storefront next door. Do try to sit in the older part of the restaurant, though, since that's where the character is. Every April, the restaurant has an Oyster Festival featuring over 30 different oyster dishes; the rest of the year there are at least six or seven oyster-based meals on the menu. The potato/leek soup (served hot) is unique—the potatoes are not mashed into a purée but left lumpy enough to give the soup texture. The restaurant also boasts one of the most attractive bars in the city. Lunch and dinner daily; reservations for five or

more recommended. (Downtown Cincinnati)

UPTOWN CINCINNATI

AMBAR INDIA RESTAURANT
350 Ludlow Ave., Clifton
513/281-7000
$
However informal the atmosphere, the food here is as elegant as Indian food in Cincinnati can get. The appetizers are a meal unto themselves; especially good are the vegetable *pakoras* and the samosas. Do ask your server to bring you the chutney selection and use them liberally on the aforementioned aps. There is also a wide vary of *nan* (Indian breads)—the *aloo nan* (potato-filled) is spicy but excellent. The entrées are spiced according to your tolerance (1 through 6) and range from lamb curry to *malai kofta* (vegetable balls in a masala sauce). Service is fast and friendly. Lunch and dinner daily. (Uptown Cincinnati)

La Normandie Taverne and Chop House, p.57

Maisonette

CACTUS PEAR
3215 Jefferson Ave., Corryville
513/961-7400
$$
This place serves up Tex-Mex at its best; the food is spicy enough to make a sweat break out on your upper lip. Menu highlights include the red pepper noodles and the shrimp marguerite. Also, the margaritas are huge and wonderfully potent. Lunch Monday through Friday; dinner daily. ♿ (Uptown Cincinnati)

CORINTHIAN RESTAURANT AND LOUNGE
3253 Jefferson Ave., Corryville
513/961-0013
$$
The cuisine here is Greek, American, and Italian—and the atmosphere is a mix of Mediterranean and South American. On Friday and Saturday nights, the bar's sizable dance floor is crowded with discophiles shaking their booties to salsa and jazz. Lunch and dinner Monday through Saturday; closed Sundays. (Uptown Cincinnati)

THE DINER
1203 Sycamore St., Over-the-Rhine
513/721-1212
$$
This is not your run-of-the-mill diner, since the food is slightly more upscale. It has the requisite burgers but also serves mussels in white wine. It's a concept restaurant, built lovingly within a genuine dining car, that caters to a cosmopolitan crowd. Lunch and dinner daily; brunch Sundays. ♿ (Uptown Cincinnati)

INN THE WOOD
277 Calhoun, Clifton Heights
513/221-3044
$

Top Ten Places to Dine with a View

Cincinnati's many riverboat and hilltop restaurants provide some awe-inspiring views of the city—especially at night. While some of these restaurants serve very good food, the primary criterion for inclusion on this list is the gorgeousness of what you can see there, not necessarily the tastiness of what you can eat.

1. **Primavista**, 810 Matson Pl., Price Hill, 513/251-6467.
2. **Seafood 32**, Regal Cincinnati Hotel, 150 W. 5th St., Cincinnati, 513/352-2160.
3. **The Waterfront**, 14 Pete Rose Pier, Covington, 606/581-1414.
4. **Chart House**, 405 Riverside Dr., Newport, 606/261-0300.
5. **Celestial Restaurant and Incline Lounge**, 1071 Celestial St., Mt. Adams, 513/241-4455.
6. **Barleycorn's Yacht Club**, Riverboat Row, Newport, 606/292-2978.
7. **Crockett's River Café and Topside Bar and Grill**, 1 Riverboat Row, Newport, 606/581-2800.
8. **Don Pablo's**, 401 Riverboat Row, Newport, 606/261-7100.
9. **Mike Fink Restaurant**, Foot of Greenup Street, Covington, 606/261-4212.
10. **Riverview Restaurant**, Quality Hotel Riverview, 668 W. 5th St., Covington, 606/491-5300.

This casual mom-and-pop–style breakfast joint attracts a diverse crowd, mostly students and professors from the nearby University of Cincinnati. The rustic decor gives Inn the Wood a down-home feel. The house special— a hearty mix of onions, green peppers, potatoes, cheese, and eggs—is a popular item, and their French toast is the best in town. Breakfast, lunch, and dinner daily; no reservations. (Uptown Cincinnati)

MAYURA INDIAN RESTAURANT
3201 Jefferson Ave., Corryville

513/221-7125
$$
This is one of the area's original Indian eateries. The atmosphere is quite pleasant and guests are made to feel welcome, due in large part to owner Swamy N. Sunkara, who loves to chat with his clientele. Past patrons include Neil Armstrong, Def Leppard, and the Rolling Stones. The tandoori chicken is recommended, and the lunch buffet is a great bargain. Lunch Tuesday through Saturday; dinner Tuesday through Sunday; closed Mondays. (Uptown Cincinnati)

MECKLENBURG GARDENS
302 E. University, Corryville
513/221-5353
$$

One of Cincinnati's oldest restaurants, the recently rehabbed Mecklenburg pays homage to its German past with menu items such as chicken spatzel and sauerbraten. Otherwise, the menu is an eclectic mix of American and Mediterranean cuisine. The patio is adorned with grapevines, and local microbrews are on tap. Lunch Monday through Friday; dinner daily. & (Uptown Cincinnati)

MEDITERRANEAN FOODS
314 Ludlow Ave., Clifton
513/961-6060
$

This mom-and-pop deli, owned by Nick and Connie Zannis, both of Greek descent, has the best hummus and *tabouli* in town. It also has a great selection of black olives and feta and has recently added gyros to the menu. Lunch daily. & (Uptown Cincinnati)

NICOLA'S RISTORANTE ITALIANO
1420 Sycamore St., Over-the-Rhine
513/721-6200
$$

An attractive, upscale Italian eatery built on two levels, Nicola's offers menu highlights including *osso bucco* (veal shank) served with a saffron risotto, and swordfish with white wine in a caper sauce. The atmosphere is airy and congenial to conversation. Lunches are much more casual than dinner. Lunch Monday through Friday; dinner Monday through Saturday; closed Sunday; reservations recommended. & (Uptown Cincinnati)

NO ANCHOVIES
324 Ludlow Ave., Clifton

513/221-2277
$

This is a hip, happenin', twenty-something joint that serves pizza whole and by the slice. The most popular item on the menu is "The Groovy," a pizza with fresh spinach, mushrooms, garlic, feta, and tomato. Lunch and dinner daily; no reservations. & (Uptown Cincinnati)

TUCKER'S RESTAURANT
1637 Vine St., Over-the-Rhine
513/721-7123
$

Family-owned and -operated since 1946, this Over-the-Rhine eatery has one of the best breakfasts in town. It also serves sandwiches, steaks, and platters. The omelets feature fresh herbs, and if you order mushrooms in your dish you'll enjoy some heavenly portabellos. Tucker's has seven booths, but if you want to watch your food being expertly prepared, sit at one of the 12 counter seats. (Uptown Cincinnati)

EAST CINCINNATI

ANAND INDIAN RESTAURANT
10890 Reading Rd., Evendale
513/554-4040
$

The authenticity of the food belies its diner atmosphere. The entrées are nothing to scoff at, but the main reason to come here is to sample the lunch buffet. The selection is vast—from tandoori chicken to lamb curry to an assortment of *nan*. Lunch and dinner daily. (East Cincinnati)

BISTRO GIGI
6904 Wooster Pike, Mariemont
513/272-4444
$$

This is the latest addition to the high-quality restaurants run by the Comisar family (of Maisonette and La Normandie fame). Most of the food—which is, of course, French—is prepared at the five-star Maisonette. Lunch and dinner Tuesday through Sunday. (East Cincinnati)

CAFÉ VIENNA
1141 St. Gregory St., Mt. Adams
513/621-6655
$$

This charming little restaurant in the heart of the quaint hilltop neighborhood of Mt. Adams offers eclectic fare, with an emphasis on German and Austrian food. Try the goulash, the best in town. Lunch and dinner Tuesday through Sunday; closed Monday; reservations recommended on the weekends. (East Cincinnati)

CELESTIAL RESTAURANT
AND INCLINE LOUNGE
1071 Celestial St., Mt. Adams
513/241-4455
$$$

A combination of continental and classic French cuisine, the Celestial is well-known for its fresh Dover sole. There's not a bad seat in the restaurant, which has a great view of the Ohio River and downtown. Lunch Monday through Friday; dinner Monday through Saturday; closed Sunday; reservations required. (East Cincinnati)

CHATEAU POMIJE
2019 Madison Rd., Walnut Hills
513/871-8788
$$

A charming restaurant with an attractive outdoor patio and an eclectic mix of world cuisines, Pomije has a wine store in the front where you select a bottle for your table. The grapes used to make the house chardonnay, cabernet, and white zinfandel are grown in their Indiana vineyards. Lunch Monday through Friday; dinner Monday through Saturday; reservations recommended for six or more. (East Cincinnati)

CHINA GOURMET
3340 Erie Ave., Hyde Park
513/871-6612
$$$

One of the best Chinese restaurants in the city, this establishment is known for its seafood—especially its steamed walleye pike in a scallion sauce. The cuisine is mostly Cantonese, but the menu includes a few Szechwan dishes. Lunch and dinner Monday through Saturday; reservations recommended on the weekends. (East Cincinnati)

FIRST WATCH
2692 Madison Rd., Norwood
513/531-7430
$

See Downtown Cincinnati entry, p. 54. (East Cincinnati)

J'S FRESH SEAFOOD
RESTAURANT
2444 Madison Rd., Hyde Park
513/871-2888
$$

J's is one of the best seafood restaurants in the city, with fish flown in fresh daily. Best bets are the charbroiled swordfish and the charbroiled salmon. Lunch and dinner Tuesday through Sunday; reservations recommended. (East Cincinnati)

LA PETITE FRANCE
3177 Glendale-Milford Rd.
Evendale
513/733-8383
$$

Outdoor dining at Mecklenburg Gardens, p. 65

Enjoy haute French cuisine with a casual flair. The poulet Oporto, served with a white wine sauce and mushrooms, was the winner of the Taste of Cincinnati award, and the chocolate crepe is sinfully delicious. Lunch and dinner Monday through Saturday; reservations recommended. ♿ (East Cincinnati)

MONTGOMERY INN BOATHOUSE
925 Eastern Ave., East End
513/721-RIBS (721-7427)
$$

This Cincinnati mainstay overlooks the Ohio River. If you're visiting friends here, you can be sure this is one of the places they'll take you. It's famous for its baby-back ribs and unique barbeque sauce. Lunch Monday through Friday; dinner daily; reservations recommended. ♿ (East Cincinnati)

PACIFIC MOON CAFÉ
8300 Market Place, Montgomery
513/891-0091
$$

Pacific Moon is by far the best Asian restaurant in town and well worth the trip. The menu, filled with Thai, Japanese, and Vietnamese items, is so extensive that it reads like a book. And if you have finicky children (or adults), there is an American section/chapter in the menu. Of particular note are the Vietnamese rolls and crab Rangoons. Lunch and dinner daily; reservations recommended. ♿ (East Cincinnati)

PETERSEN'S RESTAURANT
1111 St. Gregory, Mt. Adams
513/651-4777

See Downtown Cincinnati listings, p. 58. (East Cincinnati)

THE PRECINCT
311 Delta Ave., Columbia-Tusculum
513/321-5454
$$

This upscale steak house frequently hosts visiting celebrities, as the walls—filled with smiling photos of the likes of George Clooney, Liza Minnelli, and Paula Abdul—confirm.

The filet strip porterhouse is a house favorite. Surf-and-turf dinners are also available. Dinner daily; reservations recommended. (East Cincinnati)

ROOKWOOD POTTERY
1077 Celestial St., Mt. Adams
513/721-5456
$$
This restaurant is worth visiting, if only for the experience of dining in a kiln. The building, as its name implies, once housed the famous Rookwood Pottery—hence the aforementioned kilns. The food is unpretentious and perhaps nothing to write home about—just your typical burger type fare—but the atmosphere is highly unusual. Lunch and dinner daily; no reservations. (East Cincinnati)

TEAK THAI CUISINE AND BAR
1051 St. Gregory, Mt. Adams
513/665-9800
$$
Teak's serves great Thai food in a tasteful, casual setting. As the name suggests, teakwood features promi-

Orchids at Palm Court, p. 58

Omni Netherland Plaza

nently in the decor. The *pad Thai* is cooked to perfection and can be made with chicken, shrimp, or vegetables. Lunch and dinner daily; reservations recommended. (East Cincinnati)

WEST CINCINNATI

BOCA RESTAURANT AND BAR
4034 Hamilton Ave., Northside
513/542-2022
$$
Beautifully decorated, this restaurant boasts a hand-carved wooden bar, a floor taken from an old gymnasium, huge front windows, and a skylight. The menu, an eclectic mix of various cuisines, is limited; but what they do, they do very well. The owners used to be professional rock-tour caterers, working for the likes of 10,000 Maniacs and Michael Bolton. The hand-seared salmon and the crispy-skin chicken are menu highlights. Lunch Monday through Saturday; dinner Tuesday through Saturday. Reservations for five or more. &. (West Cincinnati)

DANTE'S RESTAURANT
I-74 and Rybolt Road, Dent
513/574-6666
$$
Dante's offers haute American cuisine in a casual but elegant atmosphere. Although they serve pasta and seafood, they're best known for their prime rib. Enjoy live music Wednesday through Saturday. Breakfast and dinner daily; lunch Monday through Saturday; reservations recommended. &. (West Cincinnati)

LA ROSA'S PIZZERIAS
2334 Boudinot Ave., Westwood
513/347-1111
$
Distinguished by its curiously sweet

tomato sauce, La Rosa's is easily the most popular local pizza chain in Cincinnati. Although it has locations throughout the area, this is the original restaurant, slightly more upscale than the rest, with an impressive wine list. Lunch and dinner daily; no reservations. & (West Cincinnati)

PRIMAVISTA
810 Matson Pl., Price Hill
513/251-6467
$$$

One of Cincinnati's finest Italian restaurants, Primavista has an awe-inspiring view of the city from atop Price Hill. When you make reservations, ask for a table next to the window—you won't regret it. Specialties include the sea bass topped with lobster pieces and the *osso buco*. Dinner daily; reservations recommended. & (West Cincinnati)

SOUTH OF THE RIVER

ANCHOR GRILL
438 Pike St., Covington, KY
606/431-9498
$

If you want some late-late-night eats, the Anchor Grill is the place to go. Admittedly, it's a greasy spoon that serves unremarkable double-deckers and cheeseburgers, but it's distinguished by its unique decor: an as-

sortment of nautical paraphernalia, complete with a miniature band that plays music at the touch of a finger. Open 24 hours. (South of the River)

BEHLE ST. CAFÉ
50 E. RiverCenter Blvd.
Covington, KY
606/291-4100
$$

Despite the TVs (always tuned to ESPN), Behle St. takes "bar food" to heights undreamed of by most bars that happen to serve food. Its menu is primarily Cajun, and the blackened chicken served with vermicelli is excellent, just spicy enough. The Greek salad is huge and could be a meal unto itself. The walls are laden with all sorts of photographs—from bygone movie stars to bygone local molls. Lunch and dinner daily; reservations recommended. & (South of the River)

COACH AND FOUR RESTAURANT
214 Scott Blvd., Covington, KY
606/431-6700
$$

With American cuisine served in an Olde English atmosphere, the Coach and Four is a lone testament to nineteenth-century Covington. The weekends tend to be packed, and the bar, reminiscent of an English pub, is a great place to work up an appetite. Menu highlights include pecan chicken with a Dijon cream sauce, risotto with prawns, and sea bass served over vermicelli. It's very dark and cozy. Lunch Tuesday through Friday; dinner Tuesday through Saturday; closed Monday; reservations recommended. & (South of the River)

COCO'S
322 Greenup St., Covington, KY
606/491-1369
$$
Coco's decor is distinguished by owner Bonnie Coe's magnificent paintings, inspired by the Southwest. Coe's sense of color makes these paintings especially noteworthy—the purple horse overlooking the stairs is a good example. Housed on two floors and with plenty of nooks and crannies, this is the perfect place for a romantic repast. The food is an eclectic form of "fusion" cuisine—mixing various culinary styles and flavors. The salads are sublime, and the wine list is exceptional. Daily specials include seafood and pasta dishes. Weekends include live music, mostly jazz. (South of the River)

DEE FELICE CAFÉ
529 Main St., Covington, KY
606/261-2365
$$
Here's Cajun food at its best. While Dee Felice offers a lunch menu, many music lovers come for dinner to enjoy the live jazz. Fridays and Saturdays are especially good, with a Dixieland jazz band. The standard New Orleans fare, such as jambalaya and crawfish etoufée, is excellent, but the highlights on the menu are the halibut sautéed in lobster butter, served with shrimp, and the garlic-seasoned oysters and shrimp on a bed of linguine. Lunch Monday through Friday; dinner

daily; reservations recommended. (South of the River)

DIJOHN RESTAURANT AND BAR
724 Madison Ave., Covington, KY
606/581-5646
$$
This location has been home to several restaurants, but DiJohn is here to stay. Despite the rather garish decor, it's a very pleasant place to while away an afternoon or evening, especially if you are seated in one of the cavernous booths. The menu is an eclectic assortment of ethnic cuisines. Highlights include the pasta *puttanesca* and Floyd's chicken, made with lemon and herbs and served with rice. On weekends there's always a long wait, so be prepared to sit at the bar and listen to the live music, usually a scat singer with piano accompaniment. Lunch and dinner Monday through Saturday; closed Sunday; reservations recommended. (South of the River)

GATEHOUSE TAVERN
Drawbridge Estate, 2477 Royal Dr.
Ft. Mitchell, KY
606/341-2800
$$
This favorite local surf-and-turf eatery is housed in a castle-like building surrounded by a moat. The interior is adorned with authentic faux-British decor. It's best to stick with the "turf" side of the menu, since the fish tends to be bland and overcooked. The châteaubriand for two is the best choice on the menu. All dinners come with a trip to the salad bar; avoid the iceberg lettuce combo and go for the Caesar salad instead. The bar is Olde English and the servers are very friendly. Dinner daily; reservations recommended. & (South of the River)

Cincinnati Chili

When people who know about such things think of Cincinnati's culinary heritage, the first thing that comes to mind is Cincinnati chili, the brainchild of Macedonian immigrant Athanas Kiradjieff, who opened his Empress Chili Parlor in 1922.

Unlike hearty Texas-style chili, Cincinnati chili is a trifle watery, and its unique taste comes from the cinnamon, Worcestershire sauce, cocoa, and allspice in the recipe. If you put it on a bun with a hot dog and mustard, that's a "coney." Add cheese to get a "cheese coney." A "three-way" is a plate of spaghetti smothered in chili with grated cheese on top; add onions for a "four-way," and beans and onions for a "five-way." And don't forget the oyster crackers.

The chili market in Cincinnati is dominated by three local chains: Skyline, Gold Star, and Empress. Dixie Chili on Monmouth Street in Newport has its share of fans; and Camp Washington Chili, located on Hopple and Colerain, is another local favorite that's open 24 hours (except on Sunday, when it's closed). Look into a chili parlor at lunchtime and you'll see people chowing down, some of them wearing bibs. This chili splatters and—believe me—you don't want to get it on your clothes.

POMPILIO'S
6th and Washington Avenue
Newport, KY
606/581-3065
$

Pompilio's is a mom-and-pop Italian restaurant whose biggest claim to fame is that a scene from the movie *Rain Man* was filmed there—the one where Dustin Hoffman's character counts the toothpicks that fall on the floor. Pictures of the cast and crew are framed for all to see, including ones of Hoffman and Cruise hugging various members of the staff. Food-wise, it's best to stick with old standbys, such as spaghetti and meatballs. The eggplant parmesan is also a good bet. Dinner salads are composed mostly of iceberg lettuce, and the vinegar in the oil and vinegar dressing is of the distilled white variety. However, the beautifully carved cherry wood bar— filled with colorful Newport characters—alone is worth the visit. Lunch and dinner daily; no reservations. ♿ (South of the River)

SCALEA'S
320 Greenup St., Covington, KY
606/491-3334
$

This mom-and-pop Italian deli is filled with all sorts of hard-to-find delicacies—from Nutella and Orangina to smoked chèvre. Bread is baked on the premises, and they offer a wide selection of sandwiches. Favorites include Scalea's Original, a heady mixture of Genoa, *cappacola*, *soprasatta*, provolone, lettuce, tomato, and roasted peppers; and the Vegetarian, with Swiss, Gouda, mozzarella, lettuce, tomato, roasted peppers, and mustard. All of them come, of course, on home-baked bread. In summer you can sit at the streetside tables. The family is in the process of opening an upscale Italian restaurant next door. Lunch daily. (South of the River)

SILVIA'S MEXICAN RESTAURANT
15 E. 7th St., Newport, KY
606/431-8110
$

It's said that you can always tell Silvia's mood by the spiciness of her salsa. The restaurant is decorated with sombreros, colorful ponchos, and corn people. The guacamole is chunky and good, and all dinners include rice and beans. Silvia's margaritas are made in the traditional manner and served in jumbo glasses or large pitchers. Lunch and dinner daily; reservations for five or more. (South of the River)

WINDOWS ON THE WATER
(The Waterfront, Spazzi)
14 Pete Rose Pier, Covington, KY
606/581-1414
$$$

This floating restaurant houses two eateries: The Waterfront, a surf-and-turf restaurant with a sushi bar; and Spazzi's, an upscale Italian restaurant run by Jimmy Gibson, one of Cincinnati's most celebrated chefs. The Waterfront serves dinner daily, but the sushi bar is closed on Sunday. Spazzi's serves dinner Tuesday through Sunday; closed Monday.

Maisonette, p. 57

Maisonette

Reservations are recommended for both restaurants. (South of the River)

YORK STREET
INTERNATIONAL CAFÉ
738 York St., Newport, KY
606/261-9675
$$

If you enjoy eating in the comfort of your own home, you'll love this place. The dining room, situated on the first floor, looks more like an oversized living room, with comfy chairs and mismatched tables. Antique bookshelves line the walls and the high ceilings and huge windows give the room an airy feel. The menu is eclectic—from gourmet pizzas to cheese platters. The second floor houses another bar and live music; the third floor doubles as an art gallery. Lunch and dinner daily; no reservations. ♿ (South of the River)

Vince Re/GCCVB

5

SIGHTS AND ATTRACTIONS

Charles Dickens, who passed through Cincinnati in 1842, raved about it in his travelogue, American Notes, *calling it "a beautiful city." Winston Churchill, visiting in 1932, agreed with his fellow countryman and proclaimed it "the most beautiful inland city in America."*

The buildings that have survived into this century are a testament to the Queen City's past, and visitors can clearly see how the European settlers tried to recreate their home towns in this American Eden. Over-the-Rhine features the largest aggregation of Italianate architecture in the nation. The city also boasts the John A. Roebling Suspension Bridge, the first permanent bridge to span the Ohio River, as well as the Ingalls Building, the first skyscraper to be supported with steel-reinforced concrete. Cincinnati is also home to Union Terminal, the largest half-dome in the Western Hemisphere, and Sunlite Pool, the largest recirculating outdoor pool in the world. Take some time to stroll through the streets of Cincinnati—there's much to be seen that way.

CITY TOURS

BB RIVERBOATS
1 Madison Ave., Covington, KY
606/261-8500
BB's pier is at the foot of Madison Street, just west of the giant floating entertainment complex, Covington Landing. If you're driving, you can have your car parked by one of the

many valets hovering around, or, if you want to save a few bucks, park farther up the street, near 5th. Of course, if you're coming from downtown and you've got the energy, it's a delightful walk: across the Suspension Bridge, down the steps to the west, and along the river. BB Riverboats has lunch, dinner, and sightseeing cruises. Its flotilla is comprised of one paddle wheeler, the *Mark Twain*, and the diesel-fueled *River Raft, River Queen,* and *Fun Liner.* Reservations must be made well in advance. ⅃ (South of the River)

CINCINNATI CARRIAGE CO.
Fountain Square, Cincinnati
513/941-4474
If you're hot to trot, a horse-drawn carriage ride might be your best mode of transportation. These horses and buggies are parked on Vine Street, west of Fountain Square. The drivers are well versed in local lore and will be happy to talk your ear off if you so desire; $25 buys you a 20-minute tour of downtown Cincinnati. (Downtown Cincinnati)

CO-OP AIRCRAFT SERVICE
Blue Ash Airport
4273 Glendale-Milford Rd.,
Blue Ash
513/791-8500
Co-Op offers scenic plane tours of Cincinnati and allows passengers to decide exactly what they want to see. Make sure you ask them to fly you over the Ohio River and past the Cincinnati skyline. Flights cost $38.50 per half-hour. (East Cincinnati)

A PERSONAL TOUCH TOUR OF CINCINNATI
256 Compton Ridge Dr.
Wyoming, OH
513/821-7929
Tour guide Tom Wertheimer wants his van tour to be "one of the nicest experiences you've ever had." You can choose your itinerary but if you're not familiar with the area, this will serve as an excellent introduction. Some of the places visited are Cincinnati's Public Landing, Union Terminal, Eden Park, and Mt. Adams, and Mainstrasse Village in Covington. $25

adults, $12 children 12 and under. (Downtown Cincinnati)

QUEEN CITY RIVERBOAT TOURS
303 O'Fallon St., Dayton, KY
606/292-8687
Lunch, dinner, and sightseeing cruises are offered on the *Spirit of Cincinnati,* a paddle wheeler, or the *Queen City Clipper,* which is pushed by a tug. But be sure to make your reservations well in advance, as these pleasure boats are very popular. ⅃ (South of the River)

SCHMIDT AVIATION
Blue Ash Airport
4335 Glendale-Milford Rd.,
Blue Ash
513/984-5880
A somewhat less leisurely tour of the city can be had by air. These four-seater airplanes can hold up to three passengers. Flights usually last 45 minutes and offer bird's-eye views of Paramount's King's Island with its faux Eiffel Tower, the Ohio River, and downtown Cincinnati. Flights usually cost $69. (East Cincinnati)

DOWNTOWN CINCINNATI

BICENTENNIAL COMMONS
805 Pete Rose Way, Cincinnati
513/352-4000
Dedicated in 1976, Yeatman's Cove Park lies on the site where the city's first European settlers disembarked in the winter of 1788. Looking across the Ohio River toward Newport, the park descends to the river in a series of steps known as the Serpentine Wall, an attractively disguised flood wall and levee that has become a Cincinnati landmark. Bicentennial Commons adjoins Yeatman's Cove to the east and contains several stages,

DOWNTOWN CINCINNATI

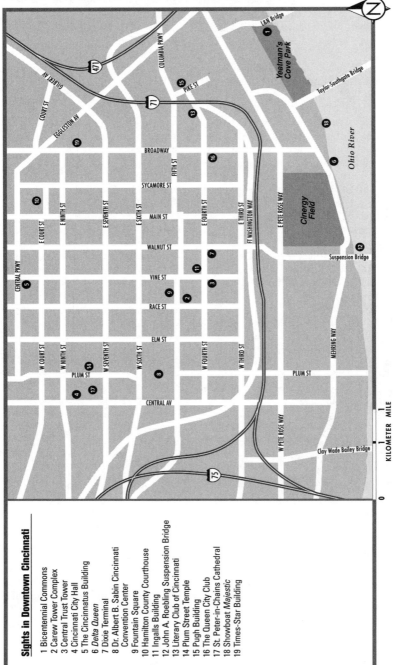

Sights in Downtown Cincinnati

1 Bicentennial Commons
2 Carew Tower Complex
3 Central Trust Tower
4 Cincinnati City Hall
5 The Cincinnatus Building
6 Delta Queen
7 Dixie Terminal
8 Dr. Albert B. Sabin Cincinnati
  Convention Center
9 Fountain Square
10 Hamilton County Courthouse
11 Ingalls Building
12 John A. Roebling Suspension Bridge
13 Literary Club of Cincinnati
14 Plum Street Temple
15 Pugh Building
16 The Queen City Club
17 St. Peter-in-Chains Cathedral
18 Showboat Majestic
19 Times-Star Building

a roller-skating rink, volleyball courts, and river overlooks. During the summer, park-goers are privy to free concerts. ♿ (Downtown Cincinnati)

CAREW TOWER COMPLEX
441 Vine St., Cincinnati
513/241-3888
Consisting of three towers rising from a five-story base, the Carew Tower complex covers half a city block and is, at 574 feet, Cincinnati's tallest building, with its observation platform providing one of the most awe-inspiring views of the city. Designed by the Chicago firm of Walter W. Ahlshlager, the "city within a city" was completed on February 10, 1931, but through the years it suffered from some misguided interior decorating choices by its tenants. The Hilton, which managed the hotel from 1956 to 1981, was the worst culprit, covering the terra-cotta walls with wallpaper and putting carpet over the terrazzo floors.

After undergoing extensive renovation in 1989, the art deco complex now houses Tower Place shopping mall and the Omni Netherland Plaza Hotel. The Rookwood ceramic floral arches on the east and west ends of the arcade are two of the largest examples of Rookwood art pottery in the world. They were designed by William E. Hentschel, who based his pattern on a repeating motif by the European metalsmith Edgar Brandt. ♿ (Downtown Cincinnati)

CENTRAL TRUST TOWER
1 W. 4th St., Cincinnati
513/621-4090
Cass Gilbert, who also designed New York's Woolworth Building, created this Italian Renaissance–style building. Upon its completion in 1913, the Central Trust Tower became the fifth-largest building in the world and

the tallest building outside New York City. It was also the tallest building in Cincinnati until 1930, when it was surpassed by the Carew Tower Complex. ♿ (Downtown Cincinnati)

CINCINNATI CITY HALL
801 Plum St., Cincinnati
513/352-3000
This red granite building, constructed in 1893, was designed by local architect Samuel Hannaford. The Council Chamber sports ceiling frescoes by Charles Pedretti and the marble stairways are adorned by stained-glass windows depicting allegorical scenes of early Cincinnati. The building was in danger of being torn down in the mid-1960s but, fortunately, the necessary destruction funds were never raised. ♿ (Downtown Cincinnati)

THE CINCINNATUS BUILDING
1025 Vine St., Cincinnati
513/762-4000

Fountain Square, p. 79

©Elder Photographic, Inc./GCCVB

Constructed in 1920 to house offices for the Brotherhood of Railway Clerks and now owned by the Kroger Company, this Second Renaissance Revival–style building is distinguished by the *trompe l'oeil* mural on the side facing Central Parkway. The mural, which replicates the building's facade, depicts Cincinnatus, the Roman General and inspiration for the Revolutionary War Order of Cincinnatus after whom the city was named. (Downtown Cincinnati)

DELTA QUEEN
Public Landing, Cincinnati
800/543-1949
Along with the *American Queen* and the *Mississippi Queen*, this old-fashioned paddle-wheel steamboat docks at the public landing several times a year during its trips up and down the Ohio River. Call to check on arrival times, since schedules vary from year to year. ♿ (Downtown Cincinnati)

DIXIE TERMINAL
41-53 E. 4th St., Cincinnati
Constructed in 1921, the Neoclassical Revival building was a terminus, first to Northern Kentucky streetcars, and then to Northern Kentucky buses. Early in 1997, Transit Authority of Northern Kentucky was effectively told to take a

hike and the ramp leading to the building from the John A. Roebling Bridge has since been torn down. Now that the building no longer attracts bus riders, business has dropped dramatically and several of the terminal's shops and restaurants have closed or moved; but the two-story glass and marble arcade, decorated with Rookwood Pottery details, is reason enough to visit. Fans of *Rain Man* might recognize the interior, which was converted into a bank for the movie. (Downtown Cincinnati)

DR. ALBERT B. SABIN CINCINNATI CONVENTION CENTER
5th and Elm Streets, Cincinnati
513/352-3750
This postmodern monstrosity, built in 1967, was named for the discoverer of the polio vaccine, who was working at Cincinnati's Children's Hospital and the University of Cincinnati at the time of his breakthrough. When the facility was enlarged in 1984, the center paid homage to the past by adding the Palladian arch from the demolished Albee Theatre to its 5th Street entrance. Trouble is, if you're in a car you can see it only in the rearview mirror, since Plum Street is a one-way street going south. Either way, the addition is a hopeless mismatch of styles and looks like a misguided afterthought. ♿ (Downtown Cincinnati)

TRIVIA

Charles Manson was born at Cincinnati's General Hospital (now University Hospital) on November 12, 1934, and was identified on his birth certificate as "No Name Maddox." His mother, Kathleen, allegedly sold her illegitimate son for a pitcher of beer but was forced to take him back by authorities.

The Delta Queen *steamboat*

FOUNTAIN SQUARE
Fountain Square Plaza, Cincinnati
800/344-3445

Fountain Square, which stands on the site of a nineteenth-century butcher's market, is located in the heart of downtown and provides a much-needed gathering space for downtown workers. In winter the Cincinnati Recreation Commission installs a small skating rink, and at Christmastime the Ku Klux Klan erects a cross, causing a flurry of indignation, several attempts to remove the offending icon, and a litany of letters to the editor. In summer the square provides free entertainment almost every day, from concerts to ballroom dancing. The fountain was designed by August von Kreling in the nineteenth century (see Museums, Galleries, and Public Art chapter). &
(Downtown Cincinnati)

HAMILTON COUNTY COURTHOUSE
1000 Main St., Cincinnati
513/632-6500

Completed in 1919, the Neoclassical Revival–style building is not the first courthouse to stand in this spot. In 1884, after William Berner was convicted of manslaughter for the murder of his employer, an angry mob stormed the building demanding justice. After three nights of pandemonium, in which the mob attacked and burned the structure, the National Guard was called in. When the mêlée died down, more than 50 protesters were dead, 200 were wounded, and the courthouse lay smoldering. A new courthouse was built, and when it was replaced in 1915, William Howard Taft laid its cornerstone. &
(Downtown Cincinnati)

INGALLS BUILDING
6 E. 4th St., Cincinnati

Built in 1903, the Ingalls Building revolutionized the architectural world: it was the first skyscraper to be supported with steel-reinforced concrete. The city, however, was so sure the structure would *not* be sound that it took two years to issue owner

Melville E. Ingalls a construction permit. Upon completion, several disbelievers waited around for the building to topple. Despite their skepticism the Ingalls, designed by local architects Elzner and Anderson, is still standing; in 1974 it was designated a National Historical Civil Engineering Landmark. (Downtown Cincinnati)

JOHN A. ROEBLING SUSPENSION BRIDGE
Foot of Race Street, Cincinnati
Even though the Kentucky legislature granted an 1846 charter to the Covington and Cincinnati Bridge Company to build a span across the Ohio River, it took several months for the Ohio legislature to do the same—with one stipulation: the bridge was not to be built in line with any Cincinnati street. Construction was plagued with setbacks, including an 1857 banking crisis and the Civil War. It was finally completed in 1867, and became the first permanent bridge to span the Ohio River. Its designer, John A. Roebling, went on to design the Brooklyn Bridge. The majestic structure, with two brick towers on each side of the river, was named to the National Register of Historic Places in 1975, and in 1988 it was painted blue to celebrate Cincinnati's Bicentennial. (Downtown Cincinnati)

LITERARY CLUB OF CINCINNATI
500 E. 4th St., Cincinnati
513/621-6589
Founded in 1848, the club claims to be the oldest one of its kind still in operation. This Federal-style building was constructed in 1820 and the club moved into the premises in 1875. Former members include William Howard Taft, Rutherford B. Hayes, artist Frank Duveneck, and

Stephanni Cohen/©Cincinnati Recreation Commission

Bicentennial Commons, p. 75

photographer Paul Briol. Ralph Waldo Emerson, Oscar Wilde, Booker T. Washington, Mark Twain, and Robert Frost all lectured here. (Downtown Cincinnati)

PLUM STREET TEMPLE
8th and Plum Streets, Cincinnati
513/579-9441
The founder of Reform Judaism, Rabbi Isaac M. Wise called this Saracenic Revival–style synagogue his "Alhambra" temple. His congregation, composed of German American Jews, first began meeting in 1846. B'nai Yeshurun invited Wise to become their rabbi in 1854, and he remained so until his death in 1900. During his time in Cincinnati, he supervised the construction of the temple (completed in 1866) and founded Hebrew Union College. (Downtown Cincinnati)

PUGH BUILDING
400 Pike St., Cincinnati
513/381-3885
This building, now known as the Polk Building, was where Achilles Pugh

printed James Birney's *The Philanthropist,* an Abolitionist paper published by the Ohio Anti Slavery Society. In July 1936, pro-slavery mobs attacked Pugh's print shop twice. On the second assault, they took part of the printing press to the foot of Main Street and threw it into the Ohio River. (Downtown Cincinnati)

THE QUEEN CITY CLUB
331 E. 4th St., Cincinnati
513/621-2708
Sinclair Lewis stayed at the Queen City Club in 1921 when he was researching his novel *Babbitt.* The club was founded in 1874 by Joseph Longworth, son of Cincinnati's first millionaire, Nicholas Longworth, for "literary purposes and for mutual improvement." The present structure was built in 1926 in the English Renaissance style. It is now a private business club. (Downtown Cincinnati)

SHOWBOAT *MAJESTIC*
435 E. Mehring Way, Cincinnati
513/241-6550
Built in 1923 by Captain Thomas Jefferson Reynolds, the *Majestic* toured the Ohio, Kentucky, Tennessee, and Green Rivers for 15 years before docking permanently at Cincinnati's Public Landing. Now run by the Cincinnati Recreation Commission, the boat's season runs from April to October and provides a stage for its own professional company as well as for college and community theater groups. ♿ (Downtown Cincinnati)

ST. PETER-IN-CHAINS CATHEDRAL
8th and Plum Streets, Cincinnati
513/421-5354
When this impressive Greek Revival cathedral was built, every Catholic in Ohio was asked to contribute no less than 12.5 cents toward its construction. Completed in 1845, it became the seat of the Roman Catholic Archdiocese of Cincinnati. The seat was moved to St. Monica's Church in Fairview in 1938, but a newly expanded St. Peter-in-Chains was rededicated in 1957. With its 12 Corinthian columns and towering steeple, it was the second permanent cathedral in the United States. ♿ (Downtown Cincinnati)

TIMES-STAR BUILDING
800 Broadway, Cincinnati
Although the *Cincinnati Times-Star* is long gone, swallowed up by the *Cincinnati Post* in 1958, its headquarters, a beautiful Gothic Revival building with art deco motifs, is still standing. Now owned by the Hamilton County Court System, it houses

TRIVIA

Holy Cross—Immaculata Church (30 Guido St., Mt. Adams, 513/721-6544) was dedicated on May 8, 1860, holding its services in both English and German. On Good Friday, its parishioners make their traditional annual ascent up the long flight of stairs from St. Gregory Street to Guido Street in Mt. Adams, praying, and puffing, all the while.

GREATER CINCINNATI

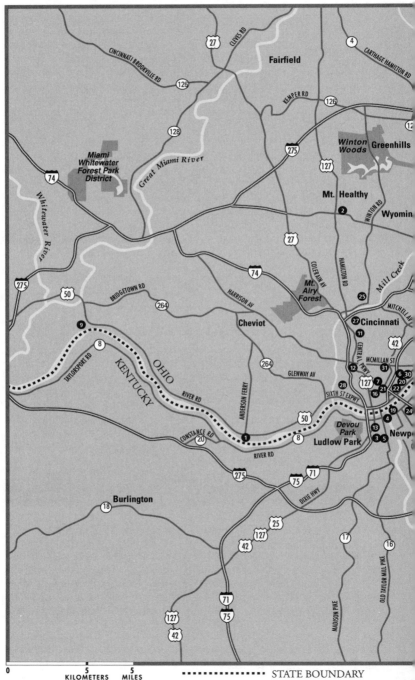

0   5   5
KILOMETERS   MILES

•••••••••••••••• STATE BOUNDARY

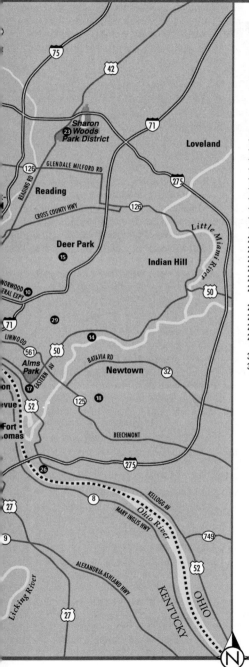

Sights in Greater Cincinnati

1 Anderson Ferry
2 Cary Cottage
3 Cathedral Basilica of the Assumption
4 Dan Carter Beard Home
5 The Duveneck Home
6 Elsinore Tower
7 Findlay Market
8 Harriet Beecher Stowe House
9 Harrison Memorial Park
10 The Indian Mound
11 Jewish Cemetery
12 John Hauck House
13 Mainstrasse Village
14 Mariemont Village
15 Meier's Wine Cellars
16 Memorial Hall
17 Memorial Pioneer Cemetery
18 Miller-Leuser Log House
19 Mimosa Museum
20 Mirror Lake
21 Music Hall
22 Rookwood Pottery Building
23 Sharon Woods Village
24 Southgate House
25 Spring Grove Cemetery and Arboretum
26 Sunlite Pool/Coney Island
27 Temple of Love
28 Union Terminal
29 University of Cincinnati Observatory
30 Water Tower
31 William Howard Taft National Historic Site

the county commissioners office and several other government bureaus. In 1983, 50 years after its construction, it was listed on the National Historical Register of Buildings. (Downtown Cincinnati)

UPTOWN CINCINNATI

FINDLAY MARKET
1800 W. Elder St., Over-the-Rhine
513/352-4638
Named for Cincinnati mayor James Findlay, a veteran of the War of 1812, this market has served Cincinnati shoppers since 1852. The enclosed building houses fish and meat shops that have been in their respective families for generations. This is a great place to buy cheap fruit and vegetables, but it's best to go very early in the morning before the produce is picked over. Taste of Findlay Market takes place in October. Open 7–6 Wed, Fri, and Sat. (Uptown Cincinnati)

HARRIET BEECHER STOWE HOUSE
2950 Gilbert Ave., Walnut Hills
513/632-5120
The famous author lived here with her father, Reverend Lyman Beecher, a Presbyterian minister and president of Lane Theological Seminar. Many of the incidents in *Uncle Tom's Cabin* were prompted by Stowe's three-year stay in Cincinnati. The house, expanded since the time of the Beechers' residence, is furnished with period pieces and contains Reverend Beecher's original desk. Books concerning all aspects of slavery are displayed throughout the abode, as are paintings depicting the inhumanity of America's "peculiar institution." Visitors can browse at their leisure, and curator Emma Cox is also available to give a guided tour of the house. Open 10–4 Tue–Thur. Free, but donations are accepted. (Uptown Cincinnati)

JEWISH CEMETERY
730 Ludlow Ave., Clifton
When Charles and Rachel Kahn were making plans to build a house on this 3-acre site, they were told by neighborhood residents that they should choose another place to make their home. According to the *Bicentennial Guide to Greater Cincinnati*, Charles Kahn told his anti-Semitic neighbors, "Very well, gentlemen. If you do not

Cincinnati's Street Fairs and Food Fests

By Dan Luebbe, music columnist for Everybody's News, Cincinnati's *weekly newspaper*

Unless you're visiting the Queen City in the dead of winter, it's very likely that you will stumble upon one of the many entertaining outdoor food fests or street fairs the Cincinnati area has to offer. Perhaps the biggest food fest is **Taste of Cincinnati**. Hundreds of area restaurants set up shop on Central Parkway during the Memorial Day weekend and offer a taste of their most famous and popular foods for $2 to $3. A new tradition was born at the Taste a few years ago when a radio station attempted to organize the world's largest chicken dance. It might sound silly, and it probably is, but when you're in a crowd of thousands of people flapping their "wings," don't be surprised if you get caught up in the moment yourself.

Both the **Klosterman Family Oktoberfest**, in the Mainstrasse Village in Covington, and **Oktoberfest-Zinzinnati**, downtown, take place, inexplicably, in September and are great fun. Both fests salute the area's rich German heritage with bratwurst, mettwurst, potato pancakes, and other traditional German fare. Beer is a must at these festivals, and the local breweries are on hand to provide it. At Oktoberfest-Zinzinnati, it's a big spectacle when the mayor taps the first keg o' beer. Covington's Mainstrasse Village is the ideal site for an Oktoberfest because of its Old World charm. The neighborhood has remained virtually unchanged through its history, yet still thrives with restaurants, pubs, and shops. Two other outstanding festivals that benefit from this Old World charm are the **Mainstrasse Mardi Gras** in February and **Maifest** in May.

The **BBQ and Blues Festival** comes to beautiful Yeatman's Cove Park along the Ohio River in June, while the **Panegyri Greek Festival** hits Finneytown during the same month. In August, look for the **Black Family Reunion** as well as the **Great Inland Seafood Festival** at Sawyer Point Park. When you arrive in Cincinnati, be sure to check the local newspaper to discover what outdoor festival awaits you.

care to have Jews living near you, you cannot object to dead Jews, and you shall have many of these for many years in no condition to offend you." True to his word, Kahn sold his plot in 1848 to the Ahabeth Achim congregation and the first of its permanent residents was buried there in 1850. (Uptown Cincinnati)

MEMORIAL HALL
1225 Elm St., Over-the-Rhine
513/621-1919
This gorgeous building, designed in the Beaux Arts Classicism style by Samuel Hannaford, was built in 1908 to memorialize Hamilton County's soldiers, sailors, Marines, and pioneers. For a brief period in the early 1980s it was home to Ensemble Theatre of Cincinnati, which has since moved two blocks over to Vine Street. Nowadays it is managed by the Cincinnati Arts Association and is used by the Cincinnati Symphony Orchestra's chamber groups and the Cincinnati Chamber Orchestra, as well as various veterans' groups. The 610-seat theater auditorium, which had fallen into disrepair, has recently been restored. & (Uptown Cincinnati)

MUSIC HALL
1241–1243 Elm St., Over-the-Rhine
513/621-1919
Completed in 1878 to provide an indoor venue for the May Festival, Music Hall—with its 3,500-seat auditorium—is one of Cincinnati's most identifiable buildings. The High Victorian Gothic–style structure, designed by Samuel Hannaford, hosted the 1880 Democratic National Convention and an 1883 industrial convention at which Thomas Edison won an award for the best incandescent light. Other tenants have included the Cincinnati Art Museum

(1882–1886) and the Technical School of Cincinnati (1886–1901). It is still used by the May Festival, as well as the Cincinnati Symphony Orchestra, the Cincinnati Opera, and the Cincinnati Ballet. & (Uptown Cincinnati)

TEMPLE OF LOVE
Mount Storm Park, Clifton
513/352-4080
All that's left of Robert Bowler's elegant estate (demolished in 1917) is this 1845 pavilion designed by Adolph Strauch, former supervisor of the Imperial Gardens in Vienna and designer of Spring Grove Cemetery. Designed to cover a not-so-romantic cistern, this ornate structure, with its Corinthian columns, is indicative of the popularity of classical styles in nineteenth-century Cincinnati. (Uptown Cincinnati)

WILLIAM HOWARD TAFT NATIONAL HISTORIC SITE
2038 Auburn Ave., Mt. Auburn
513/684-3262
William Howard Taft, this nation's twenty-seventh president and tenth Chief Justice, grew up here. The two-story Greek Revival–style brick Taft House, built in 1853 by his father, Alphonso, was divided into apartments for a while but has since been restored to its original condition. Open 10–4 daily. Free. (Uptown Cincinnati)

EAST CINCINNATI

ELSINORE TOWER
Gilbert Avenue and Elsinore Place, Walnut Hills
513/352-4080
A local production of *Hamlet* inspired this Romanesque Revival–style building, designed by Charles B. Hannaford in 1883 as a valve house

Museum Center at Union Terminal, p. 90

for the Cincinnati Water Works. It continues to serve its original purpose. (East Cincinnati)

THE INDIAN MOUND
Indian Mound Avenue, Norwood
Built by the Adena Indians, the Indian Mound is the highest spot in the Mill Creek Valley and was most likely used as a burial chamber. Two water towers stand adjacent to the mound, all of which are situated on a small park. (East Cincinnati)

MARIEMONT VILLAGE
Mariemont
513/271-3246
This English-style village was the brainchild of Mary Emery; in 1922 she planned to create an ideal community for Cincinnati's working class. Ironically, the project was so successful that by 1927 real-estate prices had risen so high that they were no longer affordable to most workers. In 1979 the community was placed on the National Register of Historic Places. (East Cincinnati)

MEMORIAL PIONEER CEMETERY
Wilmer Road, Linwood
513/352-4080
More than 135 of Cincinnati's first European settlers are buried here, making it the oldest European burial site in Hamilton County. The earliest gravestones date back to 1790. The tall Corinthian column, originally part of the old *Cincinnati Post* building, was placed here in 1888. (East Cincinnati)

MILLER-LEUSER LOG HOUSE
6540 Clough Pike,
Anderson Township
513/231-2114
It's not quite certain when this house was built, but the earliest reference to it was in 1796, when Ichabod Benton Miller bought the property from the son of Captain Matthew Jouitt, a Virginia officer who was granted 600 acres of land for his services during the Revolutionary War. Purchased by the Anderson Township Historical Society in 1971, it now serves as a living museum. Open 1–3 on the second

and fourth Sundays of the month (May–Sept). Free. (East Cincinnati)

MIRROR LAKE
Eden Park, Mt. Adams
513/352-4080
Beneath this shallow lake lie the ruins of an 1866 reservoir, but these days it's used by Cincinnatians to cool off during the long, humid summer months. This is aided by a geyser that shoots water 60 feet into the air. South of the lake are the ruins of a second reservoir that was partly demolished in 1962. (East Cincinnati)

ROOKWOOD POTTERY BUILDING
1077 Celestial, Mt. Adams
513/721-5456
Maria Longworth Storer founded Rookwood Pottery in 1880 and it soon acquired an international reputation. Henry Farny, famous for his paintings of Native American scenes, was once on staff. The original building was located on Eastern Avenue, but the pottery moved to the Mt. Adams location in 1892 and stayed until it ceased production in 1949. In 1976 the building became a restaurant, with some of its tables set inside the kilns. (East Cincinnati)

SUNLITE POOL/CONEY ISLAND
6201 Kellogg Ave. at I-275,
Anderson Township
513/232-8230
Sunlite Pool is the largest outdoor circulating pool in the world. To be exact, it measures 400 feet by 200 feet and holds 3 million gallons of water, with five diving boards and two water slides (the Zoom Flume and the Pipeline Plunge). A small amusement park is adjacent to the pool. Open Memorial Day–Labor Day; swimming pool 10–8 daily; amusement park noon–9 daily. $13.95 adults, $10.95

children 4–11, $3 extra for amusement park. (East Cincinnati)

MEIER'S WINE CELLARS
6955 Plainfield Rd., Silverton
513/891-2900
If you want to see how wine is made, Meier's offers guided tours (leaving on the hour) that demonstrate the wine-making process. Open 10–3 Mon–Sat June–Oct. Free. (East Cincinnati)

UNIVERSITY OF CINCINNATI OBSERVATORY
3489 Observatory Pl.,
Mt. Lookout
513/321-5186
The observatory, first located in Mt. Adams, was moved to this site in 1873 when pollution from the city obscured the original view. The current building, designed by Samuel Hannaford, is now used by the University of Cincinnati. Open by appointment. Free. (East Cincinnati)

WATER TOWER
Eden Park, Mt. Adams
513/352-4080
Water from this tower used to flow downward to the Walnut Hills supply mains. Built in 1894, the 172-foot-high facility was closed in 1907 and served as an infantry guardhouse during World War I. It's now used by the city as a communications facility. (East Cincinnati)

WEST CINCINNATI

CARY COTTAGE
7000 Hamilton Ave.,
North College Hill
513/522-3860
Built in 1832 by Robert Cary, this Federal-style two-story brick house

was the childhood home to sisters and poets Alice and Phoebe Cary, both blind. Now a museum, the house stands on the grounds of the Clovernook Home and School for the Blind, which has become a Braille publishing company and rehabilitation center. Open 1–4 on the first Sunday of the month. Free, but donations are accepted. (West Cincinnati)

JOHN HAUCK HOUSE
812 Dayton St., West End
513/721-3570
Situated on what used to be called "Millionaire's Row," this 1880s Italianate townhouse—with carved stone facade, painted ceilings, mosaic floors, marbled mantels, hand-grained woodwork, a Victorian garden with a cast-iron fountain, and a carriage house—was built by George W. Skaats, a coal dealer and politician, and purchased ten years later by Cincinnati brewer John Hauck. Open 1–5 Fri–Sun. $2 adults, $1 seniors, 50 cents children. (West Cincinnati)

Temple of Love in Mt. Storm Park, p. 86

Cincinnati Park Board

HARRISON MEMORIAL PARK
Brower and Cliff Roads,
North Bend
513/941-0610
William Henry Harrison (1773–1841), this nation's ninth president, came to Cincinnati in 1791 as an ensign stationed at Fort Washington, fought at the Battle of Fallen Timbers, and, at the ensuing Treaty of Greenville, was aide to General Anthony Wayne. In 1795 Harrison married Anna Symmes, daughter of John Cleves Symmes, and built a home in North Bend. His inaugural address, the longest on record (a hefty two hours), was delivered on a drizzly day, and he died of pneumonia a month later, on April 4, 1841. His body was returned to North Bend and laid to rest here. (West Cincinnati)

SHARON WOODS VILLAGE
Sharon Woods Park, S.R. 42,
Sharonville
513/563-9484
This re-created nineteenth-century village consists of five buildings that were moved to this location when they were threatened with destruction at their original sites. Visitors are guided by trained interpreters. The buildings consist of the Elk Lick House, a mid-nineteenth-century Carpenter Gothic–style house with period furnishings; the Vorhes Home, an early nineteenth-century Federal-style brick country house built in 1825; the Kemper Log House, a two-story, double pen log house built in 1804 by the Rev. James Kemper for his family of 15; the Gatch Barn; and Dr. Langdon's Medical Office. Open 10–4 Fri–Sun (Apr); 10–4 Wed–Fri, 1–5 Sat and Sun (May–Oct); 1–5 the last weekend in November and every weekend in December. $5 adults, $3 seniors, $2 children 7–12, children under 7 free. (West Cincinnati)

The Heimlich maneuver, credited with saving the lives of countless choking victims, was developed in 1974 in Cincinnati by Dr. Henry J. Heimlich.

SPRING GROVE CEMETERY AND ARBORETUM
4521 Spring Grove Ave.
Winton Place
513/681-6680

The original 167-acre cemetery, dedicated in 1845, was the brainchild of a group of Cincinnati businessmen tired of subpar burial grounds. Now 733 acres, it's the largest "rural" cemetery in the country, and serves as an arboretum, bird sanctuary, and park. Adolph Strauch, a German-born landscaper who served as gardener and then superintendent, was primarily responsible for its becoming an arboretum. Buried here are many of the city's most influential citizens, including Dr. Daniel Drake; Alexander and William McGuffey; Israel Ludlow; Salmon P. Chase; Nicholas Longworth II; George Hunt Pendleton; George B. Cox; and Charles P. Taft II. (West Cincinnati)

UNION TERMINAL
1301 Western Ave., Queensgate
513/287-7000

Built between 1931 and 1933, the Union Terminal is a magnificent art deco structure highlighted by an enormous half-dome, reputedly the largest in the Western Hemisphere. It served as a railway station until October 28, 1972, and was in danger of being torn down by its new owners, Southern Railway. The city, however, refused to issue a demolition permit and eventually bought the structure for a mere $2 (the land cost $2 million). After a failed attempt at turning it into a mall in the early 1980s, the terminal was converted into the Museum Center and houses the Cincinnati History Museum, the Museum of Natural History and Science, the Robert D. Lindner Family Omnimax Theater, and an Amtrak station. The rotunda alone is worth the visit, with its murals by German-born artist Winold Reiss, some of which are installed in the Cincinnati–Northern Kentucky Airport. & (West Cincinnati)

SOUTH OF THE RIVER

ANDERSON FERRY
4030 River Rd., Constance, KY
606/485-9210

Opened on August 30, 1817, by George Anderson, the ferry was the setting for *Silas Jackson's Wrongs; or a Romance of Anderson Ferry*, an 1898 novel by Joseph Longworth. It's now owned and operated by Paul and Deborah Anderson (no relation). Open 6 a.m.–9:30 p.m. (May–Oct); 6 a.m.–8 p.m. (Nov–Apr); 7 a.m. Sun and holidays; closed Christmas Day. $2.75 cars, 50 cents bicycles, 25 cents foot passengers, $1 motorbikes. & (South of the River)

CATHEDRAL BASILICA OF THE ASSUMPTION
1140 Madison Ave., Covington, KY
606/431-2060

Built in 1894, the medieval French Gothic–style cathedral's facade resembles that of Notre Dame in Paris and boasts murals by Frank Duveneck, statues by Cincinnati sculptor Clement J. Barnhorn, and 82 stained-glass windows (one of which, measuring 24 by 67 feet, is one of the largest in the United States). ♿ (South of the River)

DAN CARTER BEARD HOME
322 E. 3rd St., Covington, KY
Set in the Historic Licking Riverside District, this house was the boyhood home of Dan Carter Beard (1850–1941), founder of the Boy Scouts of America. The two-story brick house, overlooking the Licking River, is privately owned, but there is a statue out front commemorating Beard. (South of the River)

THE DUVENECK HOME
1226 Greenup St., Covington, KY
Painter Frank Duveneck (1848–1919) was born and raised here. After working as a church painter, he moved to Munich in 1869 to study at the Royal Academy of Fine Arts. He returned to Covington after graduation but soon moved to Boston, where he held a successful 1875 exhibit. He spent the next several years in Europe with a group known as the "Duveneck Boys," and came back to the States in 1888 after his wife, Elizabeth Boott, died in Florence, Italy. In 1900 he became a permanent faculty member at the Art Academy of Cincinnati and painted a large mural in Covington's Cathedral Basilica. Many of his works can be seen in the Cincinnati Art Museum. The house is now privately owned. (South of the River)

MAINSTRASSE VILLAGE
Covington, KY
This restored nineteenth-century German neighborhood, complete with charming shops and restaurants, takes up a five-block area on Covington's west side. Of particular interest is Eleftherios Kardoulias' *Goose Girl Fountain*, depicting a young *fräulein* taking two geese to market. The Greek sculptor destroyed the mold, making this life-size sculpture the only one of its kind. A 43-bell carillon stands on the west side of the village, distinguished by a set of mechanical figures that act out the Pied Piper of Hamelin at seven minutes past each hour. Annual events include March's Spring Stroll, May's Maifest, June's Summer Sunfest, and September's Oktoberfest. (South of the River)

MIMOSA MUSEUM
412 E. 2nd St., Covington, KY
606/261-9000
Built in 1853 as an Italianate villa, it was remodeled in 1900 to a Colonial Revival–style mansion and has been lovingly restored by Dean Howe and Robert Moldowan, even down to the original finishes. The house also contains gas lights, carbon-filament Edison bulbs, a Mason and Hamlin reproducing grand piano, and an

A 45-foot Ferris wheel at Coney Island, p. 88

Coney Island

unparalleled collection of antique Christmas trees and Victorian furnishings. Open 1–6 Sat and Sun (Jan–Nov); 1-8 Sat and Sun (Dec). $4. (South of the River)

SOUTHGATE HOUSE
24 E. 3rd St., Newport, KY
606/431-2201
Built between 1814 and 1821 by Kentucky politician Richard Southgate (1776–1857), the Southgate House stayed in the family for several generations and was the boyhood home of John Taliaferro Thompson, inventor of the Thompson submachine gun (the "tommy-gun" so favored by 1930s American gangsters). Zachary Taylor, Henry Clay, and James Polk were house guests, and it is said that Abraham Lincoln and Mary Todd once attended a party there. In 1914, it was sold to the Campbell County Knights of Columbus, and since 1976 it has been one of the area's premiere nightclubs. (See "Nightlife" chapter for more information.) & (South of the River)

©Mike Dulaney/Cincinnati Zoo

6

KIDS' STUFF

Cincinnati is a family-oriented city with plenty of activities to keep children amused. What would a summer be without a trip to Paramount's King's Island or a day at Coney Island's Sunlite Pool? And winter wouldn't be complete without a visit to Cincinnati Gas & Electric's Model Train Display or the Cincinnati Ballet's annual performance of The Nutcracker. Cincinnati has a children's theater, and Cincinnati's Playhouse in the Park presents a series of Saturday-morning shows for youngsters. The Museum Center at Union Terminal offers a wealth of activities for the younger set, and area museums have special programs designed to foster an interest in the arts. The city also has fun stores geared for kids. Whenever you're in Cincinnati, there's plenty for you and your children to do.

ANIMALS AND THE GREAT OUTDOORS

THE CINCINNATI ZOO AND BOTANICAL GARDENS
3400 Vine St., Avondale
513/281-4700
Opened to the public in 1875 and the second-oldest in the United States, the zoo houses more than 700 species of live animals. It's considered the finest-landscaped zoo in the nation, featuring more than 3,000 species and varieties of ornamental plants. Must-see exhibits include Jungle Trails, a re-creation of the rain forests of Asia and Africa with orangutans and Bonobo chimpanzees; Gorilla World; Komodo dragons; and Wings of the World. Children will particularly enjoy the Joseph H. Spaulding Children's Zoo; camel, train, and tram rides; and the Wildlife Theater. The annual Festival of Lights takes place in December, transforming the zoo into a winter wonderland. Open 9–8 (gates close

The last surviving passenger pigeon in the world, Martha, died at the Cincinnati Zoo on September 1, 1914. Her stuffed carcass is now on display at the Smithsonian, and a Passenger Pigeon Memorial, located on the zoo's grounds, pays tribute to her.

at 6). $8 adults, $5.75 seniors, $4.75 children 2–12, children under 2 free; $4.75 parking. ₠ (Uptown Cincinnati)

GORMAN HERITAGE FARM
3035 Gorman Heritage Farm Ln., Evendale
513/563-6663

Set on 100 acres, the Farm was established in 1835. It's still a working farm, with animals, historic buildings, and hiking trails. The site is run by the Cincinnati Nature Center, an environmental organization founded by a group of naturalists in 1965 to encourage understanding, appreciation, and responsible stewardship of the environment through education and pledges to preserve the heritage and integrity of its natural and agricultural lands. Educational programs are offered year-round. Open 9–5 Wed–Sat, 1–5 Sun. Free Wed–Fri; $3 adults, $1 children 12 and under on Sat and Sun. (East Cincinnati)

KROHN CONSERVATORY
Eden Park, Mt. Adams
513/421-4086

This botanical garden features 36,000 square feet of plants, including a tropical rain forest and a desert garden. Children will particularly enjoy the 20-foot waterfall that flows into the wishing pool. Annual shows include a summer Butterfly Display and the ever-popular winter Holiday Display, with a menorah and a living tableau of the Nativity scene complete with sheep, cows, donkeys, and a Christmas tree. Open 10–5 daily. Free, but donations appreciated. ₠ (East Cincinnati)

SUNROCK FARM
103 Gibson Ln., Wilder, KY
606/781-5502

This 63-acre farmstead, built in 1849, gives children a chance to interact with goats, pigs, sheep, emus, llamas, and donkeys. Kids can hand-feed the animals, gather chicken eggs, visit the pumpkin patch, go on hayrides, and watch sheep being sheared. Be sure to register in advance. By appointment only. $3 per person for one-hour weekday family tours, $5.50 per person for weekend two-hour family tours. (South of the River)

FUN AND EDUCATIONAL

CINCINNATI FIRE MUSEUM
315 W. Court St., Cincinnati
513/621-5553

Housed in the former Court Street Firehouse, the Cincinnati Fire Museum's mission is to teach children about fire prevention and safety by making it fun. In the Safe House they learn "stop, drop, and roll" techniques; the importance of smoke detectors; how to plan an escape route; when to call 911; and what to do if trapped by a fire. Permanent displays include a mural of Cincinnati's earliest firefighters, the Bucket Brigade; life-size firemen operating a nineteenth-century hand pumper; a steam pumper with two horses; two Ahrens-Fox motorized engines; and a miniature replica of a modern fire department. Children will have the most fun sliding down the pole, operating a replica of the hand pumper, and exploring an engine cab. Open 10–4 Tue–Fri, 12–4 Sat and Sun. $3 adults, $2 children. (Downtown Cincinnati)

CINCINNATI GAS & ELECTRIC MODEL TRAIN DISPLAY
139 E. 4th St., Cincinnati
513/632-2767
This display has been a local holiday tradition since it was first established in 1946. Three exquisitely landscaped tracks, complete with tiny people, animals, stations, and miniature trains, never cease to fascinate even the most fidgety kids. Open the day after Thanksgiving through December 31. Open 8–5 Mon–Fri, 8–noon Sat, closed Sun. Free. ♿ (Downtown Cincinnati)

SHARON WOODS VILLAGE
U.S. 42, Sharonville
513/563-9484
Children can experience nineteenth-century life firsthand in this re-created village. Although none of the houses were originally located here, they are all authentic and were moved to this site to save them from demolition. Each building—Elk Lick House, the Vorhes Home, Kemper Log House, Gatch Barn, and Dr. Langdon's Medical Office—is staffed by a trained interpreter in period costume. The village holds special events throughout the year, including a Civil War reenactment, old-fashioned baseball games, a Scarecrow and Pumpkin Festival, the Harvest Festival, and Christmas in the Village. Open 10–4 Fri–Sun (April); 10–4 Wed–Fri, 1–5 Sat and Sun (May–Oct); 1–5 the last weekend in November and every weekend in December. $5 adults, $3 seniors, $2 children 7–12, children under 7 free. (East Cincinnati)

MUSEUMS AND LIBRARIES

BEHRINGER-CRAWFORD MUSEUM OF NATURAL HISTORY
1600 Montague Rd., Covington, KY
606/491-4003
Nestled in the heart of Devou Park, the museum's displays are specially geared toward children and almost every room has some kind of "touch me" table. Many of the artifacts on display were collected by William Behringer and were donated to the city of Covington after his death. The Paleontology Gallery contains numerous fossils, including a particularly

TRIVIA

Cincinnati native Bill Paul holds the world record for the longest egg-balancing act—an astounding 36 hours!

Holiday toy train display at the Behringer-Crawford Museum, p. 95

awe-inspiring mastodon mandible. The Archaeology Gallery is dedicated to Native American tools and pottery. Upstairs, the Nineteenth Century History Gallery contains a period kitchen and the saddle belonging to John Hunt Morgan. The River Heritage Gallery is devoted to the history of steamships, and another upstairs room has a multitude of stuffed animals, including a black bear and a golden eagle. Less squeamish children will be delighted by the shrunken head and the stuffed two-headed calf in the glass case near the foot of the stairs. Open 10–5 Tue–Fri, 1–5 Sat and Sun. $3 adults, $2 seniors and children. (South of the River)

CINCINNATI ART MUSEUM
Eden Park, Mt. Adams
513/721-5204
Located in beautiful Eden Park, the Cincinnati Art Museum is considered one of the top 12 museums in the United States and has more than 100 galleries (see Museums, Galleries, and Public Art chapter). For Curious Kids is a series of educational programs specially designed to introduce children to the visual and performing arts using interactive tours, storytelling, workshops with performing artists, and hands-on art projects. The Doane Collection of Musical Instruments is accompanied by a tape recording duplicating the sounds of the rare antiques. Open 10–5 Tue–Sat, 11–5 Sun. $5 adults, $4 students and seniors; free to all on Sat. & (East Cincinnati)

CINCINNATI MUSEUM CENTER AT UNION TERMINAL
1301 Western Ave., Queensgate
513/287-7000
Three museums and an Omnimax theater are housed in this magnificent art deco building that used to serve as Cincinnati's railroad terminus, and plans are in the works for the addition of the Children's Museum, which was forced to move from its riverside location because of flooding. The Cincinnati Museum of Natural History is geared especially towards children,

with more than 50,000 square feet of exhibit space, including a re-creation of Cincinnati's Ice Age. Costumed interpreters liven up the Cincinnati History Society Museum and Library, whose permanent exhibits include a re-creation of Cincinnati's Public Landing in the late 1850s and a 94-foot sidewheel steamboat. And the African American Museum has a permanent exhibit, *Bein' Around Natti Town*, which is free.

Children will love the Robert D. Lindner Omnimax Theater—a five-story, 72-foot diameter tilted domed screen with a state-of-the-art digital sound system—but make time to line up for the good seats, which are right in the middle. If you end up near the top or the bottom, your nausea quotient goes right up. Also, be sure to experience the "Whispering Fountains," located in the corners of the dome's front wall. Because of the acoustically perfect design of the building, sound will travel from one corner's drinking fountain, up along the dome, and down to the other corner's fountain, thus making it possible to "whisper" to a companion on the other side of the building. Great fun for kids of all ages. The Museum Center is open 9–5 Mon–Sat; 11–6 Sun. $5.50 adults, $4.50 seniors, $3.50 children 3–12 for either the Natural History Museum, the History Society, or the Omnimax;

$12 adults, $11 seniors, $8 children for all three.

PUBLIC LIBRARY OF CINCINNATI AND HAMILTON COUNTY
800 Vine St., Cincinnati
513/369-6900
The library has just added a second building on the north side with the ground floor almost exclusively dedicated to children. The Children's Learning Center is a large, open, brightly colored room with an aquarium, computers, and comfortable seats. In the garden children can eat their lunches and read. The library also hosts story times, puppet shows, and children's book-talks. There is a read-aloud at 10:30 on Monday and story times at 7 p.m. Friday and 11 a.m. Saturday. Open 9–9 Mon–Fri, 9–6 Sat, 1–5 Sun. Free. (Downtown Cincinnati)

RAILWAY EXPOSITION COMPANY
315 W. Southern Ave.
Covington, KY
606/491-RAIL
More than 50 antique locomotives and railroad cars are on display in this 3-acre railroad yard. Highlights include a 1906 open-platform business car, a diner car, a Pullman troop sleeper, and a rail post office. Open 1–4 Sat and Sun (May–Oct). $2 adults, $1 children under 12; $5 family pass. (South of the River)

TRIVIA

The nation's first train robbery took place at North Bend, Ohio, 14 miles west of Cincinnati, on May 5, 1865. Ever courteous to the opposite sex, the robbers stole wallets only from male passengers.

Daniel Carter Beard and the Boy Scouts of America

Daniel Carter Beard (1850–1941) grew up in Covington, Kentucky, just across the Ohio River from Cincinnati. Inspired by tales of early pioneer life, he organized the Sons of Daniel Boone to introduce boys to the joys of woodworking and the great outdoors. When Englishman Sir Robert Baden-Powell created the Boy Scouts of England, he utilized Beard's organizational method. In 1910, when Boy Scouts of America was created, Beard's organization was taken into the fold. His boyhood home, situated at the confluence of the Ohio and Licking Rivers, still stands at 322 East 3rd Street in Covington.

TAFT MUSEUM
316 Pike St., Cincinnati
513/241-0343
Built in 1820, this Federal-style house became a museum in 1932. Its collection includes Qing dynasty Chinese porcelains, French Renaissance Limoges enamels, and paintings by Turner, Gainsborough, Constable, Millet, Rembrandt, Sargent, Duveneck, Whistler, Goya, Hals, and Farny. The best time to bring children is on Saturdays and Sundays when Walk-in Family programs are usually held. These include hands-on activities, treasure hunts, puzzles, and self-guided tours. Open 10–5 Mon–Sat, 1–5 Sun. Closed New Year's Day, Thanksgiving, Christmas. $4 adults, $2 seniors and students; free to all on Wed. (Downtown Cincinnati)

PERFORMING ARTS

THE CHILDREN'S THEATRE
Taft Theatre
5th and Sycamore Streets, Cincinnati
513/569-8080
The Children's Theatre has been bringing plays and musicals to the younger generation for more than 50 years. Besides the outreach performances it offers to area schools, the company presents about three public shows a year at the Taft Theater. Typical shows include *Aesop's Fables*, *Little Red Riding Hood*, and *The Secret Garden*. $5–$12. (Downtown Cincinnati)

CINCINNATI BALLET
Music Hall
1241–1243 Elm St., Over-the-Rhine
513/621-5219
The ballet presents around six shows per season, which runs October through May. If you're in Cincinnati during Christmastime, be sure to bring the kids to the ballet's annual presentation of *The Nutcracker*, a perennial favorite and local tradition. $9–$37. (Uptown Cincinnati)

CINCINNATI PLAYHOUSE IN THE PARK
962 Mt. Adams Circle, Mt. Adams
513/421-3888

Located high on the hill in Mt. Adams, the Playhouse is one of the nation's premiere regional theaters and produces about 11 shows a year in a season that runs from September to May. There are two stages: the 629-seat Robert S. Marx Theatre and the Thompson Shelterhouse, an intimate three-quarter theater that seats 220. Of particular interest to children is the Rosenthal Next Generation Theatre Series, an informal program of Saturday-morning theater held in the plaza area. Ticket prices range from $2.50 to $4. Ticket prices for other shows range from $20–$36. (East Cincinnati)

ENSEMBLE THEATRE OF CINCINNATI
1127 Vine St., Over-the-Rhine
513/421-3555

The Ensemble stages a children's pantomime during the holidays, a tradition that began in 1990. For the uninitiated, a pantomime is a traditional fairy tale where the hero is played by a woman and the comic roles are played by men in drag. The audience is encouraged to answer performers' rhetorical questions. For

Goodnight Moon Room at the Blue Marble Children's Bookstore

instance, if a character looks out at the audience and says, "Oh, no I can't," the audience is supposed to retort, "Oh, yes you can," and so on. ♿ (Uptown Cincinnati)

STORES KIDS LOVE

BLUE MARBLE CHILDREN'S BOOK STORE
1356 S. Ft. Thomas Ave.,
Ft. Thomas, KY
606/781-0602

The Blue Marble has more than

T I P

Kids love ice cream, and Cincinnati has some of the finest parlors in the nation. *Aglamesis Brothers* (3046 Madison Rd., Oakley, 513/631-0518) has that old-style charm; and *Graeter's*, another local mainstay with locations throughout the city, has chocolate chips bigger than the cows can make them.

20,000 titles in stock and an unusually knowledgeable staff. But what makes this children's bookstore unique is its Goodnight Moon Room, set up to look just like the room in the famous children's book by Margaret W. Brown. In fact, *Good Morning America* recently shot a segment there. The Blue Marble also sells toys and cassettes, hosts author signings, and special orders hard-to-find titles. Open 10–6 Mon–Thur, 10–5 Fri and Sat; closed Sun. (South of the River)

THE KIDS SHOP AT THE MUSEUM CENTER
1301 Western Ave., Queensgate
513/287-7052

When you visit Cincinnati's Museum Center with your family, you'll want to take your children to the Kids Shop. The store is geared especially toward children, with T-shirts, books, experimental science kits, dinosaur figures, stuffed animals, polished gemstones, magic sets, and the like. Most of the merchandise is educational, but if you don't tell the youngsters, they'll never know. Open 10–5 daily. (West Cincinnati)

KING ARTHUR'S COURT
3040 Madison Ct., Oakley
513/531-4600

This charming independent toy store is located on Oakley Square. It has everything you would expect from a good toy store, including model trains and airplanes, magic sets, dolls, juggling balls, and all sorts of board games and knickknacks. Open 10–6 Mon, Wed, Fri, and Sat; 10–8 Tue and Thur; 12–5 Sun. (East Cincinnati)

THEME PARKS

AMERICANA
5757 Middletown-Hamilton Rd., Middletown
513/539-7339

Americana, which celebrated its 75th year in 1997, is an old-fashioned theme park that has managed to stay open while its contemporaries closed down. Popular rides include the Screeching Eagle Roller Coaster, the Raging Thunder Log Flume, and The Serpent roller coaster. Other attractions include an Olympic-size swimming pool, a smaller pool for toddlers, video arcades, and picnic areas.

The Screechin' Eagle at Americana

Coney Island

Open Memorial Day–Labor Day; 11–9 Tue–Fri, 11–10 Sat, 11–9 Sun; closed Mon. $15.95 adults, $13.95 children under 52 inches, free for children 1–3 or under 3 feet. (outside West Cincinnati zone)

PARAMOUNT'S KING'S ISLAND
6400 King's Island Dr.,
King's Island
513/398-5600

This world-class amusement park is the closest thing to Disney World in this part of the country, with an incredible selection of rides. Highlights include The Racer, two roller coasters side-by-side, one facing forward, one backward; The Beast, a roller coaster that thunders into a tunnel from way up high; King Cobra, a stand-up roller coaster; and the Vortex, an exceptionally twisty roller coaster. The latest addition to the park is WaterWorks, 30 acres of water and slides. Ice and dance shows run several times a day and Paramount characters stroll around the park greeting visitors. Open Memorial Day–Labor Day; 10–10 Sun–Fri, 10 a.m.–11 p.m. Sat. Gates open at 9 a.m. $30.95 ages 7–59, $16.95 seniors and children 3–6. (East Cincinnati)

SURF CINCINNATI WATERPARK
11460 Sebring Dr., Forest Park
513/742-0620

This family-oriented waterpark's attractions include the 25,000-square-foot Super Surf Wave Pool, three winding body flumes, two five-story speed-slides on which you can race the clock, the Runaway Rapids, the Drifter Lazy River where you can relax and float in an inner tube, and a children's pool that bubbles and squirts. Other activities include sand volleyball, miniature golf, the Sebring

Annie Oakley

Annie Oakley, née Phoebe Anne Oakley Moses, was born in Darke County, Ohio, in 1860. Her father died when she was only four years old, and she took up shooting to provide food for her mother and six siblings. When she was 15, she met her future husband, Frank Butler, at a Cincinnati shooting match. Although she won the day, he won her heart. She joined Buffalo Bill's Wild West Show in 1885 and performed with them for 17 years. Her most famous stunt was shooting a cigarette dangling from the lips of Kaiser Wilhelm II of Germany.

She died in 1926, but "Little Sure Shot"'s memory lives on. Barbara Stanwyck played her on the silver screen in Annie Oakley *(1935), and Betty Hutton starred in Rodgers and Hammerstein's musical* Annie Get Your Gun *(1940).*

Play-Doh was invented in Cincinnati in the 1950s by Tien Lui and Joseph McVicker.

Raceway go-kart track, and bumper boats. Open 10:30–8 daily. $10.95 adults, $6.95 children 4 feet or less, children under age 3 free. (West Cincinnati)

PLACES TO PLAY

BICENTENNIAL COMMONS
Sawyer Point and Yeatman's Cove
805 Pete Rose Way, Cincinnati
513/352-4000
Located next to the Ohio River, just south of the downtown business district, these two parks offer a variety of kids' play areas, with swings, a roller-skating rink, and volleyball and tennis courts. In summer children delight in the spray pool and the Cincinnati Recreation Commission presents free concerts. The Serpentine Wall, which winds around the bend of the river in a series of steps, is a great place to sit, relax, and watch the boats go by. Open dawn to 10 p.m. daily. Free. (Downtown Cincinnati)

CONEY ISLAND/SUNLITE POOL
6201 Kellogg Ave. at I-275,
Anderson Township
513/232-8230
Before the advent of modern-day amusement parks, Cincinnati's Coney Island was *the* place to go for entertainment. People used to board the *Island Queen* at the Public Landing downtown and travel east on the Ohio River, debarking here. Although those days are long gone, this is still a great place to bring the kids. There are a few rides left, including a Ferris wheel, a merry-go-round, and paddle boats. The main reason to come here, though, is for Sunlite Pool, the largest outdoor circulating pool in the world, and its three water slides. Other attractions include a children's playground, volleyball courts, horseshoe pits, softball diamonds, grills, and picnic tables. Open Memorial Day–Labor Day; swimming pool 10–8 daily; amusement park 12–9 daily. $13.95 adults, $10.95 children 4–11, $3 extra for amusement park. (just outside East Cincinnati zone)

LUNKEN AIRPORT
PLAYFIELD COMPLEX
4750 Playfield Ln., East End
513/321-6500
The variety of attractions here will keep the kids busy. The Land of Make Believe has swings and several handicapped-accessible rides, as well as an old fighter jet, train engine, and caboose for children to explore. There's also an 18-hole miniature golf course, an inline skate area, and a 5.6-mile hiking and biking trail. Open 11–9 daily. $3 for miniature golf course; 75 cents for children 12 and under for the Land of Make Believe; $5/hour for a single-speed-bike rental, $2 extra for baby trailers. (East Cincinnati)

Contemporary Arts Center

7

MUSEUMS, GALLERIES, AND PUBLIC ART

The Queen City is home to some venerable arts institutions, including the Cincinnati Art Museum, nestled in Eden Park; the Contemporary Arts Center, which came to national prominence in 1990, when it was prosecuted for showing the works of photographer Robert Mapplethorpe; and downtown's Taft Museum, the legacy of Charles Phelps Taft and his wife, Anna Sinton. In addition to these fine art institutions, the city has some good history and science museums, as well as several smaller, specialized museums, such as Northern Kentucky's little-known Vent Haven Museum—the world's most extensive collection of ventriloquist dummies—and the American Museum of Brewing History and Arts—the world's largest display of brewing artifacts.

Cincinnati's low cost of living has attracted a plethora of artists, many of whom live in and around Over-the-Rhine, and quite a few galleries have sprung up around Main Street. Openings usually take place on Friday evenings, and hardly a week goes by without one. On the last Friday of each month, they celebrate by staying open until 10 p.m., giving revelers and passersby a chance to see new works.

Statues, sculptures, and fountains can be found on the streets and in the city's many parks, including George Grey Bernard's Abraham Lincoln in Lytle Park, a Nam June Paik work outside the 5th Street entrance to the Contemporary Arts Center on 5th Street, and, of course, Cincinnati's beloved Tyler Davidson fountain—The Genius of Water—in the heart of downtown on Fountain Square.

ART MUSEUMS

CINCINNATI ART MUSEUM
Eden Park, Mt. Adams
513/721-5204
Incorporated in 1881 and opened to the public in 1886, the Cincinnati Art Museum is considered one of the ten best in the nation, with over 100 galleries and a collection spanning more than 5,000 years—from Native American artifacts to pop art. Warhol, Picasso, Van Gogh, Cassatt, Hals, Titian, Rembrandt, Van Dyck, and Gainsborough are but a few of the artists represented. The Frank Duveneck collection is the best in the world. Open 10–5 Tue–Sat, 11–5 Sun. $5 adults, $4 students and seniors, 18 and under free; free to all on Sat. (East Cincinnati)

CONTEMPORARY ARTS CENTER
115 E. 5th St., Cincinnati
513/721-0390
Although the CAC and its then-director Dennis Barrie were finally acquitted of obscenity charges for exhibiting works by the late photographer Robert Mapplethorpe in 1990, the incident proved most embarrassing for Cincinnati, marking it as reactionary and prudish. But despite this setback (which turned out to be a major publicity coup for the center itself), the CAC has continued to provide the city with quality exhibitions. A Nam June Paik sculpture stands on the 5th Street side of the building, and the gallery is on the second floor. The space is open and inviting, and its opening receptions are always big social events. Plans are in the works for the CAC to move across the street from the Aronoff Center. Open 10–6 Mon–Sat, 12–5 Sun. $3.50 adults, $2 seniors and children, children under 12 free; free to all on Mon. (Downtown Cincinnati)

TAFT MUSEUM
316 Pike St., Cincinnati
513/241-0343
This Federal-style house, built in 1820 for Martin Baum, was once home to Nicholas Longworth, Cincinnati's first millionaire. Its last residents, Anna Sinton and Charles Phelps Taft, donated their home and collection of some 600 artworks to the city in 1927. The Taft Museum was opened in 1932, and its collection includes works by Rembrandt, Hals, Gainsborough, Turner, Sargent, Ruisdael, and Corot. It also has a collection of Chinese ceramics (primarily porcelains of the Kangxi reign), French Renaissance Limoges enamels, and seventeenth-century watches. Open 10–5 Mon–Sat, 1–5 Sun. $4 adults, $2 seniors and students; free to all on Wed. (Downtown Cincinnati)

SCIENCE AND HISTORY MUSEUMS

BEHRINGER-CRAWFORD MUSEUM OF NATURAL HISTORY
1600 Montague Rd., Covington, KY
606/491-4003
The museum is nestled in the heart of Covington's Devou Park. The majority of its artifacts were collected by William Behringer and donated to the city of Covington after his death. The Paleontology Gallery contains numerous prehistoric fossils, including a mastodon mandible. The Archaeology Gallery is dedicated to Native American tools and pottery. Upstairs, the Nineteenth Century History Gallery contains a period kitchen, and the saddle belonging to Confederate raider John Hunt Morgan. The River Heritage Gallery is devoted to the history of steamships, and another upstairs room has a multitude of stuffed

animals, including a black bear and a golden eagle. A shrunken head and a stuffed, two-headed calf are a few of the oddities in the glass case near the foot of the stairs. Open 10–5 Tue–Fri, 1–5 Sat and Sun. $3 adults, $2 seniors and children. (South of the River)

CINCINNATI MUSEUM CENTER AT UNION TERMINAL
1301 Western Ave., Queensgate
513/287-7000

This magnificent art deco building that once served as Cincinnati's railroad terminus houses three museums and an Omnimax theater. The Cincinnati Museum of Natural History has more than 50,000 square feet of exhibit space, and visitors can stroll through a limestone cavern and experience Cincinnati's Ice Age of 19,000 years ago. The Cincinnati Historical Society Museum and Library has several permanent exhibits hosted by costumed interpreters, including a re-creation of Cincinnati's Public Landing in the late 1850s, a 94-foot sidewheel steamboat, and an actual 1840s streetcar. The African American Museum highlights Cincinnati's African American heritage with its permanent exhibit, *Bein' Around Natti*

Town. It has no admission fee and is open from 1 to 5 p.m. Wednesday through Sunday.

The Robert D. Lindner Omnimax Theater, one of 19 in the United States, has a 5-story, 72-foot-diameter tilted domed screen and the most sophisticated digital sound system in the world. Plans are also in the works for the addition of the Children's Museum, whose riverside location was damaged by the 1997 flood. The Museum Center is open 9–5 Mon–Sat; 11–6 Sun. $5.50 adults, $4.50 seniors, $3.50 children 3–12 for either the Natural History Museum, the History Society, or the Omnimax; $12 adults, $11 seniors, $8 children for all three.

HEBREW UNION COLLEGE MUSEUM/SKIRBALL
3101 Clifton Ave., Clifton
513/221-1875

Founded in 1875 by Rabbi Isaac Mayer Wise to train American Reform Rabbis, Hebrew Union College is the largest and oldest institution of higher Jewish learning in the Western Hemisphere, with four campuses: New York City, Los Angeles, Jerusalem, and Cincinnati. The core exhibit, *An Eternal People*, explores the cultural heritage of the Jewish people using

TRIVIA

Cincinnati became front-page news in 1990, when a group of policemen stormed into the Contemporary Art Center and shut it down. The offending art? Photographs by the late photographer Robert Mapplethorpe. The city proceeded to prosecute the center and its then-director, Dennis Barrie, on charges of pandering obscenity. The case became a cause célèbre, the defendants were acquitted, and Cincinnati earned itself a new nickname—"Censornatti."

Taft Museum, p. 104

artwork, memorabilia, coins, jewelry, and textiles drawn from the Skirball Museum collection in Los Angeles. Open 11–4 Mon–Thur, 2–5 Sun, 1–4 Sat and Sun. Closed Fri, Sat, and Jewish and national holidays. $2 adults, $1 children under 12, $5 family pass. (Uptown Cincinnati)

OTHER MUSEUMS

AMERICAN MUSEUM OF BREWING HISTORY AND ARTS
Exit 186 off I-75; the Buttermilk Pike Exit, Ft. Mitchell, KY
606/341-2802
Housed in the Oldenberg complex, this museum has the largest collection of beer paraphernalia in the world, from bottles to caps to trays to signs. Tours are conducted every hour. Open 1–5 daily. $4 includes tour and tasting. (South of the River)

THE BETTS HOUSE RESEARCH CENTER
416 Clark St., West End

513/651-0734
The oldest surviving brick building in the city, this two-story farmhouse was constructed in 1804 and is dedicated to studying building materials and traditions. A permanent exhibit demonstrates how this particular building was made. Open 11–3 Tue, Wed, and Thur; 11–2 Sat. $2. (Uptown Cincinnati)

THE GRAY HISTORY OF WIRELESS
1223 Central Pkwy, Cincinnati
513/381-4033
Cincinnati's Powell Crosley Jr. put Cincinnati on the map in the 1930s when he broadcast WLW at 500,000 watts, making it the world's most powerful radio station. If you want to see the transmitter amplifier tubes that enabled WLW to become the "nation's station," visit this museum, assembled from radio memorabilia collected by one Jack Gray. A Baldwin piano that probably accompanied the dulcet sounds of the Mills Brothers and Rosemary Clooney is also on display. Open 9–5 Mon–Fri; closed Sat and Sun. Free. (Uptown Cincinnati)

UNITED STATES PLAYING CARD MUSEUM
Beech and Park Avenues, Norwood
513/396-5731

The United States Playing Card Company, the world's largest manufacturer of playing cards, established this museum soon after its founding, and from the 1920s to 1984 the collection was housed in the Cincinnati Art Museum. On display are card decks, ranging from turn-of-the-century Apache cards (hand-painted on hide) to Union Playing Cards, circa 1862. A German deck from 1460 is the oldest in the collection and the library contains over 1,000 esoteric volumes on cards.

Powell Crosley: The Man with the Midas Touch

Powell Crosley, whose father owned Cincinnati's Pike's Opera House, was an inventive man, to say the least. In 1921 he designed a small, affordable radio set, then realized that if he wanted people to buy his sets they would have to want to listen to them. So he founded his own radio station, WLW. By 1934 WLW had become the world's most powerful station, broadcasting at an astounding 500,000 watts. The signal was soon cut back, however, because of complaints from around the country. The "nation's station" gave many entertainers their first big break, including Rosemary Clooney, Fats Waller, Red Skelton, Rod Serling, and the Mills Brothers. In 1934 Crosley bought the financially troubled Cincinnati Reds. Redland Field became Crosley Field, the first major league baseball field to host a night game.

Crosley never tired of tinkering. Among his inventions were the Shelvador, a refrigerator that used the door's recess for shelves; the Koolrest bed, with a canopy cover and an installed refrigeration unit to keep the sleeper cool; the Go-By-By, a baby stroller/go-kart; and the X-er-Vac, a machine that stimulated the scalp, supposedly causing it to regrow hair. His least successful invention was the 1939 Crosley Car. Smaller and more fuel-efficient than its competitors, the $850 automobile was far ahead of its time. Crosley sold the car plant in 1952 but remained the Reds' owner until his death in 1961.

World War II aficionados will be particularly interested in the "Escape Map Card" deck that conceals a map within the cards themselves. No copies of the original mock-up exist, but the company produced a replica of this historic deck in 1990 to give to veterans of a POW camp. Curator Ron Decker, co-author of the recently published *A Wicked Pack of Cards*, is on hand for visitors who'd like a guided tour. Open 12–4 Tue and Thur. Free. (Uptown Cincinnati)

VENT HAVEN MUSEUM
33 W. Maple Ave., Ft. Mitchell
606/341-0461
This unobtrusive museum, housed on a quiet Ft. Mitchell street, is one of this area's best-kept secrets. The house once belonged to William Shakespeare Berger, a remarkable individual who turned his interest in ventriloquism into perhaps the largest collection of "vent" memorabilia in the world. There are more than 500 figures in the three galleries and hundreds of volumes on the subject, some dating back to the eighteenth century. $2 adults, $1 children ages 8–12. (South of the River)

GALLERIES

ART ACADEMY OF CINCINNATI
Eden Park, Mt. Adams
513/562-8777
Located adjacent to the Cincinnati Art Museum in Eden Park, the Art Academy is one of four museum schools in the country. Frank Duveneck once taught here. Two galleries—the Chidlaw and the Exo—display works by students, faculty, and visiting artists. Open 9–5 Mon–Fri. (East Cincinnati)

ATTIC GALLERY
York Street International Café
8th and York, Newport, KY
606/491-ARTS
Housed on the third floor of the York Street International Café in Newport, the gallery is one of many attractions in this building, which also offers dining on the first floor and live music on the second. It has a heavy focus on local art and is a great place for an opening since there are three floors from which to choose. Open 12–11 daily. (South of the River)

BASE ART GALLERY
1311 Main St., Over-the-Rhine
513/721-BASE
This Main Street gallery is a cooperative of 18 local artists and presents paintings, photography, and sculpture. On the final Friday of each month the gallery is open until 10 p.m. Openings are always a good time, with food, wine, and live music, which can also be enjoyed in the adjoining courtyard. Open 1–6 Thur,

Carnegie Visual & Performing Arts Center

Bob Cutl/Carnegie Art Center

12–9 Fri and Sat, 12–4 Sun. (Uptown Cincinnati)

CARL SOLWAY AND MICHAEL SOLWAY GALLERIES
424 Findlay St., Over-the-Rhine
513/621-0069

Located 2.5 blocks west of Findlay Market, this is essentially two galleries in one. The Carl Solway Gallery, run by Michael's father, assists in fabricating sculptures for Nam June Paik. Son Michael runs the exhibition program, featuring contemporary conceptual art with some emphasis on new technology. Past shows have highlighted works by Joel Otterson, Alan Rath, and Ben Patterson. Open 9–5 Mon–Fri, Sat by appointment. (Uptown Cincinnati)

CARNEGIE VISUAL & PERFORMING ARTS CENTER
1028 Scott Blvd., Covington, KY
606/491-2030–galleries
606/655-8112–theater

Built in 1902 with matching funds from Andrew Carnegie's Library Fund, the Carnegie served as the Covington Public Library until 1974. The Beaux Arts building now houses four galleries exhibiting works by local and regional artists. Connected to the galleries is a theater built in the style of an eighteenth-century European opera house. The theater provides a venue for small professional theater groups and also offers concerts, dance performances, and educational shows for area schools. Open 10:30–5:30 Tue–Fri, 1–4 Sat. Admission by donation. (South of the River)

CINCINNATI ART GALLERIES
635 Main St., Cincinnati
513/381-2128

This downtown gallery carries the largest selection of nineteenth- and early-twentieth-century American and European paintings in the city, with works by the likes of Henry Farny and John Twachtman. Its annual auction of Rookwood Pottery (see sidebar) takes place in June. The gallery also publishes several books on pottery. Open 9–5 Mon–Fri, 10–5 Sat; closed Sun. (Downtown Cincinnati)

CLOSSON'S GALLERY
601 Race St., Cincinnati
513/762-5510

Housed in a downtown fine-furniture store, this gallery claims to be the oldest west of the Alleghenies. It carries originals and limited edition prints by nineteenth- and twentieth-century European and American painters as well as works by wildlife artist John Ruthven and maritime artist John Stobart. Open 10–6 Mon–Sat; closed Sun. (Downtown Cincinnati)

FREEMAN GALLERY
406 Central Ave., West End
513/579-0005

The Freeman features works by local

Rookwood Pottery

by Dr. Robert Vitz, Professor of History, Northern Kentucky University

Influenced by ceramic ware exhibited at the 1876 Philadelphia Centennial Exhibition (the nation's first world's fair), Maria Longworth Nichols, daughter of the wealthy and socially prominent Joseph Longworth, founded Rookwood Pottery to produce aesthetically pleasing pottery. William Watts Taylor was soon hired as the pottery manager and later as president. Under Taylor's firm direction, Rookwood quickly established itself as a leader in the art pottery movement that was spreading across the country. Rookwood ware received a gold medal at the 1889 Paris Exposition Universelle, the first of many national and international awards. Success, coupled with periodic Ohio River floods, led Nichols (who had since become Mrs. Bellamy Storer) and Taylor to move the pottery in 1890 from the river's edge just east of downtown to the brow of Mt. Adams, where its Tudor-style building is a city landmark.

Rookwood's excellence stemmed from a group of extraordinary designers, many of whom trained at the nearby Art Academy of Cincinnati. Among the pottery's most distinguished artists were the Japanese-born Kataro Shirayamadani, who worked there from 1887 until his death in 1948, and Edmund T. Hurley, whose work received national recognition in the first decades of the twentieth century. Other prominent designers included Sara Sax, William P. McDonald, Albert Valentien, Harriet Wilcox, Sara Toohey, and Carl Schmidt. After 1930, changes in aesthetic taste, increased mass production, and the onset of the Great Depression led to Rookwood's gradual decline. In 1960 the pottery moved to the Mississippi, and several years later it closed.

and national African American artists. John Biggers has had works exhibited here, as have several book illustrators. Open 4–6 Fri, 1–6 Sat. (West Cincinnati)

THE GALLERY AT WELLAGE AND BUXTON
1431 Main St., Over-the-Rhine
513/241-9127
This Main Street gallery exhibits regional contemporary work. New shows always open on Final Friday (the last Friday of the month), when the gallery stays open until 10. Open 10–5 Mon–Fri, 10–3 Sat; closed Sun. (Uptown Cincinnati)

ONLY ARTISTS
1315 Main St., Over-the-Rhine
513/241-6672
Specializing in Mexican and American folk art and contemporary crafts, Only Artists stays open until 10 on Final Fridays. Open 11–5 Wed and Thur, 11–7 Fri, 10–5 Sat. (Uptown Cincinnati)

WESTON ART GALLERY
650 Walnut St., Cincinnati
513/977-4166
Housed in the Aronoff Center for the Arts, downtown, the Weston is a two-level gallery with a revolving exhibition season of emerging regional and national artists. Previous shows include works by Tim Hawkinson and Todd Slaughter. The gallery also hosts a film series. Open 1–6 Tue–Sat, 12–6 Sun, 6–8 on performance nights at P & G Hall. $1. (Downtown Cincinnati)

YWCA WOMEN'S ART GALLERY
898 Walnut St., Cincinnati
513/241-7090
This downtown gallery is on the second floor of the YWCA and displays works by local and regional artists, with a special emphasis on art by women. Open 9–8 Mon–Fri, 9–5 Sat; closed Sun. (Downtown Cincinnati)

PUBLIC ART

ABRAHAM LINCOLN STATUE
Lytle Park, Cincinnati
This 11-foot bronze statue of the Great Emancipator was commissioned by the Charles P. Taft family and took sculptor George Grey Bernard five years to finish. When it was dedicated in 1917, former U.S. president William Howard Taft delivered the address. Lincoln visited Cincinnati on February 12, 1861, on his way to Washington. Coincidentally, the night Lincoln was

TRIVIA

Famous wildlife artist John James Audubon moved to Cincinnati in 1819, worked as a taxidermist for the Western Museum for six months, and then tried to make a living as a portrait painter and art teacher. Dissatisfied with his prospects, he boarded a flatboat headed for New Orleans and never returned. A statue of Audubon stands at the confluence of the Licking and Ohio Rivers on Covington's Riverside Drive.

assassinated by John Wilkes Booth, Booth's brother Junius Brutus was appearing at the now-demolished Pike's Opera House downtown. Upon hearing the news, Junius fell to the ground in a faint and high-tailed it out of the city at the first opportunity. (Downtown Cincinnati)

AGGRAVATION DE L'ESPACE
Central Parkway, Cincinnati
French artist Jean Boutellis created this abstract steel sculpture, and it was originally installed in front of City Hall at 9th and Plum Streets in 1980. Its name, however, rang all too true, and when pedestrians complained that it got in their way it was moved to the current location. (Downtown Cincinnati)

ATMAN
Eden Park, Mt. Adams
Mark di Suvero created this piece in 1986, and it was installed in front of the Cincinnati Art Museum. The 32-foot-high, 10-ton abstract sculpture made from steel girders used to have a redwood swing suspended from its frame, but this was removed for fear of liability. Suvero, who was born in Shanghai, China, named the sculpture *Atman*, which means "world soul." (East Cincinnati)

"THE BOY AND THE BOOK"
Stanbery Park, Mt. Washington
Italian-born artist Arturo Ivone created this sculpture, popularly known as "The Boy and the Book." Commissioned by the Mt. Washington Civic Club and American Legion Post 484, it originally stood in Campus Lane Park but was moved to its present location in 1941. (East Cincinnati)

CAPITOLINE WOLF SCULPTURE
Eden Park, Mt. Adams

Atman *in Eden Park*

Cincinnati Park Board

This bronze wolf is a replica of the Etruscan wolf on the Capitoline Hill. The two infants, Romulus and Remus, are Renaissance additions. The sculpture was given to Cincinnati by the Order of the Sons of Italy. The inscription on the plaque, "Anno X," refers to 1931, the tenth year of Benito Mussolini's regime and the year it was presented to the city. (East Cincinnati)

CORMORANT FISHERMAN SCULPTURE
Eden Park, Mt. Adams
A gift from Cincinnati's sister city of Gifu, Japan, the bronze sculpture depicting a Japanese fisherman bending over a cormorant was created by Kosei Tateno and installed in 1992. (East Cincinnati)

H.H. RICHARDSON MONUMENT
Burnet Woods, Clifton
When the Cincinnati Chamber of Commerce Building burned down in a 1911 fire, the fragments that survived were salvaged by the Cincinnati Astronomical Society for an observatory

that was never built. The pieces were transmogrified into a Stonehenge-like sculpture by Stephen Carter, who won a design contest sponsored by the University of Cincinnati's architectural school. The 27-foot-diameter circle was installed in 1967. (Uptown Cincinnati)

JAMES ABRAMS GARFIELD MONUMENT
Piatt Park, Cincinnati
Garfield, who made his living as a Cleveland preacher, canal boat operator, and president of Hiram College before his ill-fated trip to the White House, was one of six U.S. presidents born in Ohio. Cincinnati sculptor Charles Henry Niehaus cast this bronze sculpture in Rome in 1885, and it was installed two years later at the intersection of 8th and Race Streets. In 1915 the statue was moved because it was causing traffic problems; in 1988, following renovation of the park, it was moved once again, almost to its original location. (Downtown Cincinnati)

KILGOUR FOUNTAIN
Hyde Park Square, Hyde Park
Cincinnati-born sculptor Joseph Cronin designed this fountain, a gift to the people of Hyde Park from real-estate magnate Charles Kilgour. The fountain, composed of a classically draped woman, lion-head water spouts, and fluted basins, was completed in 1900 and redesigned in 1975 by Eleftherios Karkadoulias, who added the surrounding pool. (East Cincinnati)

STEPHEN FOSTER STATUE
Alms Park, Linwood
Composer Stephen Foster moved to Cincinnati when he was 19 to clerk in his brother's office on 4th Street. He wrote and sold several songs during his four years here, including "Oh, Susanna." The statue, which took Arthur Ivone nearly two years to create, was cast at the Antioch Art Foundry in Yellow Springs, Ohio, and unveiled in 1937. (East Cincinnati)

TYLER DAVIDSON FOUNTAIN/ *THE GENIUS OF WATER*
Fountain Square Plaza, Cincinnati
Designed by August von Kreling and cast in 1867 by the Royal Bavarian Foundry in Munich, this fountain was given to the city by Henry Probasco in memory of his business partner and brother-in-law, Tyler Davidson. The square was redesigned and enlarged in the 1960s, and the fountain, which originally faced east, was turned 180 degrees to face west. (Downtown Cincinnati)

Cincinnati-Born Artists

Jim Borgman
Jim Dine
Robert S. Duncanson
Frank Duveneck

Henry Farny
Edward Potthast
John Rettig
John Twachtman

VIETNAM VETERANS MEMORIAL
Eden Park, Mt. Adams
Dedicated in 1984, Kenneth Bradford's bronze sculpture of two mournful-looking soldiers stands on pink granite base inscribed with the map of Vietnam. A 60-foot-high memorial flagpole, relocated from the nearby Galbraith Memorial, stands beside it. (East Cincinnati)

WILLIAM HENRY HARRISON MONUMENT
Piatt Park, Cincinnati
Created by Louis T. Rebisso, an Art Academy instructor, this is the only equestrian statue in Cincinnati. The bronze sculpture of this nation's ninth president was erected in 1896 and commemorates Harrison's involvement in the Battle of Tippecanoe and the War of 1812. (Downtown Cincinnati)

WORLD WAR I MEMORIAL
Valley Park, Camp Washington
Chicago artist John Paulding designed this bronze sculpture of an infantry soldier, or doughboy, as a memorial to those soldiers from the Camp Washington community who died in World War I. It was installed in 1920 and has since had dedications to Korean and Vietnam soldiers added to the remaining sides of the pedestal. (West Cincinnati)

8
PARKS, GARDENS, AND RECREATION AREAS

If you fly into Cincinnati, take a look out the window on your approach; you'll be amazed at the amount of greenery throughout the city. Even driving around town, you'll be struck by the abundance of trees that are the result of the large number of hills too steep for buildings and also of the area's beautifully landscaped parks. In 1911 Mt. Airy Forest became the site of the first municipal reforestation project in the nation, and more than a million trees were planted on what were once meadows.

Parks have always been integral to Cincinnati. The best example is Eden Park, which, in addition to its greenery, houses some of the city's most venerable institutions: the Cincinnati Art Museum, Cincinnati Art Academy, Krohn Conservatory, and Cincinnati Playhouse in the Park. The city is still committed to conserving and developing its park system; this decade has seen a new planning effort, aptly titled "Planting the Future—The Cincinnati Parks and Greenways Plan."

AULT PARK
Observatory Avenue, Hyde Park
513/352-4080

This 223-acre park, run by the Cincinnati Park Board, is set on a ridge overlooking the Little Miami Valley. Levi Addison Ault, park commissioner from 1908 to 1926, donated the initial 142 acres of land to the park; a memorial to him stands on the terrace of the Ault Park Pavilion, a magnificent structure inspired by the Italian Renaissance. Irises, tulips, and flowering trees can be seen in the ornamental gardens, a perfect setting for the Greater Cincinnati Flower and Garden Show which takes place there each May. Open 6 a.m.–10 p.m. daily. (East Cincinnati)

BICENTENNIAL COMMONS
Sawyer Point and Yeatman's Cove
805 Pete Rose Way, Cincinnati
513/352-4000
Located next to the Ohio River just south of the downtown business district, these adjacent city parks offer a variety of recreational facilities, including a playground, roller-skating rink, and volleyball and tennis courts. The Boathouse, located on the eastern side of the park, is home to one of Cincinnati's most popular restaurants, Montgomery Inn Boathouse, as well as an Olympic rowing center. The Serpentine Wall, a series of steps that doubles as a levee, is a great place to watch the boats go by and there's also a fishing pier (just don't eat the fish you catch!). Free concerts take place here throughout the summer, and this is a great place to watch the Labor Day fireworks. Open 6 a.m.–10 p.m. daily. (Downtown Cincinnati)

DEVOU PARK
800 Park Ln., Covington, KY
606/431-2577
This 550-acre park was donated to the city of Covington in 1910 and has one of the most spectacular views of the city. The vista from Devou Park's overlook was used for the opening shots of the television sitcom *WKRP in Cincinnati*, as well as for the soap opera *Edge of the Night*. The 1.25-mile-long Sierra Club Nature Trail, home to deer, raccoons, badgers, foxes, and a wide variety of birds and wildflowers, is located close to Devou Golf and Tennis Club. The park has an amphitheater where the Devou Summer Classics Theater company performs, and is also home to the Behringer-Crawford Museum, a lake, and the remains of a Civil War gunnery. Open dawn to dusk. (South of the River)

Entrance to Bicentennial Commons at Sawyer Point

Stephanni Cohen/©Cincinnati Recreation Commission

EDEN PARK
Eden Park Drive, Mt. Adams
513/352-4080
This 186-acre park just to the east of downtown in Mt. Adams was once a huge vineyard owned by Nicholas Longworth. Now it's one of the most beautiful parks in the city system, with a magnificent view of the Ohio River Valley. In summer, visitors can splash around in Mirror Lake and its 60-foot-high geyser; in winter, they can ice-skate on the lake. The lake covers an old reservoir, and ruins of another lie to its south.

Eden Park is also home to the Cincinnati Art Museum, Cincinnati Playhouse in the Park, and the Krohn Conservatory. Other attractions include the Vietnam Memorial, Elsinore Tower, the Capitoline Wolf (donated by the city of Rome during Mussolini's regime), the Cormorant Fisherman sculpture (donated by Cincinnati's sister city of Gifu, Japan) and the Ohio River monument, a

Top Ten Cincinnati Vistas

1. From the observation deck on the Carew Tower
   —*David Brown, curator of the Contemporary Arts Center*

2. From the hills of Newport, Kentucky
   —*Stacy Owen, music director of 89.7 WNKU*

3. The trains from Fairview Park
   —*Josip Novakovich, writer* (Apricots from Chernobyl)

4. From the steps in front of Holy Cross Immaculata in Mt. Adams
   —*John Fox, editor and publisher of* Citybeat

5. From the overlook at Mt. Echo Park
   —*Jeff Hillard, writer* (Pieces of Fernald: Poems and Images of a Place)

6. From a boat on the Ohio River
   —*Thom Atkinson, playwright*

7. Traveling toward Cincinnati on the John A. Roebling Suspension Bridge at night
   —*Kelly Germain, comedienne, member of Carnivores in Action*

8. Driving north toward Cincinnati on I-71/I-75
   —*Austin Wright, novelist* (Disciples)

9. From the Devou Park overlook
   —*Robert T. Rhode, Professor of English at Northern Kentucky University*

10. Driving west toward Cincinnati on Columbia Parkway
    —*Kim Wood, Cincinnati Bengals' strength coach*

30-foot-high obelisk commemorating the canalization of the Ohio River between Pittsburgh, Pennsylvania, and Cairo, Illinois. Outdoor concerts take place in the Seasongood Pavilion. Open 6 a.m.–10 p.m. daily. (East Cincinnati)

**EMBSHOFF WOODS
AND NATURE PRESERVE
4050 Paul Rd., Delhi Township
513/521-PARK**

This 316-acre park, sprawled on a ridge top in Delhi Township, was donated by the Embshoff family and is now run by the Hamilton County Park District. Although 90 percent of the park is set aside as a natural area, there are plenty of recreational facilities, including a Parcours Fitness Trail, Frisbee golf course, playground, picnic and shelter areas, and the River Mount Pavilion. The park— from which you can spot red-tailed

The Spring House Gazebo in Eden Park, p. 116

hawks, bald eagles, barred and great horned owls, raccoons, opossums, and gray squirrels—also provides a great view of downtown. Open dawn to dusk daily. $1 motor vehicle permit. (West Cincinnati)

FAIRVIEW PARK
West McMillan Street, Fairview
513/352-4080
On October 10, 1843, William Miller climbed to this spot in anticipation of the Second Coming of Christ, but to no avail. It's easy to see why Miller chose this site. Fairview Park has a spectacular view of the valley and the trains below. An incline, leading to McMicken Avenue, was here from 1894 to 1923. The park has a playground and a pool. Open 6 a.m.–10 p.m. daily. (Uptown Cincinnati)

HAUCK BOTANIC GARDENS
2625 Reading Rd., Avondale
513/352-4080
Cornelius J. Hauck, who served on the Park Board for 18 years and developed a new strain of lilac, planted more than 900 types of trees, shrubs, and evergreens on the grounds of his 8-acre estate and donated it to the city of Cincinnati in his will. Of particular interest is the Tudor-style English Tea House, a replica of a 1939 World's Fair building. Open 6 a.m.–10 p.m. daily. (Uptown Cincinnati)

KROHN CONSERVATORY
1501 Eden Park Dr., Mt. Adams
513/421-4086
This glassed-in botanical garden features 36,000 square feet of plants, including a tropical rain forest, a desert garden, and a 20-foot waterfall that flows into the wishing pool. Annual events include a summer Butterfly Display and a Holiday Display, with a menorah; a living Nativity scene complete with sheep, cows, and donkeys; and a Christmas tree. Open 10–5 daily. Free, but donations appreciated. (East Cincinnati)

LAKE ISABELLA
10174 Loveland-Madeira Rd.,
Symmes Township

513/521-PARK

This 77-acre park, run by the Hamilton County Park District, has a 28-acre fishing lake with a full-service boathouse, rowboat rentals, a pier, an outdoor deck, and an indoor dining area. There are also picnic areas, a playground, a wildlife viewing area, and canoe access to the Little Miami River. Lake Isabella—stocked with adult channel, blue, and shovelhead catfish, and rainbow trout—is a pay fishing lake. An Ohio State fishing license is not required, but anglers should purchase a daily ticket and fish from the bank or from a rental boat. Open dawn to dusk daily. $1 motor vehicle permit. (East Cincinnati)

LUNKEN AIRPORT PLAYFIELD COMPLEX
4750 Playfield Ln., East End
513/321-6500

Built on a floodplain on the site of Columbia, one of Cincinnati's first three European settlements, Lunken Airport was the largest municipal airport in the nation when it was dedicated in 1932 and was American Airlines' first home. Its flat terrain makes it perfect for bicycling and the 5.6-mile hiking and biking trail is one of the most popular in the area. The complex also features an 18-hole miniature golf course, 16 tennis courts, and a playground called the Land of Make Believe. Open 11–9 daily. $3 for miniature golf course; 75 cents for children 12 and under for the Land of Make Believe; $5/hour for a single-speed-bike rental, $2 extra for baby trailers. (East Cincinnati)

LYTLE PARK
4th and Lawrence Streets, Cincinnati
513/352-4080

This attractive downtown park is a peaceful oasis in an otherwise busy metropolis. It's surrounded by nineteenth-century structures and gives visitors the feeling of being transported back in time. Of particular interest is an 11-foot-high bronze statue of Abraham Lincoln by George Grey Barnard. (Downtown Cincinnati)

MITCHELL MEMORIAL FOREST
5401 Zion Rd., Miami Township
513/521-PARK

The Hamilton County Park District runs this heavily wooded, 1,340-acre park with a fishing pond, several picnic areas, a playground, and a stone memorial shelter. Winding through the woods is Wood Duck Trail, from which you can spot warblers, woodpeckers, white-tailed deer, raccoons, and possums. Open dawn to dusk daily. $1 motor vehicle permit. (West Cincinnati)

MT. AIRY FOREST
5083 Colerain Ave., Mt. Airy

TRIVIA

Hamilton native Charles F. Richter developed the Richter Scale in 1935. This logarithmic scale represents the energy released by an earthquake.

Three Great Parks

Three of the Cincinnati area's best parks lie a little further out but are certainly worth the drive. **Miami Whitewater Forest** (9001 Mt. Hope Rd., Harrison, 513/521-PARK) is the largest park in the Hamilton County Park District. Its 3,906 acres, featuring a variety of managed habitats and an 85-acre lake, offer a wealth of recreational activities, including horseback riding, golf, Frisbee golf, and fishing. There are three beautiful nature trails, and the boathouse rents rowboats, pedal boats, canoes, hydrobikes, bicycles, and inline skates. Take Exit 3 off I-74, the Dry Fork Road Exit.

East Fork State Park (2505 Williamsburg-Bantam Rd., Afton, 800/BUCKEYE) is an 8,420-acre park with a 2,160-acre lake, a hunting area, and 58 miles of hiking trails, including a 4.6-mile mountain-bike trail. It also has 68 miles of bridle trails, boat ramps, and a campground. In early June, local radio station WGRR puts on a free Oldies Fest. Take Exit 65 off I-275 the OH 125, Amelia, Beechmont Avenue Exit.

During the Ice Age, as the ice caps inched their way south, huge herds of giant mastodons, mammoths, bison, primitive horses, and sloths moved to what is now **Big Bone Lick State Park** (3380 Beaver Rd., Union, KY, 606/384-3522). The prehistoric beasts were attracted to the salt found in what were then swamps but got stuck and died in great numbers, leaving their bones behind. Today, all that is left of the salty marsh is one sulfur spring, but many of the bones are still here, on display in the Big Bone Lick Museum. The park also has a 7.5-acre lake, 2.4 miles of hiking trails, an 18-hole mini-golf course, a swimming pool, tennis and basketball courts, a playground, and campground facilities. Take Exit 175 off I-75, the KY 388, Richwood Exit.

Mirror Lake at Eden Park, p. 116

513/352-4094

This 1,466-acre park, established in 1911, was the site of the first municipal reforestation program in the United States. Its 120-acre arboretum, constructed in 1953, has more than 1,600 species of trees and shrubs and attracts a large number of birds. This is a great place to hike, and Mt. Airy Forest has several miles of nature trails: Furnas Trail, Ponderosa Trail, Quarry Trail, Red Oak Trail, and Twin Bridge Trail. Open 6 a.m.–10 p.m. daily. (West Cincinnati)

MT. ECHO PARK
Elberon Avenue, Price Hill
513/352-4094

This 73-acre park is set on a ridge high above the Ohio River Valley, and its overlook provides a panoramic view of the Ohio River, Kentucky, and the downtown Cincinnati skyline. There are two trails—the 1-mile Nature Trail Loop and the 1.25-mile Park Loop—and a playground, baseball field, tennis courts, basketball courts, and

picnic shelters. Open 6 a.m.–10 p.m. daily. (West Cincinnati)

MT. STORM PARK
700 Lafayette Ave., Clifton
513/352-4080

Robert Bonner Bowler, owner of the Kentucky Central Railroad, built his estate on a hill overlooking the city, with a panoramic view of the Millcreek Valley, and his heirs sold it to the city of Cincinnati after his death. Adolph Strauch, famed superintendent of Spring Grove Cemetery, designed the grounds and the Temple of Love, a fanciful round dome with eight Corinthian columns. Open 6 a.m.–10 p.m. daily. (Uptown Cincinnati)

PIATT PARK
Garfield Place, Cincinnati
513/352-4080

This peaceful downtown park lies between 7th and 9th Streets, running from Vine to Elm Streets. Trees and seasonal flowers adorn each side of the strip, almost making you forget that there's a road on each side of you. In summer the city presents a series called Acoustic Lunch in Piatt Park that showcases the talents of local musicians. The park is book-ended on the west by a statue of James Garfield, the twentieth U.S. president, and on the east by an equestrian statue of William Henry Harrison, the ninth U.S. president. (Downtown Cincinnati)

SHARON WOODS PARK
11450 Lebanon Rd., Sharonville
513/521-PARK

The Hamilton County Park District runs this 755-acre park comprising a re-created nineteenth-century village, deciduous forest, meadows, grasslands, picnic areas, and a man-made 35-acre lake, considered one of the best bass lakes in the county. The park opened in 1932, the lake was created four years later, and in 1938 golf legend Bobby Jones inaugurated the park's 18-hole golf course.

Pedal boats, rowboats, canoes, bikes, and tandem bikes can be rented at the boathouse, along with bait and tackle supplies. Fishing is by rental boat only, but there's a bank-fishing area along the pier for seniors, children, and handicapped individuals. The harbor has an Ice Age–theme wet playground and a path with a geological timeline. There is also a 2.6-mile hike/bike trail that winds around the lake, and a 1-mile Parcours Fitness Trail with 18 exercise stations. The 1.25-mile Richard H. Durrell Trail along the 90-foot Sharon Creek Gorge is part of a scenic nature preserve and is well known for its wealth of Ordovician fossils. Open dawn to dusk daily. $1 motor vehicle permit. (East Cincinnati)

SHAWNEE LOOKOUT
2008 Lawrenceburg Rd., Miami Township
513/521-PARK
The Hamilton County Park District runs this 1,026-acre park that was once home to the Hopewell culture, mound-builders who left behind the remains of a fortress, mounds, and burial grounds. The area, with its commanding views of the Ohio and Great Miami River Valleys, was later settled by Shawnee and Miami tribes. Visitors can also visit the restored Springhouse School and Log Cabin House to see how the early pioneers lived.

There are three nature trails— 1.3-mile Blue Jacket Trail, 1.4-mile Miami Fort Trail, and 2-mile Little Turtle Trail—along with an 18-hole golf course, a clubhouse, and a pro shop with a year-round archaeological exhibit. If you stand on the tee of the twelfth hole, you can see three states: Ohio, Kentucky, and Indiana. There are also playgrounds, an athletic field, picnic areas, a reservable shelter, and a boat-launch ramp with access to the Great Miami and Ohio Rivers. Open dawn to dusk daily. $1 motor vehicle permit. (West Cincinnati)

SPRING GROVE CEMETERY AND ARBORETUM
4521 Spring Grove Ave., Winton Place
513/681-6680
This 733-acre cemetery, dedicated in 1845, is the largest "rural" cemetery

in the country, and serves as an arboretum, bird sanctuary, and park. Adolph Strauch, a German-born landscaper who served as gardener and then superintendent, was primarily responsible for its becoming an arboretum. Many of the city's most influential citizens are buried here. (West Cincinnati)

WINTON WOODS
10245 Winton Rd.,
Springfield Township
513/521-7275
This 2,628-acre park, run by the Hamilton County Park District, has several natural habitats: meadows and forests in various stages of growth, with an assortment of beech, oak, and maple trees. Recreational facilities include Frisbee golf, playgrounds, picnic areas, shelters, and athletic fields. There is also a 20-station Parcours Fitness Trail and two nature trails: 1-mile Kingfisher Trail and .75-mile Great Oaks Trail. Parky's Farm, a 100-acre demonstration farm with orchards, gardens, crops, goats, pigs, sheep, and horses, is also in Winton Woods. The Winton Woods Riding Center offers classes for beginners and advanced equestrians. The 188-acre lake is undergoing an extensive restoration that should be completed by the spring of 1998. Open dawn to dusk daily. $1 motor vehicle permit. (West Cincinnati)

9

SHOPPING

Although the Queen City has many suburban shops and malls, the accessibility and variety of its downtown retail establishments is what sets this city apart. From Batsakes Hat Shop (which has made hats for the likes of Luciano Pavarotti and Tony Bennett) to Closson's (which houses the oldest art gallery west of the Alleghenies), all the downtown stores are within walking distance of each other, and some are even connected by a second-level skywalk, which comes in handy on a cold and rainy day.

SHOPPING AREAS

City Center
This shopping district—bounded by 4th Street on the south and 6th Street on the north—is centered around Fountain Square, in the very heart of downtown Cincinnati. Many of the shops are connected by the skywalk system and are within easy walking distance of each other. Some of the older establishments have been around since the nineteenth century.

BANKHARDT'S LUGGAGE SHOP
6 W. 4th St., Cincinnati

513/421-2121
Bankhardt's Luggage Shop has been providing the Queen City with fine leather goods since it first opened in 1868. It specializes in top-of-the-line luggage and offers such brands as Hartmann, Tumi, and Samsonite. It also carries an unusual selection of chess sets, travel clocks, handbags, attaché cases, and portable travel bars. Open 10–5:30 Mon–Sat; closed Sun. (Downtown Cincinnati)

BATSAKES HAT SHOP
& DRY CLEANERS
605 Walnut St., Cincinnati
513/721-9345

SHOPPING NEAR THE SKYWALK

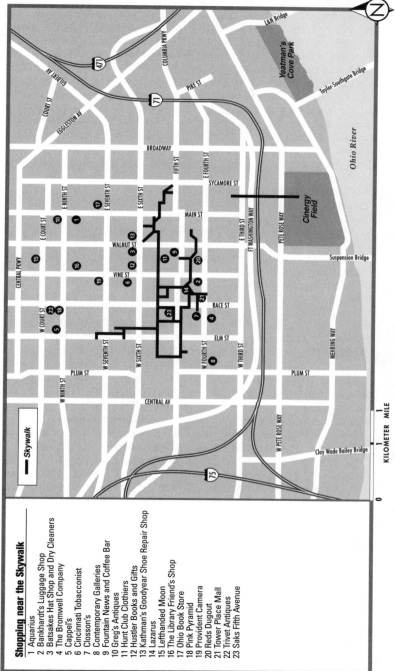

Shopping near the Skywalk

1 Aquarius
2 Bankhardt's Luggage Shop
3 Batsakes Hat Shop and Dry Cleaners
4 The Bromwell Company
5 Cappel's
6 Cincinnati Tobacconist
7 Closson's
8 Contemporary Galleries
9 Fountain News and Coffee Bar
10 Greg's Antiques
11 Hunt Club Clothiers
12 Hustler Books and Gifts
13 Kathman's Goodyear Shoe Repair Shop
14 Lazarus
15 Lefthanded Moon
16 The Library Friend's Shop
17 Ohio Book Store
18 Pink Pyramid
19 Provident Camera
20 Reds Dugout
21 Tower Place Mall
22 Trivet Antiques
23 Saks Fifth Avenue

This Cincinnati mainstay is across the street from the Aronoff Center for the Arts. The store was opened in 1907 by Pete Batsakes, a first-generation Greek immigrant, and the business has remained in the family. The hat shop and shoeshine stand are owned by Pete's nephew, Gus Miller, and the dry-cleaners is owned by Pete's sons, George and James. Batsakes Hat Shop is best known for its illustrious list of customers—such as Luciano Pavarotti, Tommy Lasorda, Tony Bennett, Burt Reynolds, Red Skelton, Anthony Quinn, Joe Pesci, George Bush, and Ronald Reagan—and photos of these and other smiling patrons adorn the walls and windows. Batsakes makes hats on the premises and offers such brands as Stetson, Dobbs, Kangol, and Borsalino. Open 7–6 Mon–Sat; closed Sun. (Downtown Cincinnati)

CINCINNATI TOBACCONIST
617 Vine St., Cincinnati
513/621-9932
Located in the old *Cincinnati Enquirer* building, an ornate art deco construction with a limestone facade, Cincinnati Tobacconist has been providing cigars, cigarettes, pipes, lighters, and gourmet coffee to Cincinnatians since 1976. It has a wide selection of cigars—more than 50 brands—including Ashtons, Dunhills, and Arturo Fuente. It also has several brands of hard-to-find foreign cigarettes, such as Rothmans and Gitanes. Open 10–5:30 Mon–Sat; closed Sun. & (Downtown Cincinnati)

CLOSSON'S
401 Race St., Cincinnati
513/762-5500
Opened in 1866, Closson's claims to be the oldest art gallery west of the Alleghenies. The gallery, housed on the second floor, features nineteenth- and twentieth-century European and American painters as well as works by wildlife artist John Ruthven and maritime artist John Stobart. Closson's specializes in fine and antique furniture and has gorgeous showcase model rooms on the first floor. It also sells Oriental rugs and fine china. Open 10–6 Mon–Sat; closed Sun. (Downtown Cincinnati)

CONTEMPORARY GALLERIES
221 W. 4th St., Cincinnati
513/621-3113
When it first opened in 1962, Contemporary Galleries was located in Mt. Washington. The furniture store moved to its downtown digs—a massive building with four floors of showcase space—in 1979 and carries an enormous selection of state-of-the-art furniture. Its very stylish merchandise ranges from sofas to futons to beds to home office equipment. Open 10–6 Mon–Fri, 10–8:30 Thur, 10–5 Sat; closed Sun. & (Downtown Cincinnati)

FOUNTAIN NEWS
AND COFFEE BAR
5th and Walnuts Streets,
Cincinnati
513/421-4049
The Fountain has been providing the Queen City with an international selection of magazines and newspapers since it first opened in 1921. Although the store has changed hands since then, it's still a family-run business. Fountain News moved from its former location on Walnut Street to a prime spot on the corner a few years ago. The store carries more than 65 newspapers, from as far afield as Brazil, and has by far the city's best selection of magazines.

Talk of the Town, p. 136

Ohio Lottery tickets are also sold here. Open 7:30–6:30 Mon–Fri, 8–6 Sat, 8–3 Sun. (Downtown Cincinnati)

HUNT CLUB CLOTHIERS
Fountain Square Plaza, Cincinnati
513/721-2004

This men's specialty store, located on the north side of Fountain Square Plaza, opened in 1973 and carries a selection of quality men's apparel, footwear, and accessories, featuring such brands as Oxford, Hickey-Freeman, Corbin, Southwick, Polo, and Burberry. It also has a tailor and two seamstresses on hand. Open 9:30–5:30 Mon–Fri; closed Sun. ♿ (Downtown Cincinnati)

HUSTLER BOOKS AND GIFTS
34 E. 6th St., Cincinnati
513/421-7323

For years Kings News announced in huge letters on the side of its building, "We Never Close." But close it did when its owner died. It has since been bought by brothers Larry and Jimmy Flynt—of *Hustler* magazine fame—and offers local and regional newspapers and more than 500 magazines, including, of course, *Hustler* magazine and other products, such as T-shirts, bags, and erotic toys. Jimmy Flynt runs the store, and Larry makes occasional guest appearances. Open 8–8 Mon–Fri, 10–8 Sat, and 10–6 Sun. (Downtown Cincinnati)

KATHMAN'S GOODYEAR SHOE REPAIR SHOP
108 W. 6th St., Cincinnati
513/621-7541

Johann Heinrich Kathman, a cobbler by trade, came to Cincinnati from Oldenberg, Germany, and received his U.S. citizenship papers in 1853, but not before he was asked to denounce the Duke of Oldenberg on paper. Five generations later the Kathmans are still in the shoe business. Although they no longer make shoes, they still specialize in repairing shoes, boots, and leather goods. They also offer garment repair and alterations. Kathman's officially incorporated in 1905 and has kept up a tradition of quality service and Old World courtesy ever since. Open 8–5:30 Mon–Fri, 8–1 Sat; closed Sun. & (Downtown Cincinnati)

REDS DUGOUT
Westin Hotel, 21 E. 5th, Cincinnati
513/241-0947
Located on the ground level of the Westin Hotel, Reds Dugout is essentially a Cincinnati Reds gift shop, with all sorts of Reds paraphernalia, including hats, T-shirts, sweatshirts, mugs, jackets, sweaters, and key rings. It's also one of the best places to buy Reds tickets: it has no TicketMaster surcharge. 10–5 Mon–Fri, closed Sat and Sun. & (Downtown Cincinnati)

Downtown/Over-the-Rhine
This shopping district—bounded by 7th Street on the south and 14th Street on the north—lies just north of the City Center district and is also within easy walking distance of downtown's hotels. Many of the shops in this district have been around for years and have built up a loyal local clientele.

AQUARIUS
831 Main St., Cincinnati
513/721-5193
When Aquarius opened in 1977, it was primarily a book shop with a Native American theme. The last few years has seen a change in direction, and the family-run business now specializes in Celtic, Pagan, and Wiccan wares, such as statues, jewelry, CDs, incense, bagpipes, drums, flutes, and books. It still carries some Native American goods and a few Egyptian wares. Open 11–5 except Wed and Sun. (Downtown Cincinnati)

THE BROMWELL COMPANY
117 W. 4th St., Cincinnati
513/621-0620
This family business, run by three successive generations of Gerwes, has been in operation since 1819 and carries a large selection of brassware, specializing primarily in fireplace fixtures. Bromwell also offers a number of unique decorative brass gifts. Open 9:30–6 Mon–Wed and Fri, 9:30–8 Thur, 9:30–5 Sat; closed Sun. (Downtown Cincinnati)

CAPPEL'S
920 Elm St., Cincinnati
513/621-0952
The Cappel family has run this arts-and-crafts store since it opened in 1945, offering an unparalleled selection of materials from silk flowers to burlap to bridal bouquets to party decorations. Cappel's also has a theatrical costume and makeup store at

TRIVIA

Gibson Greetings, Inc., the nation's oldest greeting-card company, was founded in 1850 by four Cincinnati brothers of Scottish descent. Its first printing press was located on Gano Alley, downtown, and, although it has since moved to larger digs, it's still headquartered in the Queen City.

Barney Kroger: Entrepreneur Extraordinaire

Bernard "Barney" Henry Kroger opened his first grocery store in 1883 on Pearl Street, three blocks from the Ohio River. To start the business, he had saved $372, and he borrowed another $350 from a friend. The partners named their store the Great Western Tea Company, and the fledgling business made a profit, despite an Ohio River flood that wiped out its stock.

Barney Kroger soon bought his partner out, renamed his store the B. H. Kroger Tea & Grocery Company, and by 1893 had expanded to 17 stores. Kroger understood the power of advertising and spent more money on newspaper ads than his competitors. In 1902 he formed the Kroger Grocery & Baking Company and became the first grocery store in the United States to bake its own bread. Kroger also added a meat department and had a devilish time trying to keep his butchers honest. This grocery entrepreneur is also credited with having the first grocery store that put price tags on its merchandise. Kroger soon opened stores in Hamilton and Dayton, and then expanded his operation throughout the Midwest.

Ever the astute businessman, Kroger sold his shares in 1928, just before the stock market crash, only to buy them back in the 1930s. By the time he died in 1938, at the age of 78, his estate was worth $22 million. Today, Kroger's is still headquartered in Cincinnati and is the largest supermarket chain in the nation—not bad for an initial investment of $722!

130 West Court Street. Open 9–5:30 Mon–Fri, 9–5 Sat; closed Sun. (Downtown Cincinnati)

GREG'S ANTIQUES
925 Main St., Cincinnati
513/241-5487
Opened in 1977, Greg's Antiques carries an unusual selection of Victorian marble-top furniture, armoires, and architectural antiques—such as stained glass, mantels, chimney pots, gates, and fences. It also has a variety of antique knickknacks—from signed baseballs to old postcards. Greg's second location (at 1400 Main

Street) specializes in antique bedroom and dining-room sets imported from France, England, and Belgium. Open 11–5 Mon–Fri, 10–4 Sat; closed Sun. (Downtown Cincinnati)

LEFTHANDED MOON
48 E. Court St., Cincinnati
513/784-1166
This downtown boutique opened in 1993 and carries unusual and unique gift items—from hand-painted tiles and hand-crafted jewelry from local artisans, to paintings by Cincinnati artists. It also offers contemporary men's clothing from small designers around the country. Open 11:30–7 Mon–Sat; closed Sun. (Downtown Cincinnati)

THE LIBRARY FRIENDS' SHOP
Public Library
800 Vine St., Cincinnati
513/369-6920
Staffed by volunteers, the Library Friends' Shop's collection of greeting cards, playing cards, stuffed toys, posters, T-shirts, and other knickknacks makes it a great place to browse for unusual gifts. It also carries a selection of used books. Open 10–4 Mon–Sat, 1–4 Sun. & (Downtown Cincinnati)

OHIO BOOK STORE
726 Main St., Cincinnati
513/621-5142
Ohio Book Store opened in 1940 and carries the largest selection of used books in downtown Cincinnati. It also has a bookbinding service in the basement and an excellent selection of old magazines on the first floor, including some very early editions of *Playboy* and *Life* (wrapped in protective plastic coverings, of course). Ohio Book Store also specializes in local history and has published more

than 15 books on the subject. Open 9–4:45 Mon–Sat; closed Sun. (Downtown Cincinnati)

PINK PYRAMID
907 Race St., Cincinnati
513/621-7465
Identified by a pink triangle on its front (a reference to the Nazis' method of identifying homosexuals), this is primarily a gay-oriented shop with an excellent selection of gay-themed books, videos, greeting cards, buttons, and magazines. Open 11 a.m.–10:30 p.m. Mon–Thur, 11 a.m.–midnight Fri and Sat, 1–8 Sun. (Downtown Cincinnati)

POLEY'S BIG AND TALL
1117 Vine St., Over-the-Rhine
513/421-6292
Since it opened in 1908, Poley's has specialized in menswear for exceptionally large people, carrying oversized trousers ranging from 42" to 80" waists as well as shoes from size 12 to 18. Open 10–5 Mon–Sat; closed Sun. (Uptown Cincinnati)

PROVIDENT CAMERA
18 W. 7th St., Cincinnati
513/621-5762
Provident Camera has been providing Cincinnati with photographic equipment since it opened in 1930. A full-service camera store, it carries both new and used camera equipment and has machines that enlarge negatives and make prints from prints, slides, and photo CDs. It also has a very knowledgeable staff, most of whom have been in the business for many years. Open 9–6 Mon–Fri, 9–5 Sat; closed Sun. (Downtown Cincinnati)

ST. THERESA'S TEXTILE TROVE
1329 Main St., Over-the-Rhine

513/333-0399

Opened in 1994, St. Theresa's was profiled by the *New York Times* as one of the businesses responsible for the revitalization of Over-the-Rhine. It carries fabrics from such far away places as Guatemala, France, Austria, and Australia, along with a wide selection of quilters' cottons, African prints and brocades, and beads from around the world—silver from Bali and Ethiopia, amber from African and Baltic countries, trade beads from Africa, and crystals from Austria. Open 11–6 Mon–Fri, 11–5 Sat; closed Sun. (Uptown Cincinnati)

TRIVET ANTIQUES
917 Race St., Cincinnati
513/421-2818

Walk into Trivet Antiques and you'll think you've gone back in time. The place is filled with posters, cardboard cutouts, beads, and, most importantly, clothing straight out of the Sixties and Seventies. And, no, the clothing has never been worn. The owner just had the foresight to order huge quantities of it back when it was available. Open 12–5 Mon–Sat; closed Sun. (Downtown Cincinnati)

WOODEN NICKEL ANTIQUES
1410 Central Pkwy.,
Over-the-Rhine

513/241-2985

Opened in 1976, Wooden Nickel is well known for its selection of Victorian and contemporary furniture, restored chandeliers, front and back bars, stained glass, fireplace mantels, beveled glass entry doors, and architectural garden items. Open 10–5 Mon–Sat; closed Sun. (Uptown Cincinnati)

Uptown

This shopping district covers the northern part of Over-the-Rhine as well as the University of Cincinnati area. The majority of establishments in this district cater to a somewhat younger crowd, due, of course, to the proximity of the college.

AVALON CLOTHING COMPANY
230 W. McMillan, Clifton Heights
513/651-3847

Avalon is near the University of Cincinnati and caters to its young patrons by offering a hip selection of shoes, clothes, and accessories, making this contemporary urban fashion boutique a local trendsetter. Open 10–8 Mon–Fri, 11–7 Sat, 12–5 Sun. (Uptown Cincinnati)

THE BOOK STORE
454 W. McMicken, Over-the-Rhine

TRIVIA

When John F. Kennedy was shot in Dallas in November 1963, he was riding in a custom-built limousine manufactured by Cincinnati-based Hess and Eisenhardt. The limo came with a variety of gadgets, including three interchangeable bulletproof roofs. Unfortunately for the president and the nation, JFK chose that day to ride with the top down.

513/621-4865

If you're not paying close attention, you might completely miss The Book Store, an Italianate house in a poor residential district. The selection, spread out over five floors, is astounding; the prices are reasonable (50 cents apiece for some of the paperback fiction); and it's easy to spend hours just browsing through the multitude of books that range from esoteric volumes on mathematics and philosophy to pulp fiction. The Book Store also has some eye-catching art deco pieces, an unusual selection of posters, and used records. Open 1–6 Sat and Sun. (Uptown Cincinnati)

DUTTENHOFER'S BOOKS AND NEWS
214 W. McMillan, Clifton Heights
513/381-1340

Duttenhofer's is a musty, used-book store close to the University of Cincinnati. Its stock is eclectic, ranging from show-biz bios to books on ancient Rome, but it's best known for its selection of first editions. Open 10–9 Mon–Fri, 10–6 Sat and Sun. (Uptown Cincinnati)

DUTTENHOFER'S MAP STORE
210 W. McMillan, Clifton Heights
513/381-0007

Duttenhofer's Map Store has the best selection of cartographic material in the city, with maps from around the world. The staff is knowledgeable and will special-order items they don't have in stock. Open 9–5:30 Mon–Fri, 10–4 Sat; closed Sun. (Uptown Cincinnati)

FINDLAY MARKET
1800 W. Elder St., Over-the-Rhine
513/352-4638

One of the Queen City's treasures,

Findlay Market has been serving Cincinnati shoppers since it opened in 1852. The enclosed building houses fish and meat shops; the surrounding esplanade has a variety of stalls hawking vegetables. Many of the stalls and booths have been in the same families for generations. Taste of Findlay Market always takes place in October. Open 7 a.m.–6 p.m. Wed, Fri, and Sat. (Uptown Cincinnati)

HANSA GUILD
369 Ludlow Ave., Clifton
513/221-4002

An attractive boutique that specializes in handmade items of natural fiber, Hansa carries imports from around the world, including sweaters from South America, Spain, and Scandinavia. It also offers women's clothing, moccasins for the whole family, men and women's hats, and an unusual selection of hand-woven dhurrie rugs and tapestries. Open 10–8 Mon–Sat; closed Sun. (Uptown Cincinnati)

LUDLOW NEWS AND VIDEOS
308 Ludlow Ave., Clifton

Lefthanded Moon, p. 130

Brian Bell

Frances Trollope's Lasting Legacy

Frances Trollope came to Cincinnati in 1827, when the city was on its way to becoming the nation's largest pork-packer. In 1828 Mrs. Trollope opened a bazaar on 3rd Street that went bankrupt two years later, mainly because she didn't buy her goods wholesale, preferring to purchase merchandise from other retail establishments and mark it up. Thoroughly disgusted with her failed business venture, Mrs. Trollope returned to England and wrote a travelogue entitled Domestic Manners of the Americans *(1832), in which she voiced her intense dislike for "Porkopolis," writing:*

"I am sure I should have liked Cincinnati much better if the people had not dealt so very largely in hogs . . . I never saw a newspaper without remarking such advertisements as the following:

" 'Wanted, immediately, 4,000 fat hogs.'

" 'For sale, 2,000 barrels of prime pork.'

"But the annoyance came nearer than this; if I determined upon a walk up Main Street, the chances were five hundred to one against my reaching the other side without brushing by a snout fresh dripping from the kennel . . ."

513/281-4082

This newsstand carries magazines and newspapers from around the world and is a great place to pick up hard-to-find 'zines. As the name implies, it also carries a selection of videos—some for sale, most for rent. Ludlow News is also one of the few places in town where you can purchase foreign cigarettes, such as Dunhills, Players, and Bidis. Ohio Lottery tickets are sold here, too. Open 8–11 Sun–Thur, 8–12 a.m. Fri and Sat. (Uptown Cincinnati)

MOLE'S RECORD EXCHANGE
2622 Vine St., Corryville

513/861-6291

Mole's, located on Short Vine in University Village near the University of Cincinnati, carries a rapidly revolving stock of used records, CDs, and tapes, with a heavy emphasis on alternative and indie rock (due its proximity to the college). It also has an excellent jazz section and will special-order hard-to-get import CDs. Open 11:30–8 Mon–Fri, 12–8 Sat, 1–5 Sun. (Uptown Cincinnati)

NEW WORLD BOOKSHOP
336 Ludlow Ave., Clifton
513/861-6100
This independent bookstore is quite

small but carries a wide selection of books for its size, specializing in New Age, spirituality, and natural health. Open 10–9 Mon–Thur, 10–10 Fri and Sat, 12–6 Sun. (Uptown Cincinnati)

OUTDOOR ADVENTURES
2910 Vine St., Corryville
513/221-6700
Outdoor Adventures, near the University of Cincinnati, features 13,000 square feet of camping and climbing equipment, including clothing, tents, and backpacks. This is *the* place to go if you're on your way to Red River Gorge or Mammoth Cave—popular weekend destinations for locals and students. Open 10–8 Mon–Fri, 10–5 Sat, 12–5 Sun. (Uptown Cincinnati)

OZARKA DISC AND TAPE
111 Calhoun St., Mt. Auburn
513/751-0345
This record, tape, and CD exchange is patronized heavily by University of Cincinnati students and hence has a large rotating selection of low-priced modern rock. It also carries used music videos. Open 12–7:30 Mon–Fri, 12–5 Sat; closed Sun. (Uptown Cincinnati)

PANGAEA
325 Ludlow Ave., Clifton
513/751-3330
Pangaea is an attractive little boutique with a singular selection of merchandise imported from Africa and Indonesia, including tie-dyed hippie clothing, unusual silver jewelry, wood carvings, masks, incense, and wall hangings. Open 10–9 Mon–Fri, 10–8 Sat, 12–5 Sun. (Uptown Cincinnati)

SPIRAL LIGHTS
344 Ludlow Ave., Clifton
513/751-5523
Located in the Ludlow Garage next to Uno's Pizzeria, this will appeal especially to Deadheads and hippies. It carries handmade jewelry, one-of-a-kind gifts, and clothing from around the world, much of it tie-dyed. Open 11–9 Mon–Sat, 12–6 Sun. (Uptown Cincinnati)

TAWANA IMPORTS
326 Ludlow Ave., Clifton
513/861-2516
The name is a holdover from the past when it was run by different management, but this little boutique still carries a unique collection of women's apparel. Most is made in this country, but some merchandise is imported from Turkey. Open 10–8 Mon–Sat, 12–6 Sun. (Uptown Cincinnati)

WIZARD RECORDS AND TAPES
2612 Vine St., Corryville
513/961-6196
This independent record store, on Short Vine in University Village, near the University of Cincinnati, specializes in hard-to-get imports and carries a large selection of vinyl. The staff, consisting mostly of musicians, is knowledgeable and will special-order items not in stock. Wizard's supports the local music scene and carries a comprehensive selection of local releases. Open 11–9 Mon–Sat, 12–5 Sun. (Uptown Cincinnati)

OTHER NOTABLE STORES

FERGUSON'S ANTIQUE MALL
3742 Kellogg Ave.,
Columbia-Tusculum
513/321-7341
If you like shopping for antiques, you'll be in heaven here. Local dealers offer a wide selection of merchandise, from antique furniture, glassware, and china, to out-of-

print books and records. Browsing at Ferguson's is a great way to spend an afternoon, and you're sure to find something to pique your interest. There's also an adjacent restaurant patronized by old-timers. Open 10–5 Wed–Fri, 9–6 Sat and Sun; closed Mon and Tue. (East Cincinnati)

JOSEPH BETH BOOKSELLERS
2692 Madison Rd., Norwood
513/396-8960

In 1996 Joseph Beth Booksellers was voted "Bookseller of the Year" by *Publisher's Weekly*—and it's easy to see why. The store is very well laid out, with attractively designed shelves, comfy chairs in which to read, and most importantly, a very wide selection of books and magazines. The children's department is separated from the main store and hosts weekly story times. Joseph Beth also has a café and a music store that specializes in classical CDs with a smattering of jazz, blues, and folk. Of all the Cincinnati-area bookstores, Joseph Beth has the most author signings, with events taking place several times a week, occasionally including live music. Open 9–10 Mon–Thur, 9–11 Fri and Sat, 10–8 Sun. (East Cincinnati)

LIQUOR DIRECT
670 W. 3rd St., Covington, KY
606/291-2550

This is one of Northern Kentucky's best-kept secrets. Don't be fooled by the no-frills operation—it has a great selection of wines, beers, and liquor at extremely reasonable prices. The staff is knowledgeable, and they even sell *Wine Spectator*. Open 9–10 Mon–Thur, 9–11 Fri and Sat; closed Sun. (South of the River)

THE PARTY SOURCE
WITH THE BREWWORKS
12th Street and I-75, Covington, KY
513/581-2739

This yellow, castle-like structure was home to the Bavarian Brewing

---

Booze News

In Ohio, liquor is sold in state-run stores. Beer and wine are available in groceries, drugstores, and convenience stores. Beer can be purchased all day, but wine can be sold only between 1 p.m. and midnight. Liquor isn't sold on Sunday.

Kentucky, however, has a multitude of superior, privately run (read: cheaper, better selection) liquor stores and is a mere bridge-trip away from Cincinnati. Liquor stores are closed on Sundays, but you can purchase beer and wine from grocery and convenience stores. You must be 21 or older to purchase liquor in Ohio and Kentucky.

Contemporary Galleries, p. 126

Company from 1870 to 1920, when Prohibition shut it down. It went back into business briefly in 1934 but eventually closed again in 1966 after a succession of owners. The plant has now been converted into the Party Source, a huge store with an awe-inspiring selection of wines, beers, liquor, and gourmet food items (another Party Source is at 95 Riviera Drive, Bellevue, KY). The former brewery has also started making beer again, served in the BrewWorks Restaurant and Pub part of the operation, a three-story restaurant with a humidor. Open 9–10 Mon–Thur, 9–11 Fri and Sat, 1–7 Sun. (South of the River)

TALK OF THE TOWN
9019 Reading Rd., Reading
513/563-8844

Just 15 minutes from downtown, Talk of the Town specializes in elegant and fun vintage apparel, accessories, and jewelry from the 1800s to the 1970s. Whether you are a serious vintage collector looking for something unique or you're just browsing for a gift, Talk of the Town has something to satisfy every taste and every budget. (East Cincinnati)

MAJOR DEPARTMENT STORES

JCPENNEY

James Cash Penney opened his Golden Rule Store in the mining town of Kemmerer, Wyoming, in 1902. His business has come a long way since then, including a 1913 name change and a nationwide mail order business. The four major JC Penney locations in the Greater Cincinnati area all contain optical shops, styling salons, and portrait studios. They are: Eastgate Mall (4621 Eastgate Boulevard, Eastgate, 513/752-2622); Florence Mall (6000 Florence Mall, Florence, Kentucky, 606/525-1170); Northgate Mall (9471 Colerain Avenue, Bevis, 513/741-9300); Tri-County Mall (11700 Princeton Pike, Springdale, 513/671-2511). There is also a catalog outlet store (8770 Colerain Avenue, Groesbeck, 513/385-9700) close to Northgate Mall. Mall stores open 10–9 Mon–Sat, 12–6 Sun; catalog outlet store open 9–9 daily.

LAZARUS

Lazarus is part of Federated Department Stores, which also owns Bloomingdale's, Macy's, and Stern's. The downtown store opened in its present location in November 1997, but, unlike its suburban counterparts, does not have furniture, electronics, and book departments, nor a beauty salon. Greater Cincinnati stores: Lazarus at Fountain Place (505 Vine Street, Cincinnati, 513/361-4200); Beechmont Mall (7500 Beechmont Avenue, Beechmont, 513/624-4280); Kenwood Towne Centre (7875 Montgomery Road, Kenwood, 513/745-5380); Northgate Mall (9531 Colerain Avenue, Bevis, 513/245-5200), and Tri-County Mall (11700 Princeton Pike, Springdale, 513/782-2395). There is also a Kenwood Furniture Gallery in Sycamore Plaza (7800 Montgomery Road, Kenwood, 513/745-8980). Open 10–9 Mon–Sat, 12–6 Sun.

McALPIN'S

This department store is part of Mercantile Stores Company, which is headquartered in Fairfield, Ohio. The company owns more than 100 stores in 17 states under a variety of names, including Bacons, Caster Knott, deLencrecies, Gayfers, Glass Block, Hennesys, J.B. White, Joslins, Lion, Maison Blanche, Root's, and Jones Store Company. McAlpin's is one of the most popular department stores in the area because of its wide selection, affordable merchandise, well-staffed beauty salons, and incredible Moonlight Sales. There are six McAlpin's locations in Greater Cincinnati: Crest-view Mall (2901 Dixie Highway, Crestview Hills, Kentucky, 606/344-2795); Eastgate Mall (4615 Eastgate Boulevard, Eastgate, 513/943-5205); Kenwood Towne Centre (7913 Montgomery Road, Kenwood, 513/745-4107); Northgate Mall (9681 Colerain Avenue, Bevis, 513/741-2405); Tri-County Mall (11700 Princeton Rd., Tri-County, 513/346-6001); and Western Hills Plaza (6000 Glenway Avenue, Western Hills, 513/244-3476). Open 9:30–9:30 Mon–Sat, 10–8 Sun.

PARISIAN

Parisian is part of the Knoxville-based Proffitt's Inc., which has more than 170 stores in 24 states under a variety of names, including Loveman's, Hess, McRae's, Parks-Belk, Younkers, and Herbergers. Parisian is probably the most upscale of the Greater Cincinnati department stores, selling fashion apparel, accessories, home furnishings, and cosmetics. There are three locations in the Greater Cincinnati area: Forest Fair Mall (300 Forest Fair Drive, Forest Fair, 513/346-3600); Beechmont Mall (7500 Beechmont Avenue, Beechmont, 513/624-5200); and Kenwood Towne Centre (7801 Montgomery Road, Kenwood, 513/792-2400). Open 10–9 daily.

SAKS FIFTH AVENUE
5th and Race Streets, Cincinnati
513/421-6800

The world-famous New York–based chain, located across from Tower Place and connected to the skywalk system, opened its Cincinnati location in 1984, adding a bit of Big Apple glamour to the Queen City's downtown retail scene. Saks offers a fine selection of men's and women's apparel, accessories, footwear, cosmetics, and perfume, and houses a full-service beauty salon. Open 10–8 Mon and Thur, 10–6 Tue, Wed, Fri, and Sat, 12–5 Sun. &
(Downtown Cincinnati)

Queen City Anarchist

Boston native Josiah Warren (1798–1874), known as the Father of American Anarchism, came to the Queen City in 1819 to work as an orchestra leader. After inventing a lamp that used lard instead of tallow, he established a "Time Store," where customers could pay for their purchases with their services. He later published an anarchist periodical titled The Peaceful Revolutionist, *which only lasted for four months. In his lifetime, he established several anarchist colonies—one of them in nearby Clermont County, idealistically named Utopia.*

SHOPPING MALLS

KENWOOD TOWNE CENTRE
7875 Montgomery Rd., Kenwood
513/745-0205
Anchored by McAlpin's, Lazarus, and Parisian, Kenwood Towne Centre is one of the ritziest malls in the greater Cincinnati area, with a multiplex cinema, a food court, and two full-service restaurants—Funky's Cafe and Ruby Tuesday. More than 180 stores are on the two levels, including Ann Taylor, Laura Ashley, Banana Republic, Warner Bros. Studio Store, the Museum Company, the Nature Company, the Sharper Image, Suncoast Motion Picture Company, and the I Love Cincinnati Shoppe. 10–9 Mon–Sat, 12–6 Sun. Holiday hours are 10–10 Mon–Sat, 12–7 Sun. (East Cincinnati)

NORTHGATE MALL
9501 Colerain Ave., Northgate
513/385-5600
This one-floor mall is anchored by Lazarus, J. C. Penney, McAlpin's, and Sears and has a food court, a Burger King, and four full-service restaurants—Applebee's Neighborhood Grill and Bar, T.G.I. Friday, Don Pablo's Ranchero Grill, and the Italian Oven. Notable stores include the Children's Palace, Frederick's of Hollywood, The Limited, Lerner New York, Paul Harris, and Victoria's Secret. Open 10 a.m.–9 p.m. Mon–Sat, 12–6 Sun. (West Cincinnati)

TOWER PLACE/CAREW TOWER
441 Vine St., Cincinnati
513/241-7700
This downtown shopping mall, located in the Carew Tower Complex and connected to the skywalk system, has revitalized downtown's retail scene since its opening in 1991. At that time downtown was suffering from the recession and had lost several major department stores, including the Carew Tower's former tenant, L. S. Ayres. Tower Place stays open later than most downtown shops and is open even on Sunday, when most downtown stores are closed. It has a

parking garage, gift-wrapping and shipping services, and stroller and wheelchair rental.

The lower level food court has a fountain in the middle, an ATM machine, a beauty salon, and a barber shop. There are more than 30 shops on the street level, including Banana Republic, The Gap, Nine West, the Nature Company, and Williams-Sonoma. The skywalk level has more than 25 stores, including Camelot Music, Victoria's Secret, Ann Taylor, Bath and Body Works, and the I Love Cincinnati Shoppe. Open 10–8 Mon–Sat, 12–5 Sun. ♿ (Downtown Cincinnati)

OUTLET CENTERS

DRY RIDGE OUTLET CENTER
1100 Fashion Ridge Dr.,
Dry Ridge, KY
616/824-9516

This outlet center is a great place to hunt for bargains, with more than 20 stores representing such brands as Liz Claiborne, Van Heusen, Mikasa, Nike, Samsonite, Dress Barn, Naturaliser, Kitchen Collection, Leather Loft, and Sugarshack. Take Exit 159, the Dry Ridge Exit off I-75. Open 10–9 Mon–Sat, 12–6 Sun. (South of the River)

River Downs Race Track

10

SPORTS AND RECREATION

The Queen City's long tradition of athletic participation dates back to 1848, when German immigrants organized turnverein societies to promote wrestling, gymnastics, and fencing. These days, there are more recreational opportunities than ever, from canoeing on the scenic Little Miami River to cross-country skiing in beautiful Mt. Airy Forest to golfing at one of greater Cincinnati's many courses.

As for spectator sports, Cincinnati is home to the Cincinnati Reds, the world's oldest professional baseball team; two-time AFC champion Cincinnati Bengals; two AAA hockey teams, the Cyclones and the Mighty Ducks; the Silverbacks, an indoor soccer team; two dynamic college basketball teams, the Xavier Musketeers and the UC Bearcats; and two thoroughbred race tracks, River Downs and Turfway Park.

Annual sporting events include July's Great American Insurance ATP Championship and Senior PGA Tour Golf Tournament, and the Cincinnati Heart Mini Marathon in March.

PROFESSIONAL SPORTS

Baseball

CINCINNATI REDS
Cinergy Field, 100 Pete Rose Way,
Cincinnati
800/829-5353
Created in 1869, the Cincinnati Reds are the world's oldest professional baseball team. They have won nine National League pennants and five World Series titles. Although the Reds only moved into the 55,000-seat Cinergy Field (then Riverfront Stadium) in 1970, talks are underway for a new baseball stadium and locals are greatly divided as to where it should be built. Some want the new stadium built on the eastern edge of

In 1910 Cincinnati native President William Howard Taft threw out the first ball on opening day of baseball season, beginning a long-standing tradition.

downtown close to Over-the-Rhine; others—mostly suburbanites who rarely go downtown—want the stadium on the riverfront. Reds owner Marge Schott has probably received more press than the team itself for her insensitive remarks about minorities. $14 blue box seats, $11 green box seats, $9 red box seats, $6 red reserved seats. (Downtown Cincinnati)

Football

CINCINNATI BENGALS
Cinergy Field,
1 Bengals Dr., Cincinnati
513/621-3550
Hall of Famer Paul Brown, the father of modern professional football, moved to Cincinnati in 1968 to found the Cincinnati Bengals after he lost control of the Cleveland Browns. The Bengals are now owned by his two sons, Mike and Pete. Two-time AFC champs, the Bengals are in the process of building a new $400-billion riverfront stadium on the western side of downtown. In the meantime they play at Cinergy Field, formerly Riverfront Stadium. Many of the best seats are sold out to season-ticket holders, so call well in advance for tickets or be prepared to pay top dollar to the scalpers on the streets. $37 mid-level, $35 lower-level, $31 upper-level seats. (Downtown Cincinnati)

Golf

SENIOR PGA TOUR GOLF TOURNAMENT
The Golf Center at King's Island, Mason
513/398-5742
Competitors on the Senior PGA golf tour have included the likes of Jack Nicklaus and Arnold Palmer. In 1997 the purse was $1 million. The event is usually held around the first week in July. (East Cincinnati)

Hockey

CINCINNATI MIGHTY DUCKS
The Cincinnati Gardens,
2250 Seymour Ave., Roselawn
513/351-3999
The Cincinnati Mighty Ducks are the newest addition to Cincinnati's hockey scene, with an inaugural season in the fall of 1997. This AAA team is part of the American Hockey League, the professional development league for the National Hockey League. The Ducks' season runs from October to April. Tickets range $5–$14. (Uptown Cincinnati)

THE CYCLONES
The Crown,
Pete Rose Way, Cincinnati
513/531-PUCK
The Cyclones, who play in the International Hockey League, recently

Cincinnati Reds Highlights . . .
and Lowlights

1869: The Cincinnati Redstockings become the world's first professional baseball team.

1919: The Reds win the World Series, but it is later discovered that eight White Sox players had fixed the series.

1935: The first night game in professional baseball takes place at Cincinnati's Crosley Field.

1938: Johnny Vander Meer pitches back-to-back no-hitters.

1940: The Reds beat the Detroit Tigers in the World Series, 4 to 3.

1970: The Cincinnati Reds take up residence in Riverfront Stadium (now Cinergy Field).

1974: Babe Ruth's all-time home run record is broken by Hank Aaron at Riverfront Stadium.

1975: The Reds, featuring Johnny Bench, Pete Rose, Joe Morgan, and Tony Perez, beat the Boston Red Sox in the World Series, 4 to 3.

1976: The Big Red Machine sweeps the New York Yankees in the World Series, 4 games to 0.

1978: Tom Seaver becomes the first Reds pitcher to throw a no-hitter at Riverfront Stadium.

1983: Johnny Bench hits his last home run, number 389, at Riverfront Stadium.

1985: Pete Rose brings the home-town crowd to their feet when he gets his 4,192nd hit, surpassing the legendary Ty Cobb's record for all-time hits. The game is delayed by the cheers of the crowd. "Charlie Hustle" is overcome by emotion and covers his eyes. Rose went on to get 64 more hits, boosting the still-standing record to 4,256.

1988: Tom Browning becomes the first Red to pitch a perfect game.

1990: The Reds sweep Oakland in the World Series, 4 to 0, after completing a wire-to-wire first-place season.

1993: Cincinnati Reds owner Marge Schott is suspended from baseball for one year for making bigoted remarks.

moved from the 10,000-seat Cincinnati Gardens to the 15,000-seat Crown, formerly known as Riverfront Coliseum. Their season runs from October to April. Tickets range $6–$15. (Downtown Cincinnati)

Horse Racing

RIVER DOWNS RACE TRACK
6301 Kellogg Ave., Cincinnati
513/232-8000
River Downs is a scenic thoroughbred racing track near the Ohio River. Live racing runs April through August, and simulcast racing takes place every day except Christmas Eve and Christmas Day. The Clubhouse has been renovated recently, with more than 300 high-resolution monitors for simulcast viewing and a restaurant. The Miller Highlife Cradle Stakes run on Labor Day, the Bassinet Stakes in late August. Take Exit 72 off I-275, the U.S 42, Kellogg Avenue, New Richmond Exit. Live racing 12:55–5 p.m. Thur–Tue. Simulcast racing 12 p.m.–12 a.m. daily. Free, $3 clubhouse seating. (outside East Cincinnati zone)

TURFWAY PARK
RACING ASSOCIATION

7500 Turfway Rd., Florence, KY
800/733-0200 or 606/371-0200
Live thoroughbred racing takes place from December through April, then again in September and October. Big-ticket races include the Jim Beam Stakes in late March and the Kentucky Cup Day in September. Turfway Park has a very large restaurant on the fifth floor that overlooks the track. Simulcast racing, from such tracks as Saratoga and Arlington Park, takes place seven days a week. Exit 182 off I-75, the KY 1017, Turfway Road Exit. Live racing 7–11 p.m. Wed–Fri, 1–11 p.m. Sat and Sun. Gates open at 11:30 a.m. for simulcast racing. $3. Free parking. (South of the River)

Soccer

THE SILVERBACKS
The Crown,
537 E. Pete Rose Way, Cincinnati
513/241-1818
This indoor soccer team that plays in the National Professional Soccer League just moved from the 10,000-seat Cincinnati Gardens to the 15,000-seat Crown. Formerly known as Riverfront Coliseum, the Crown recently underwent $14 million in renovations and is also home to the Cincinnati Cyclones, who play in the International Hockey League. The Silverbacks' season begins in October and ends in March. Tickets range $7–$12. (Downtown Cincinnati)

Tennis

GREAT AMERICAN INSURANCE
ATP CHAMPIONSHIP
ATP Stadium, Mason
513/651-0303

Cincinnati native Eddie Arcaro rode 4,779 winners during his career. He won the Kentucky Derby five times and the Preakness and Belmont Stakes six times each.

This is the sixth-largest men's professional tennis tournament in the world. More than 56 top-ranked players compete for more than $2 million in prize money. The tournament, a Mercedes Super Nine event on the World ATP Tour, is held during the first two weeks in August; the Senior tournament takes place late July. The stadium is located across from Paramount's King's Island. Take Exit 25 AB off I-71, the OH 741 North, King's Mills Road, Mason Exit. (East Cincinnati)

RECREATIONAL ACTIVITIES

Biking

Cincinnati roads are not very hospitable to cyclists, although the city's many hills provide challenging climbs and speedy descents. For those who don't want to grapple with traffic without the benefit of a roadside berm, most area parks offer hike/bike trails. There is also a 22-mile paved trail that winds along the Little Miami River between Milford and Morrow. And if you're in Cincinnati during the month of August you'll want to participate in the annual Morning Glory Ride, a challenging 20-mile trek that tackles some of the Queen City's numerous hills.

LUNKEN AIRPORT PLAYFIELD COMPLEX
4750 Playfield Ln., East End
513/321-6500
Lunken Airport is situated on a huge floodplain alongside the Ohio River, and its 5.6-mile hike/bike trail is one of the most popular in the area. Other Lunken attractions include tennis courts, a golf course, skateboarding facilities, and a children's playground. Open 11–9 daily. $5/hour for a single-speed-bike rental, $2 extra for baby trailers. (East Cincinnati)

SHARON WOODS PARK
11450 Lebanon Rd., Sharonville
513/521-PARK
This 755-acre park, comprising deciduous forest, lush meadows, and grasslands, has a 2.6-mile hike/bike trail that circles around Sharon Woods Lake. Rentals are $5 an hour for a single-speed or tandem bicycle. And if you've come this far you have to check out Sharon Woods Gorge—its spectacular 90-foot cliff is home to a wealth of Ordovician fossils. Open dawn to dusk. $3 yearly pass, $1 daily user fee. (East Cincinnati)

Boating

SHARON WOODS LAKE
11450 Lebanon Rd., Sharonville
513/521-PARK
The 35-acre Sharon Woods Lake, set amid a scenic 755-acre park, has a variety of boating activities available to the public. Its boathouse, open from early March to late October, rents rowboats, canoes, pedal boats, and hydrobikes. Rental fees: $4.01 per half-hour or $6.13 per hour. If you rent a rowboat for six hours, you pay a flat fee of $8.01; if you take it out all

day, it costs $11.32. Open dawn to dusk. $3 yearly pass, $1 daily user fee. (East Cincinnati)

Bowling

MADISON BOWL
4761 Madison Rd., Madisonville
513/271-2700

Madison Bowl stays open 24 hours with plenty of lanes—32 in all—for bowlers to use. If you get hungry there's a restaurant within the bowling alley (9 a.m.–11 p.m.), and if you get thirsty there's also a full-service bar (9 a.m.–2:30 a.m.). For bowlers who have trouble keeping score, Madison offers automatic scorekeeping. Bowling costs $2.50 per game; shoe rental is $1 extra. (East Cincinnati)

WESTERN BOWL
6383 Glenway Ave., Bridgetown
513/574-2222

Western Bowl stays open 24 hours, but during evenings or on weekends you'll have trouble finding a lane—all 68 are usually in use by incredibly good bowlers competing for the Hoinke Classic which, by the way, is

the largest bowling tournament in the world. The event takes up ten months of the year so if you like to watch bowling on TV, stop by between the third week in January and late September and catch it live. If you want to play, come late at night or on a weekday. Bowling $2.80 adults, $1.80 seniors and ages 17 and under; shoe rental $1.75 adults, $1.25 ages 17 and under. (West Cincinnati)

Camping/Backpacking

WINTON WOODS CAMPGROUND
10245 Winton Rd.,
Springfield Township
513/521-PARK

Winton Woods Campground is set alongside a picturesque pine grove next to Winton Woods Lake. The lake is currently undergoing a massive renovation and has been completely drained but should be finished and much improved by the time you read this. All the camping sites have parking pads, fire rings, and picnic tables. Not all have electrical hookups, so be sure to ask in advance. (West Cincinnati)

Is it a Ball or a Strike?

William "Dummy" Hoy—a deaf baseball player who started his career in Oshkosh, Wisconsin, and ended up in Cincinnati—complained that it was impossible for him to tell the difference between a strike and a ball. His suggestion that umpires raise their right hands for a strike, began the use of hand signals by umpires in professional baseball.

Cincinnati Mighty Ducks

Chris Mason of the Cincinnati Mighty Ducks, p. 141

Canoeing

The Little Miami River is one of only 19 rivers in the nation that hold both state and national Scenic River status. It's also monitored by Little Miami, Inc., an environmental group of local citizens. The majority of canoe liveries are based further upstream—in Morrow, Fort Ancient, and Waynesville.

BRUCE'S CANOE RENTAL
200 Crutchfield Pl., Loveland
513/683-4611
Bruce's will take you farther upstream so that you can paddle back downstream in a two-person canoe and end

up back where you started. Children ages 18 and under must get their parents to sign for the canoe. The 5-mile trip begins at Glen Island State Park, the 10-mile trip at South Lebanon, and the 15-mile trip at Morrow. Open 9–7 daily. $20 per canoe (5-mile); $24 per canoe (10-mile); $28 per canoe (15-mile). (East Cincinnati)

Day Hikes

MT. AIRY FOREST
5083 Colerain Ave., Mt. Airy
513/661-4094
This 1,466-acre forest sits on Hamilton County's highest ridge and has the distinction of being the first urban reforestation project in the nation. More than 1 million trees were planted here in 1911. The trail names are descriptive in themselves and include the Ponderosa, Quarry, Red Oak, Twin Bridge, and Overlook. Open 6 a.m.–10 p.m. daily. Free. (West Cincinnati)

SHARON WOODS PARK
11450 Lebanon Rd., Sharonville
513/521-PARK
The Sharon Woods Gorge Area of this 755-acre park was named as a State Dedicated Natural Area in 1977, due mainly to its 90-foot cliff rich in Ordovician fossils. The 1.6-mile Richard H. Durrell Gorge Trail

TRIVIA

Quarterback Roger Staubach, nicknamed "Roger the Dodger," was born in Cincinnati in 1942. He won the Heisman Trophy in 1963, played for the Dallas Cowboys, retired after the 1979 season, and was inducted into the Football of Fame in 1985.

Cincinnati Sports Greats

Cincinnati has produced many sports greats, including boxers Ezzard Charles and Bud Smith; baseball players Pete Rose, Barry Larkin, Ken Griffey Jr., Miller Huggins, Jim Bronson, and Dave Justice; football Hall of Famer Roger Staubach; tennis players Tony Trabert and Bill Talbert; and five-time Kentucky Derby–winner Eddie Arcaro.

winds through this heavily wooded area. Open dawn to dusk. $3 yearly pass, $1 daily user fee. (East Cincinnati)

SHAWNEE LOOKOUT
**2008 Lawrenceburg Rd.,
Miami Township
513/521-PARK**
This 1,026-acre park, set alongside the Ohio River, was once home to Native Americans; traces of their civilization remain in the form of Miami Fort, a great earthen mound. There are three trails: 1.3-mile Blue Jacket Trail, 2-mile Little Turtle Trail, and 1.4-mile Miami Fort Trail. Park attractions include the Springhouse School and Log Cabin (open May–Sept), and a visitor center, which has an archaeological display. Open dawn to dusk. $3 yearly pass, $1 daily user fee. (West Cincinnati)

Fishing
Visiting fisherfolk may purchase a three-day nonresidential license for $15. Children ages 15 and under and members of the U.S. Armed Forces on furlough do not require fishing licenses. For more information, contact Wildlife District Five (1076

Old Springfield Pike, Xenia, OH, 937/ 372-9261).

LAKE ISABELLA PARK
**10174 Loveland-Madeira Rd.,
Symmes Township
513/791-1663**
This 77-acre park, situated alongside the Little Miami River, has a 28-acre lake with full-service boathouse, rowboat rentals, a pier, an outdoor deck, and an indoor dining area. Lake Isabella is a pay-fishing lake. Its catfish season begins in early April and ends in early October. It has two trout seasons, one running early March through mid-April; the other during October. An Ohio State fishing license is not required, but anglers must purchase a daily ticket. You must be 16 or older to rent a boat.

From Memorial Day to Labor Day, the park stays open on weekends for all-night fishing. The boathouse is open early March to late October. When it's closed, Hamilton County Park Rangers collect fishing fees. Children 12 and under fish for free. Seniors fish for free on Wednesdays. There's also a bank from which to fish, open dawn to dusk. $3 yearly pass, $1 daily user fee. Catfish-season fishing ticket: $8 adults, $5 children 13–15. Trout-season fishing ticket: $8 adults, $6 children 13–15. Rowboats rentals: $6.50 for six hours. (East Cincinnati)

SHARON WOODS PARK
11450 Lebanon Rd., Sharonville
513/521-PARK
This 755-acre park is home to an artificial 35-acre lake, considered one of the best bass lakes in the county. Pedal boats, rowboats, canoes, bikes, and tandem bikes can be rented at the boathouse, along with bait and tackle supplies. Fishing is by rental boat only, but there is a bank-fishing area along the pier for seniors, children, and handicapped individuals. A fishing license is required; it can be purchased at the boathouse and costs $15 a year. Open dawn to dusk daily. $1 motor vehicle permit. (East Cincinnati)

Fitness Clubs

CAREW TOWER HEALTH AND FITNESS CLUB
441 Vine St., Cincinnati
513/651-1442
Housed beneath the Omni Netherland Hotel in the Carew Tower, this downtown fitness club has an indoor swimming pool, a full line of Cybex exercise machines, NordicTracks, treadmills, stationary bikes, and rowing machines, in addition to a sauna, steambath, and whirlpool. 5:30–9:30 Mon–Fri, 8–6 Sat and Sun. Daily passes $10. (Downtown Cincinnati)

CINCINNATI RECREATION COMMISION'S ROWING AND FITNESS CLUB
925 Eastern Ave., East End
513/352-3660

Located east of downtown's adjacent riverside parks, Bicentennial Commons at Sawyer Point, this fitness club is run by the Cincinnati Recreation Department and has a wide variety of exercise equipment, including Hammer Strength and Nautilus free weights, bikes, steppers, treadmills, and rowing machines. Open 6 a.m.–9:30 p.m. Mon–Fri, 8–4 Sat, 12–4 Sun. Daily passes $3. (Downtown Cincinnati)

YWCA
898 Walnut St., Cincinnati
513/241-7090
Across from the public library downtown, the YWCA has an indoor pool, treadmills, step machines, stationary bikes, free weights, and a Nordic-Track. Open 6 a.m.–8:30 p.m. Mon–Fri, 9–5 Sat; closed Sun. Daily passes $5. (Downtown Cincinnati)

Golf

AVON FIELDS GOLF COURSE
4081 Reading Rd., Avondale
513/281-0322
This 18-hole, 5,051-yard, par-66 public course is the oldest municipal golf course west of the Allegheny Mountains, with rolling terrain and small target greens. It also has a driving range. (Uptown Cincinnati)

CALIFORNIA GOLF COURSE
5920 Kellogg Ave., California
513/231-6513
This 18-hole, 6,236-yard, par-70 course is built around two reservoirs and overlooks the Kentucky hills. (East Cincinnati)

DEVOU PARK GOLF COURSE
1344 Audubon Rd., Covington, KY
606/431-8030

Cincinnati Silverbacks Soccer Club, p. 143

This 18-hole, par-70 public course is set in the rolling hills of Covington's Devou Park with adjacent tennis courts and a scenic trail. (South of the River)

**DUNHAM COMPLEX
GOLF COURSE
4400 Guerley Rd., Price Hill
513/251-1157**

This nine-hole, 1,396-yard, par-29 public course has many hills and valleys. (West Cincinnati)

**GLENVIEW GOLF COURSE
West Sharon Road and
Springfield Pike, Glendale
513/771-1747**

This 18-hole, 7,024-yard, par-72 public course was voted one of America's top 50 public golf courses by *Golf Digest* magazine. A new nine-hole course has been added recently. It also has a driving range. (West Cincinnati)

**GOLF CENTER AT KING'S ISLAND
6042 Fairway Dr., Mason**

513/398-7700

This world-class course is home to the Senior PGA Golf Tournament. It has two 18-hole courses: the 6,731-yard, par-71 Grizzly; and the 3,428-yard, par-61 Bruin. (East Cincinnati)

**INDIAN VALLEY GOLF COURSE
3950 Newtown Rd., Newtown
513/561-9491**

This 18-hole, 5,973-yard, par-70 public course is nestled alongside the scenic Little Miami River. It also has a putting green. (East Cincinnati)

**LITTLE MIAMI GOLF CENTER
ADDRESS TK
513/561-5650**

This nine-hole, par-35 public course has a driving range and an 18-hole miniature-golf course. (East Cincinnati)

**NEUMANN GOLF COURSE
7215 Bridgetown Rd.,
Green Township
513/574-1320**

This public course has 27 holes over

GOLF COURSES IN GREATER CINCINNA

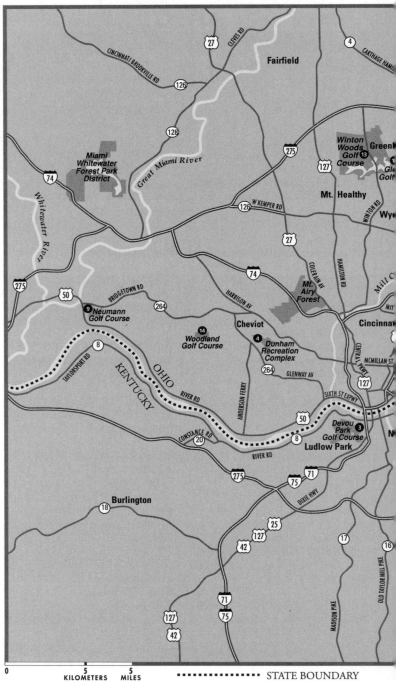

27
CLEVES RD
4
CARTHAGE HAMIL
Fairfield
CINCINNATI BROOKVILLE RD
126
128
275
Miami Whitewater Forest Park District
127
Great Miami River
Winton Woods Golf Course **13** **Green**
Gle Golf
74
Mt. Healthy
126 W KEMPER RD
WINTON RD
27
Wye
Whitewater River
74
Mill C
HAMILTON RD
275
50
COLERAIN AV
BRIDGETOWN RD
HARRISON AV
Mt. Airy Forest
MIT
Cincinna
264
9 *Neumann Golf Course*
8
TAYLORSPORT RD
14 *Woodland Golf Course*
Cheviot
4 *Dunham Recreation Complex*
CENTRAL PKWY
MCMILLAN ST
127
KENTUCKY
OHIO
RIVER RD
264 GLENWAY AV
ANDERSON FERRY
SIXTH ST EXPWY
50
Devou Park Golf Course **3**
N
CONSTANCE RD
20
8
RIVER RD
Ludlow Park
275
75
71
Burlington
DIXIE HWY
18
25
127
42
17
16
OLD TAYLOR MILL PIKE
71
75
MADISON PIKE
127
42

0   5   5
KILOMETERS   MILES
●●●●●●●●●●●●●● STATE BOUNDARY

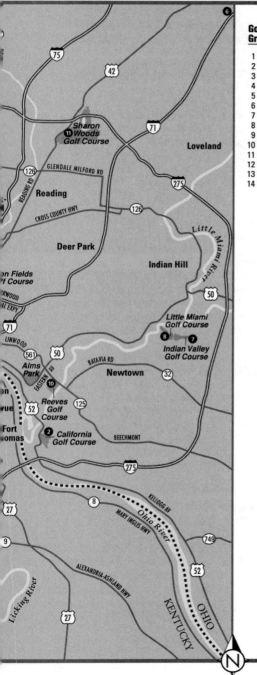

Golf Courses in Greater Cincinnati

1 Avon Fields Golf Course
2 California Golf Course
3 Devou Park Golf Course
4 Dunham Complex Golf Course
5 Glenview Golf Course
6 Golf Center at King's Island
7 Indian Valley Golf Course
8 Little Miami Golf Center
9 Neumann Golf Course
10 Reeves Golf Course
11 Sharon Woods Golf course
12 Winton Woods/Meadow Links
13 Winton Woods/Mill Course
14 Woodland Golf Course

The largest Chicken Dance ever took place at Cincinnati's 1994 Oktoberfest, with 48,000 dancers waddling their way into the *Guinness Book of Records*.

rolling, wooded terrain and a practice range. The Red 9 is 2,943 yards, par 35; the White 9 is 3,046 yards, par 36; and the Blue 9 is 3,172 yards, par 35. You can also play 18 holes. (West Cincinnati)

REEVES GOLF COURSE
Lunken Airport Playfield, Wilmer and Beechmont Avenues, East End
513/321-2740
This 18-hole, 6,371-yard, par-70 public course also has a nine-hole, par-27 course suitable for the whole family. The course is also completely flat, making it ideal for novices. The practice range is lighted and has some heated tees. (East Cincinnati)

SHARON WOODS GOLF COURSE
11355 Swing Rd., Sharonville
513/769-4325 or 521-PARK
Sharon Woods is an 18-hole, par-70 public course. (East Cincinnati)

WINTON WOODS/
MEADOW LINKS
10999 Mill Rd., Forest Park
513/825-3701
This nine-hole, par-31 public course also has a driving range. (West Cincinnati)

WINTON WOODS/MILL COURSE
1515 W. Sharon Rd., Forest Park
513/825-3770
This is an 18-hole, par-71 course. (West Cincinnati)

WOODLAND GOLF COURSE
5820 Muddy Creek Rd., Covedale
513/451-4408
This nine-hole, 2,194-yard, par-34 public course is set on rolling terrain and is good for family play. (West Cincinnati)

Hunting
Tourists wishing to hunt small game can purchase a three-day tourist small-game hunting license for $25. To hunt bigger game, such as deer and wild turkey, first you have to purchase an annual nonresident hunting license for $91, then you have to get a deer permit for $20 and/or a wild turkey permit for $20. Hunting is permitted in certain state parks within select areas, and seasons vary from park to park. For more information, call 800/BUCKEYE. Bears, badgers, bobcats, hawks, owls, and eagles are protected.

Ice Skating

EDEN PARK, MT. ADAMS
513/352-4080
This picturesque park has a shallow, knee-high lake built over an old reservoir. In summer it's used as a wading pool; when winter comes and it freezes over, it becomes a skating rink. Open dawn to dusk daily. Free. (East Cincinnati)

FOUNTAIN SQUARE ICE RINK
Fountain Square, Cincinnati
513/684-4945
The Cincinnati Recreation Commission sets up this ice rink in the heart of downtown Cincinnati during the holiday season. Although rather small, it's a lot of fun and a great way to keep the kids occupied on a cold day. During the *holiday season*, Santa's Elf House goes up right next door, turning Fountain Square into a winter wonderland. $1 admission, $1 skate rental. Hours vary. (Downtown Cincinnati)

Riverboat Gambling

ARGOSY CASINO
1 Walnut St., Lawrenceburg, IN
800/700-4477
Argosy Casino, located on the Ohio River in Lawrenceburg, Indiana, is only 20 minutes away from Cincinnati and offers a wide variety of gaming choices, including slot machines, Caribbean stud poker, blackjack, roulette, craps, video poker, and video Keno. The three decks hold 1,700 passengers and Argosy's Buffet provides breakfast, lunch, and dinner. Cruises leave every two hours on the odd-numbered hours. $5–$9. (just outside West Cincinnati zone)

GRAND VICTORIA
CASINO AND RESORT
600 Grand Victoria Dr.,
Rising Sun, IN
800/GRAND-11
Grand Victoria's 322-foot-long, 40,000-square-foot paddle-wheel casino offers several two- to three-hour cruises daily. It's 45 minutes away from Cincinnati and has more than 1,300 slot machines, 80 table games, and a smoke-free playing area. Hyatt has

also built a 200-room hotel that overlooks the Ohio River and an 18-hole golf course. The 300-acre resort also contains a steak house, buffet restaurant, sports bar, and health club with an indoor pool and outdoor terrace. Cruises begin boarding at 9 a.m. and leave every two hours. Sun–Thur, the last cruise leaves at 1 a.m.; Fri and Sat, the last cruise leaves at 3 a.m. $5–$9. (just outside West Cincinnati zone)

Rollerblading

BICENTENNIAL COMMONS AT SAWYER POINT AND YEATMAN'S COVE
805 Pete Rose Way, Cincinnati
513/352-6316
These two adjoining riverside parks, within walking distance of downtown, make for a picturesque inline skating experience. Just make sure that you don't let the view of the Ohio River and the Kentucky shore distract you too much! If you're in the mood to boogie, there's a disco rink for inliners and roller skaters on the eastern end of the park. Park open dawn to dusk. Rink open 4–9 p.m. Mon–Thur, 4–10 p.m. Fri, 12–10 p.m. Sat, 12–6 p.m. Sun. (Memorial Day–Labor Day); 4-10 Fri, 12–10 Sat and Sun, closed Mon–Fri (Labor Day–Memorial Day). $2.50 ages 13 and older, $1.50 children 12 and under. $1 skate rental. (Downtown Cincinnati)

Skiing

MT. AIRY FOREST
5083 Colerain Ave., Mt. Airy
513/352-2607
If you have a pair of skis and you want to test out the lay of the land, Mt. Airy Forest makes for picturesque and

Fishing on Lake Isabella, p. 147

challenging skiing. Although there are no set trails in this 1,466-acre forest, cross-country skiing is permitted throughout the park, which sits on Hamilton County's highest ridge. 6 a.m.–10 p.m. daily. Free. (West Cincinnati)

horseshoe pits, softball diamonds, grills, and picnic tables. Open Memorial Day–Labor Day. Swimming pool open 10–8 daily, amusement park open 12–9 daily. Admission $13.95 adults, $10.95 children 4–11, $3 extra for amusement park. (East Cincinnati)

Swimming

SUNLITE POOL/CONEY ISLAND
6201 Kellogg Ave. at I-275, Cincinnati
513/231-7801

Sunlite Pool is the largest outdoor circulating pool in the world. To be exact, it measures 400 by 200 feet and holds 3 million gallons of water. It has five diving boards and two water slides: the Zoom Flume and the Pipeline Plunge. Next to the pool is a small amusement park with a Ferris wheel, some kiddie rides, a merry-go-round, and paddle boats. Other attractions include a children's playground, volleyball courts,

Tennis

DEVOU PARK TENNIS COURTS
1344 Audubon Rd., Covington, KY
606/431-8030

Nestled amid the undulating hills of Devou Park, next to Devou Park Golf Course, lie six blacktop and three clay public tennis courts. Open dawn to dusk. $4 an hour. (South of the River)

LUNKEN AIRPORT PLAYFIELD COMPLEX
4750 Playfield Ln., East End
513/321-6500

These eight clay courts and eight

hard courts are said to be some of the best in town. They are lit at night. Open 9 a.m.–9:30 p.m. daily. $7–10. (East Cincinnati)

SAWYER POINT
TENNIS PAVILION
Bicentennial Commons at Sawyer Point and Yeatman's Cove
805 Pete Rose Way, Cincinnati
513/352-6317
These eight hard courts, set alongside the Ohio River, are within an easy walk of downtown. Open 9 a.m.–9:30 p.m. daily. $3 an hour. (Downtown Cincinnati)

11

PERFORMING ARTS

In 1873 Cincinnati became the first city in the United States to host a singing festival, which was so successful that an auditorium was built to accommodate it. Music Hall is now a major local landmark and still home to the May Festival, now an annual event. The Queen City is also home to the Cincinnati Symphony Orchestra, the fifth-oldest in the nation, and the Cincinnati Opera, the nation's second oldest, not to mention the world-famous University of Cincinnati College Conservatory of Music.

Cincinnati's two professional resident theater companies—Cincinnati Playhouse in the Park and Ensemble Theater of Cincinnati—regularly present new and old works. Musicals and old standbys are very popular in the Queen City, making it hard for the smaller theater groups to present original material. The few successful local theater companies have survived by sticking to the tried-and-true productions, with the exception of the improvisational Carnivores in Action.

The Aronoff Center for the Arts has greatly enlivened downtown's theater scene by bringing in traveling Broadway shows as well as other national and international acts. The Cincinnati Ballet presents its season at the Aronoff, except for its annual holiday production of The Nutcracker, which takes place at Music Hall. The Contemporary Dance Theater brings in national dance troupes, and several local theater companies have made the smaller stages their home bases.

THEATER

ARONOFF CENTER FOR THE ARTS
650 Walnut St., Cincinnati

513/621-2787
This massive new arts center straddles half of a downtown block and houses three theaters and an art

gallery. It's managed by the Cincinnati Arts Association, which brings in an extremely wide variety of music, theater, and musicals. Procter & Gamble Hall seats 2,700 and was designed to house the lavish productions of the Broadway Series. The Contemporary Dance Company and the Cincinnati Ballet present part of their season here. Local theater groups, such as the Cincinnati Shakespeare Festival and Downtown Theater Classics, rent the smaller theaters, and the Westin Art Gallery hosts a small film festival. The Jarson-Kaplan Theater seats 440 and the Fifth Third Black Box Theater seats 150. (Downtown Cincinnati)

CARNEGIE CENTER FOR THE PERFORMING AND VISUAL ARTS
1028 Scott Blvd., Covington, KY
606/655-8112, Ext. 1

The Carnegie Center began as one of the first Carnegie Foundation libraries and now houses a 700-seat theater and four galleries. The center encourages home-grown theater companies and is used by such groups as Foxrock Theatre Company, the Genesius Players, and Carnivores in Action, an improv troupe. The magnificent Beaux Arts building has just received a much-needed grant to restore its former glory and to make it handicapped accessible. (South of the River)

CINCINNATI PLAYHOUSE IN THE PARK
Eden Park, Mt. Adams
513/421-3888

Cincinnati Playhouse in the Park, nestled near the top of Mt. Adams with a panoramic view of downtown Cincinnati, was hailed by the *New York Times* as "one of the most picturesque settings of any American regional theatre." Since it opened in 1960 the Playhouse has become one of the Midwest's premier regional theaters and has seen many illustrious actors (such as Anthony Perkins, Lynn Redgrave, Cicely Tyson, Estelle Parsons, Patty Duke, John Hillerman, and Cleavon Little) tread the boards of its two theaters—the 629-seat Robert S. Marx Theatre and the more intimate 220-seat Thompson Shelterhouse.

In 1987 the Lois and Richard Rosenthal New Play Prize was established to encourage quality work from around the nation. The Rosenthal Next Generation Theatre Series, a program of Saturday-morning shows designed to heighten young people's interest in theater, began in 1994. About 11 shows are presented each season. Annual traditions include the holiday production of *A Christmas Carol* and the October presentation of *Abracadabra*, a popular family magic show. The building recently underwent a $6-million renovation and construction project. ♿ (East Cincinnati)

TRIVIA

Dancer George Chakiris, born in Norwood, Ohio, won an Oscar for Best Supporting Actor for his role as Bernardo in *West Side Story*.

TRIVIA

Cincinnati television legend and news anchor Al Schottelkotte was the voice of the radio announcer in one of the very first episodes of *Gilligan's Island.*

CINCINNATI SHAKESPEARE FESTIVAL
719 Race St., Cincinnati
513/381-BARD

Cincinnati Shakespeare Festival is a local theater company devoted to presenting the works of the Bard and his contemporaries. The company offers five main-stage performances a year in the Aronoff Center's Fifth Third Theater, and its season runs from September to the end of June. The name change is fairly recent; you may already know this group by its former moniker, Fahrenheit Theater. ♿ (Downtown Cincinnati)

DOWNTOWN THEATRE CLASSICS
4 W. 4th Street, Cincinnati
513/621-3822

Downtown Theatre Classics is a newly formed local company that presents old chestnuts—mostly comedies and musicals—at the Aronoff Center's Jarson Kaplan Theater and the Taft Theatre. The company usually puts on about five shows a year. ♿ (Downtown Cincinnati)

ENSEMBLE THEATRE OF CINCINNATI
1127 Vine St., Over-the-Rhine
513/421-3555

Within walking distance of downtown, this Over-the-Rhine theater was established in 1983 and first took up residence in Elm Street's Memorial Hall. The Ensemble Theatre moved to its present digs in 1988, and since that time has received both national and regional accolades. The Ohio Theatre Alliance voted it 1992's "Distinguished Theatre of the Year" and ETC's 1994 production of Brad Fraser's *Poor Superman* was selected as one of *Time* magazine's "Top Ten Theatre Productions" in America.

ETC has a resident company and presents about six main-stage shows a season—many of them new works. It also stages a pantomime during the

Cincinnati Shakespeare Festival's 1997 production of Hamlet

Stephen Collins Foster

by Dr. Robert Vitz, Professor of History, Northern Kentucky University

Stephen Collins Foster, an "idle dreamer" in the mind of his family, came to Cincinnati in 1846, at the age of 20. During the three years he lived in the Queen City, he worked as a bookkeeper in his brother's commission firm on Cassilly Row and lived in a boarding house on 4th Street, just east of Broadway (now the site of the Old Guildford School). Just as Harriet Beecher Stowe acquired background in Cincinnati for Uncle Tom's Cabin *during these years, Foster frequented the levee by day, where he heard the singing of African American roustabouts, and in the evenings he visited the nearby National Theatre or Melodeon Hall, absorbing the rhythms of the newly popular but often coarse minstrel music.*

Within months of his arrival, he was submitting polished compositions to William C. Peters, a local music publisher whom he had known in Pittsburgh, and during his Cincinnati years, Foster wrote or had published several of his most popular songs, including "Oh! Susanna," "Uncle Ned," "Away Down South," and possibly "Gwine to Run All Night (the Camptown Races)."

Fearing a prejudicial reaction, Foster did not want his name attached to these early so-called plantation melodies, and they were advertised in local papers simply as "Songs of the Sable Harmonists" or "Ethiopian Melodies." Later, particularly after "Oh, Susanna" became popular during the California Gold Rush, Foster allowed his name to be identified with his material, and these sentimental songs of home, family, and love made him the best-loved songwriter of the nineteenth century. By early 1850 Foster had achieved considerable recognition for his songwriting, along with enough financial success to leave his position as bookkeeper, and he returned to Pittsburgh, the place of his birth. Ten years later he moved to New York City, where, despite declining health, he continued to compose until his untimely death in 1864.

holidays, a tradition that began in 1990. The Off Center On Stage series presents around five shows a season and gives ETC a chance to mount less mainstream productions. The theater seats 202, and the seats are raked. The season runs from September to May. & (Uptown Cincinnati)

SHOWBOAT *MAJESTIC*
435 E. Mehring Way, Cincinnati
513/241-6550
"The Last of the Floating Theaters" was built in 1923 by Captain Thomas Jefferson Reynolds and toured the Ohio, Kentucky, Tennessee, and Green Rivers for 15 years before docking permanently at Cincinnati's Public Landing. Now run by the Cincinnati Recreation Commission, the Showboat presents about six shows a year—mostly musicals and comedies—in a season that runs from April to October. Four shows are produced by the Showboat, and the other two slots are usually filled by community theater groups. The boat has a concession stand and seats 233. & (Downtown Cincinnati)

THE TAFT THEATRE
5th and Sycamore, Cincinnati
513/562-4949
The Taft was built in 1929 and is part of a larger complex that serves as headquarters for Cincinnati's Masonic groups. Named for Charles P. Taft II, it managed to survive the demolition of downtown's many theaters during the 1960s and '70s. It is leased to Nederland Concerts and provides a downtown venue for some Broadway Series shows, comedians, gospel shows, and national musical acts. The auditorium seats 2,500 and its season runs from September to early May. & (Downtown Cincinnati)

CLASSICAL MUSIC AND OPERA

CINCINNATI OPERA
Music Hall
1241 Elm St., Over-the-Rhine
513/241-ARIA
Founded in 1920 as the Summer Opera Association, the second-oldest opera company in the nation had a most unusual performance space: the Cincinnati Zoo. The company performed there until the 1970s, but has since moved to less noisy digs at Music Hall. & (Uptown Cincinnati)

CINCINNATI POPS ORCHESTRA
Music Hall
1241 Elm St., Over-the-Rhine
513/321-3300
Although the Cincinnati Pops has a different name from the Cincinnati

TRIVIA

In 1894 Cincinnati's James H. Hennegan and Dayton's W. H. Donaldson founded an eight-page monthly titled *Billboard Advertising*. In May of 1900, it changed its name to *The Billboard*. Its editorial offices moved to New York in the 1940s, but its Cincinnati printing plant remained in operation until 1983. Now referred to simply as *Billboard*, it rightly bills itself as "the International Newsweekly of Music, Video and Home Entertainment."

In 1862 Dwight Hamilton Baldwin used his life savings, a mere $2,000, to found Baldwin Piano & Organ Co. He built his first Baldwin piano in 1891 and went on to establish a worldwide name.

Symphony, it's essentially the same orchestra but with a different conductor, Erich Kunzel. From September through May the Pops performs at Music Hall; in June and July, it moves outdoors to Riverbend. Shows are often highlighted by famous guests, such as Rosemary Clooney and Dudley Moore. ♿ (Uptown Cincinnati)

CINCINNATI SYMPHONY
Music Hall
1241 Elm St., Over-the-Rhine
513/381-3300

The Cincinnati Symphony was established in 1895, made up mostly of music faculty from the University of Cincinnati and the then-separate College Conservatory of Music (CCM is now part of UC). The fifth-oldest orchestra in the nation, it has had many great conductors, including Leopold Stokowski and Ernst Kunwald. The current music director is Jesus Lopez Cobos. ♿ (Uptown Cincinnati)

MEMORIAL HALL
1225 Elm St., Over-the-Rhine
513/533-4667

Built in 1908 and designed by Samuel Hannaford, Memorial Hall is managed by the Cincinnati Arts Association and used by various musical groups, including the Cincinnati Symphony Orchestra. The 610-seat theater auditorium, which had fallen into disrepair, has recently been restored. ♿ (Uptown Cincinnati)

MUSIC HALL
1241 Elm St., Cincinnati
513/381-3300

Music Hall, designed by Samuel Hannaford, is one of Cincinnati's most identifiable buildings and has been described most aptly as "Sauerbraten Gothic." It was completed in 1878 to provide an indoor venue for the May Festival and hosted the 1880 Democratic National Convention and several industrial expositions. It seats 3,397 and is still used by the May Festival as well as the Cincinnati Symphony Orchestra, the Cincinnati Opera, and the Cincinnati Ballet. ♿ (Downtown Cincinnati)

Cincinnati Opera's 1997 production of Verdi's Falstaff

Phillip Groshong Photography/Cincinnati Opera

Cincinnati-Born Celebrities

Marty Balin, *founder of Jefferson Airplane*
Theda Bara, *film vamp, née Theodosia Goodman*
Thomas Lewis Berger, *novelist* (Little Big Man)
Stephen Birmingham, *novelist* (The Auerbach Will)
Ray Combs, *host of* Family Feud
Doris Day, *singer and film star, née Doris Kappelhoff*
Elizabeth Drew, *columnist*
Suzanne Farrell, *ballerina*
Nikki Giovanni, *poet* (Cotton Candy on a Rainy Day)
The Isley Brothers, *soul music group*
Louis Kronenberger, *drama critic for the* New York Times
James Levine, *musical director of the New York Metropolitan Opera*
Robert Lowry, *novelist* (Find Me In Fire)
Robert McCloskey, *children's author* (Make Way For Ducklings)
Adolph Simon Ochs, *publisher of the* New York Times
Sarah Jessica Parker, *actress* (Honeymoon in Vegas)
Tyrone Power, *film star*
Roy Rogers, *cowboy star*
Stephen Spielberg, *film producer and director*
Ted Turner, *media magnate*
Jonathan Valin, *novelist* (Extenuating Circumstances)
Lew Wallace, *novelist* (Ben Hur)
Andy Williams, *singer*
Austin Wright, *novelist* (Telling Time)

DANCE

CINCINNATI BALLET
Aronoff Center for the Arts
650 Walnut St., Cincinnati
513/621-5219
Cincinnati Ballet's first major performance took place at the University of Cincinnati's Wilson Auditorium. It moved to the Taft Theatre in 1975, then to Music Hall three years later. Its performances now take place in the newly built Aronoff Center for the Arts (with the exception of its popular holiday show *The Nutcracker*, which is still presented at Music

Liz Lerman Dance Exchange at the Contemporary Dance Theater

Hall). Carmen DeLeone, who was appointed music director in 1969, was nominated for a Pulitzer Prize in 1995 for his original score to *Peter Pan*. The company stages about five productions a season, which runs from October through May. (Downtown Cincinnati)

CONTEMPORARY DANCE THEATER
The Dance Hall
2778 Vine St., Cincinnati
513/751-2800

Contemporary Dance Theater was founded in 1972 by Jefferson James, whose mission was to promote and produce modern dance performances of local, regional, and national artists and to foster the growth of dance through education. Since then, she has consistently fostered local talent while presenting top-notch visiting dance companies, including Bill T. Jones/Arnie Zane, and Company, AFROCUBA, Lewitzky Dance Company, Parsons Dance Company, and Liz Lerman Dance Exchange. Dance and movement classes are offered in the Dance Hall, which also hosts the Performance and Time Arts Series, Choreographers Without Companies, and other local shows. Visiting companies perform at the Aronoff Center's Jarson-Kaplan Theater. (Uptown Cincinnati)

TRIVIA

Actress Sarah Jessica Parker was once a member of the Cincinnati Ballet. She went on to dance with the American Ballet Theater, played the title role in the Broadway production of *Annie*, and has starred in several movies, including *Footloose* and *Honeymoon in Vegas*.

CONCERT VENUES

ARONOFF CENTER FOR THE ARTS
650 Walnut St., Cincinnati
513/721-3344
The Aronoff Center hosts several big-name musical acts a year; past performers have included Tony Bennett, Chaka Khan, and Herbie Hancock. Procter & Gamble Hall seats 2,700, the Jarson-Kaplan Theater seats 440, and the Fifth Third Black Box Theater seats 150. (Downtown Cincinnati)

BOGART'S
2621 Vine St., Corryville
513/281-8400
Bogart's is one of the Midwest's premier rock clubs, hosting an impressive roster of bands since it opened in the mid-1970s—from Warren Zevon to Ladysmith Black Mombazo and the Red Hot Chili Peppers. It holds 1,400 people and has four full-service bars, not to mention a pizza-and-popcorn stand. The front is always plastered with posters of upcoming bands. The box office is in the front, too, and is open 11 a.m.–5 p.m. Mon–Fri. If there's a show, it stays open later. Tickets can also be purchased through Select-a-Seat. (Uptown Cincinnati)

CINCINNATI GARDENS
2250 Seymour Ave., Roselawn
513/631-7793

Although Cincinnati Gardens is home to the AAA hockey team (the Cincinnati Mighty Ducks) and houses the occasional wrestling tournament, it also imports some musical acts. Tickets for the 10,000-seat facility can be purchased through the box office or TicketMaster. (Uptown Cincinnati)

THE CINCINNATI ZOO AND BOTANICAL GARDENS
Coors Peacock Pavilion
3400 Vine St., Avondale
513/281-4700
The Cincinnati Zoo is no stranger to music. For years, it was the summer home of the Cincinnati Opera and now it brings in national rock acts during spring and summer. The outdoor venue holds up to 3,000 people, but there are no seats, so bring a blanket. (Uptown Cincinnati)

THE CROWN
100 Broadway, Cincinnati
513/241-1818
The Cyclones hockey team, which also owns the Silverbacks indoor soccer team, recently bought Riverfront Coliseum, invested $14 million in renovations (including the installation of 15,000 new seats), and renamed it The Crown. Shows are now being booked by Nederland Concerts, which inaugurated the refurbished facility with a Fleetwood Mac concert. (Downtown Cincinnati)

TRIVIA

Cincinnati native Doris Day, née Doris Kappelhoff, grew up in Price Hill. She made her singing debut on WLW radio and moved to Hollywood to star in movies such as *Pillow Talk*, *Jumbo*, and *Please Don't Eat the Daisies*.

TRIVIA

Cincinnati native Lee Bowman played Ellery Queen in the 1950s TV series.

RIVERBEND MUSIC CENTER
I-275 and Kellogg Avenue, Anderson Township
513/232-6220

Riverbend Music Center lies right beside a curve in the Ohio River and holds 16,000 people—6,000 in the pavilion, 10,000-plus on the lawn. Its proximity to the river often results in winter floods, but these don't affect its season, which begins at the end of May and ends in September. If you get lawn seats, bring a blanket and, if you have them, binoculars. Otherwise you'll have to rely on the giant monitors that can be seen only when it gets dark. The season usually consists of big-name acts, as well as various multiple-act festivals (H.O.R.D.E., Lollapalooza, etc.). The Cincinnati Symphony Orchestra performs here every Friday and Saturday in June and July. Take Exit 72 off I-275, the U.S. 52, Kellogg Avenue, New Richmond Exit. & (East Cincinnati)

SYCAMORE GARDENS
1133 Sycamore St., Over-the-Rhine
513/621-1100

Sycamore Gardens is a state-of-the-art rock club that hosts both local and national acts and some stand-up comedians. There's a huge dance floor in the front, a raised level with tables and chairs further back, two full-service bars, two pool tables, and a beer garden. Most of the shows are for ages 19 and over. & (Downtown Cincinnati)

BUYING TICKETS

ALL SEATS
513/241-4849

Tickets for sports and music events.

FRONT ROW TICKETS
513/792-9993

Tickets for sports and music events.

SELECT-A-SEAT
513/721-1000

Outlets at Elgin Office Equipment (810 Main Street, downtown) and Tower Place Mall (28 West 4th Street, downtown) offer tickets for sports, music, and theater events.

TICKETMASTER
513/749-4949

Outlets at all Thriftway grocery stores offer tickets for sports, music, and theater events.

The Barrelhouse Brewing Co.

12

NIGHTLIFE

The last decade has seen a renewed vitality in Cincinnati's nightlife. The cover bands of yesteryear have given way to a slew of up-and-coming groups performing original material. Because of the recent successes of bands like Blessid Union of Souls, the Ass Ponys, and the Afghan Whigs, record execs seem to be checking out local shows now more than ever. The Main Street Entertainment District has brought this vibrant music scene closer to downtown, and on weekend nights the streets take on a carnival atmosphere as revelers hop from bar to bar. Corryville, near the University of Cincinnati, is another hot nightspot, with clubs such as Top Cats and Sudsy Malone's (a laundromat/bar) bringing in national acts as well as showcasing home-grown talent. Mt. Adams, home to Cincinnati's Playhouse in the Park and many charming restaurants and bars, also draws big crowds. The hilltop community, with its higgledy-piggledy streets, has limited parking space, so it's best to take a taxi unless you enjoy driving around looking for vacant spots.

Microbreweries are all the rage these days, and several have sprung up in the last few years, harkening back to the days when the Queen City was the nation's largest producer of beer and home to a multitude of beer gardens.

LIVE MUSIC

Jazz

ARNOLD'S BAR AND GRILL
210 E. 8th St., Cincinnati
513/421-6234

Simon Arnold opened his restaurant and tavern in 1861. Today it's owned by Jim Tarbell and has the distinction of being Cincinnati's oldest continuously operated tavern. There's live music six days a week—a mix of jazz, folk, bluegrass, and blues—performed by seasoned musicians.

The bar, immediately to your left upon entering, looks into an adjoining room where the bands play in winter. In summer they set up in a sheltered bandstand in the corner of the patio, one of the best places in the city to hear music. At night the patio is illuminated by Christmas lights, and during the day it's sheltered underneath the canopy of a very, very tall tree. Highly recommended. The kitchen closes at 9 p.m. Mon–Thur and at 11 p.m. on Fri and Sat. Open 11–1 p.m. Mon–Sat; closed Sun. (Downtown Cincinnati)

BLUE WISP JAZZ CLUB
19 Garfield Pl., Cincinnati
513/721-9801

The Blue Wisp offers music seven nights a week. The entrance to this local institution may seem inconspicuous, but jazz buffs will be in heaven once they walk down the steps, past the signed photos, and into the softly lit basement club. The house band, aptly titled the Blue Wisp Big Band, plays on Wednesdays. Previous acts include the Phil Woods Quartet, Herb Ellis, and Ray Brown. Open 4 p.m.–2:30 a.m. daily; music starts at 9 p.m. Mon–Wed, 10 p.m. Fri–Sun. $3–$7. (Downtown Cincinnati)

CELESTIAL
1071 Celestial St., Mt. Adams
513/241-4455

This upscale Mt. Adams restaurant serves French cuisine and also is known for its spectacular view of the city. On Fridays and Saturdays the lounge, which shares the vista, has jazz in the form of such artists as singer Mary Ellen Tanner and her three-piece band. Open 11:30 a.m.–2 a.m. Mon–Fri; 5:30–9:30 Mon–Thur; 5:30–10 p.m. Fri–Sat. (East Cincinnati)

DEE FELICE CAFÉ
529 Main St., Covington, KY
606/261-2365

This Cajun restaurant, in the heart of Covington's Mainstrasse village, also has music on the menu. From the elevated bandstand, Dee Felice serves up Dixieland on Friday and Saturday nights; jazz on Wednesday, Thursday, and Sunday nights; and a solo pianist on Monday and Tuesday. Be sure to make a reservation; this is one of Northern Kentucky's most popular nightspots. Open 11 a.m.–10 p.m. Mon–Tue, 11–11 Wed–Thur, 11–midnight Fri, 5–midnight Fri, 5–10 Sun; music starts at 8 Wed and Thur, 7:30 on weekends. No cover charge. (South of the River)

TRIVIA

Born in Cincinnati on September 23, 1928, Frank Benjamin Foster began his musical career by playing the clarinet and alto sax. Eventually, he switched to the tenor sax and became the tenor soloist for the Count Basie orchestra from 1953 to 1954. In the late 1960s he joined Elvin Jones' band, and in the 1970s he fronted an ensemble titled the Loud Minority. In 1986 he became the leader of the Count Basie Band.

HAVANA MARTINI CLUB
580 Walnut St., Cincinnati
513/651-2800

This recently opened club, located opposite the Aronoff Center, is one of downtown's newest nightlife attractions. So pristine that it's somewhat reminiscent of a hotel bar, the club stocks a huge humidor with more than 175 kinds of cigars. Monday through Saturday you can hear live jazz, mostly three-piece bands. Open 3:30 p.m.–12:30 a.m. Mon–Thur; 3:30 p.m.–2:30 a.m. Fri and Sat; 4:30 p.m.–12:30 a.m. Sun. Music usually starts at around 8:30. No cover charge. (Downtown Cincinnati)

KALDI'S COFFEEHOUSE AND BOOKSTORE
1202 Main St., Over-the-Rhine
513/241-3070

Kaldi's was one of the first businesses to gamble on this old part of town and is now very much the anchor of the emerging Main Street Entertainment District. It usually has live music every day except Sunday; jazz Thursday through Saturday, filling out the week with acoustic folk and bluegrass. Local acts to watch out for here are the Ron Enyard Trio and Steve Schmidt on piano and organ. If you want a place with character, this is it. The two front rooms are lined with shelves upon shelves of books that serve as ample decoration, conversation pieces—and they're for sale, too! Open 8 a.m.–1 a.m. Mon–Thur, 8 a.m.–2:30 a.m. Fri, 10 a.m.–2:30 a.m. Sat, 10 a.m.–12 a.m. Sun; music starts at 9 p.m. on weekdays, 9:30 p.m. on weekends. No cover charge. (Uptown Cincinnati)

THE PROMONTORY
1111 St. Gregory St., Mt. Adams
513/651-4777

Part of Petersen's Restaurant, this Mt. Adams club has jazz four nights a week, mostly standards, and occasionally some funk. Open 11:30 a.m.–1 a.m. Mon–Tue, 11:30 a.m.–2:30 a.m. Wed–Sat; closed Sun. Music starts at 8:30 Wed, 9 Thur, 10 Fri and Sat. No cover charge. (East Cincinnati)

Blues

JEFFERSON HALL SALOON
1150 Main St., Over-the-Rhine
513/723-9008

This Main Street hangout hosts a number of premier local, regional, and national rock and blues artists. Open 4 p.m.–2:30 a.m. Tue–Fri, 7 p.m.–2:30 a.m. Sat and Sun; closed Mon. Cover charge varies. (Uptown Cincinnati)

MAD FROG
1 E. McMillan St., Mt. Auburn

513/784-9119

Formerly Cory's, Mad Frog is near the University of Cincinnati on the corner of Vine and McMillan, with live music seven days a week. Hear blues on Fridays and Saturdays; local rock bands, open-mike nights, and cover bands fill the bill the rest of the week. Open 4 p.m.–2:30 a.m. daily. No cover charge. (Uptown Cincinnati)

Rock

BOGART'S
2621 Vine St., Corryville
513/281-8400

One of the Midwest's premier rock clubs, Bogart's is in the University Village on Short Vine, near the University of Cincinnati. It holds 1,400 people and has four full-service bars and a pizza-and-popcorn stand. Practically every big-name band has played here, from the Ramones to Richard Thompson to the Circle Jerks. You can get tickets from the club itself or from Select-a-Seat.

Shows usually start around 8. Cover charge varies. (Uptown Cincinnati)

BUZZ COFFEESHOP AND CD-O-RAMA
2900 Jefferson Ave., Corryville
513/221-3472

Located just off Short Vine in the University Village, Buzz has a coffee shop on the first floor (with an eclectic assortment of comfortable furniture) and a CD store on the second. Besides selling, buying, and trading CDs until midnight, it brings in national acts about three times a month—an intimate setting to see live music. Open 9 a.m.–2 a.m. Mon–Fri, 11 a.m.–2 a.m. Sat–Sun. Cover charge varies. (Uptown Cincinnati)

SOUTHGATE HOUSE
24 E. 3rd St., Newport, KY
606/431-2201

The Southgate House was the boyhood home of John Taliaferro Thompson, inventor of the Thompson submachine gun (the fabled tommygun). It became a nightclub in 1976

Live jazz at The Promontory

Greg Friedman

On August 10, 1920, Cincinnati native Mamie Smith (1883–1946) became the world's first vocalist to record a blues song, Perry Bradford's "Crazy Blues."

and has been bringing quality acts to town since then. Past performers include Townes Van Zandt, NRBQ, John Gorka, and Sleepy LaBeef. Shows usually begin at 8. Cover charge varies. ⅃ (South of the River)

SUDSY MALONE'S ROCK 'N' ROLL LAUNDRY AND BAR
2626 Vine St., Corryville
513/751-2300
This Corryville hot-spot, in the University Village near the University of Cincinnati, has the distinction of being a laundromat, a bar, and one of Cincinnati's premier clubs for cutting-edge music. This is the place that books bands before they get really big, along with up-and-coming local bands. If you bring in a bag of laundry on show nights there's no cover charge—unless it's a popular national act. One of the greatest dumps in the city. Open 7 a.m.–2 a.m. daily; music usually starts around 10. Cover charge varies. (Uptown Cincinnati)

SYCAMORE GARDENS
1133 Sycamore St., Over-the-Rhine
513/621-1100
A state-of-the-art rock club with a huge dance floor in the front, a raised level with tables and chairs further back, two full-service bars, and two pool tables. Sycamore Gardens hosts both local and national acts. The music is a mix of standard alternative rock, funk, blues, jazz, reggae, and

disco—and they even bring in comedy. The beer garden holds more than 300 people. Most of the shows are for ages 19 and over. Open 5 p.m.–2:30 a.m. Fri, 8–2:30 Sat. Shows usually start around 9 p.m. Cover charge varies. (Uptown Cincinnati)

TOP CATS
2820 Vine St., Corryville
513/281-2005
Located on Short Vine in the University Village near the University of Cincinnati, Top Cats provides an intimate setting for local, regional, and national acts. The nightclub is upstairs; in summer Top Cats opens its picturesque patio, which has an outdoor bar. The downstairs bar, Fat Cats, is part of the same complex and has two pool tables, enough dartboards for league play, and a great selection on its jukebox. Open 7 p.m.–2:30 a.m.; closed Sun. Top Cat's opens at 9 p.m., Fat Cats at 7 p.m. Cover charge varies. (Uptown Cincinnati)

Country and Western

COYOTE'S MUSIC AND DANCE HALL
Drawbridge Estate,
2477 Royal Dr., Ft. Mitchell, KY
606/341-5150
There aren't too many places in town to hear country music, and Coyote's has filled the void, bringing in such

performers as Waylon Jennings and Willie Nelson. The music is not limited to country, though; acts such as Blue Oyster Cult have played here, too. Coyote's also offers dance lessons. 18 and over; ID required. Open 7 p.m.–2 a.m. Wed–Sat. Cover charge varies. (South of the River)

Other

UPSTAIRS AT CAROL'S
825 Main St., Cincinnati
513/333-4299
Situated above Carol's Corner Café, Upstairs at Carol's is an intimate cabaret club that's open only on Fridays and Saturdays. Although its main offering is cabaret, it also presents improv comedy, the occasional percussion group, and solo pianists. Open 8 p.m.–2 a.m. Fri and Sat. Shows usually start at around 8, depending on the act. Cover charge varies. (Downtown Cincinnati)

YORK ST. INTERNATIONAL CAFÉ
738 York St., Newport, KY
606/261-9675
York St. has a restaurant on the ground floor, a nightclub on the second, and an art gallery on the third. The cozy nightclub presents live music—an eclectic assortment of rock, blues, bluegrass, and folk—four nights a week (Wed–Sat). The majority of the acts are local, with occasional regional and national acts. Open 11 a.m.–10 p.m. Mon–Thur, 11 a.m.–12 a.m. Sat, 11 a.m.–9 p.m. Sun; music begins at 10. (South of the River)

DANCE CLUBS

ELEVATION
1005 Walnut St., Cincinnati
513/333-0995
Elevation is open just three days a week, but if something's going on inside you'll know it as soon as you walk past the door. Ravers and technophiles hang around the front, which is illuminated by a purple neon light and soundscaped by the thumping techno beats coming from within. Once inside you'll be treated

The humidor at Havana Martini Club, p. 168

Top Ten Places for Drinks with a View

1. **High Spirits**, Regal Cincinnati Hotel, 150 W. 5th St., downtown, 513/352-2100.

2. **The Celestial**, 1071 Celestial St., Mt. Adams, 513/241-4455.

3. **Prima Vista**, 810 Matson Place, Price Hill, 513/251-6467.

4. **City View Tavern**, 403 Oregon St., Mt. Adams, 513/241-8439.

5. **Mt. Adams Pavilion**, 949 Pavilion St., Mt. Adams, 513/721-7272.

6. **The Albee**, Westin Hotel, Fountain Square, downtown, 513/621-7700.

7. **The Palm Court Lounge**, Omni Netherland Hotel, 5th and Race Streets, downtown, 513/421-9100.

8. **Covington Landing**, foot of Madison Street, Covington, KY, 606/291-9992.

9. **Willie's Sports Café**, 401 Crescent Ave., Covington, KY, 606/581-1500.

10. **Rock Bottom Brewery**'s outdoor patio, Fountain Square, downtown, 513/621-1588.

to a great light show and energetic dance music. Open 10 p.m.–2:30 a.m. Thur; 10–4 Fri–Sat; closed Sun–Wed. Free before midnight; $4 thereafter. (Downtown Cincinnati)

LONGWORTH'S
1108 St. Gregory St., Mt. Adams
513/579-0900
The hippest of the yuppies hang out at this popular Mt. Adams spot. No dress code, but you'll feel right at home wearing your chinos and Dockers. The bar downstairs serves food until 9:45 p.m. and has a patio. For   the more energetic, there's a dance club upstairs. This is definitely not a techno club—disco, funk, and pop

reign here. These are the songs you listened to in high school, if you're in your twenties or thirties, along with the requisite mirror ball. The dance club admits ages 21 and up. Bar open 11:30 a.m.–2 a.m. daily. Dance club open 10 p.m.–2 a.m. Wed–Sat. Cover charge $3. (East Cincinnati)

VERTIGO
University Plaza Shopping Center
1 West Corry St., Corryville
513/751-2642
An unlikely place for a dance club, Vertigo is nestled between a Walgreen's drugstore and a Kroger's grocery in a strip mall. It is, however, near the University of Cincinnati and gets a lot of business from

UC students. DJs play a mix of industrial, retro Eighties, alternative, disco, and funk, depending on the night. Admits ages 19 and up, but don't forget your ID—they won't let you in without it. Open 9 p.m.–2:30 a.m. Mon–Thur; 9 p.m.–4 a.m. Fri–Sat; closed Sun. $2 over 21; $4 under 21. (Uptown Cincinnati)

WAREHOUSE
1313 Vine St., Over-the-Rhine
513/684-9313
Vampires, raver chicks, and chain-wallet punkies dance to the thumping techno beat in this Over-the-Rhine dance club. A little New York on the fringe of the heartland, it's a definite Goth scene. 18 and over. Open 10 p.m.–2 a.m. Wed–Thur, 10 p.m.–4 a.m. Fri–Sat; closed Sun–Tue. (Uptown Cincinnati)

YUCATAN LIQUOR STAND
Foot of Madison, Covington Landing, Covington, KY
606/261-0600
Part of the gargantuan Covington Landing riverboat complex, Yucatan Liquor Stand is a 21-and-up dance club that caters to a young crowd. If you like swimsuit competitions, this is the place for you. Most nights have some sort of theme—Ladies' Night,

College ID Night, etc.—and the music is a mix of disco, country, and rock-and-roll. Open 4 p.m.–2:30 a.m. daily. No cover. (South of the River)

PUBS AND BARS

ALLYN'S CAFÉ
3538 Columbia Pkwy., Columbia-Tusculum
513/871-5779
This Cajun restaurant serves up local jazz and blues acts nightly. The music usually starts around 10; kitchen closes at 10:30. Open 11:30 p.m.–2 a.m. daily. Cover charge varies. (East Cincinnati)

THE BARRELHOUSE BREWING CO.
22 E. 12th St., Over-the-Rhine
513/421-BEER
This Over-the-Rhine microbrewery, part of the Main Street Entertainment District, specializes in Bavarian wheat beers, German lagers, English and Belgian ales, stouts, porters, and pilsners. If you're with a group, a good way to taste the beers is to buy a sampler. The menu is upscale bar food. It also has live music—a mix of rock, salsa, funk, blues, and reggae—on Friday and Saturday nights. Pool tables are in the back. Open 11 a.m.–2 Tue–Fri, 12

TRIVIA

Jazz pianist Mike Longo was born in Cincinnati on March 19, 1939. When he was 20, he won a *Down Beat* Hall of Fame scholarship, then moved to Toronto, Canada, to study under Oscar Peterson. He played with Dizzy Gillespie from 1966 to 1973, becoming his musical director and arranger.

Cincinnati's Rich Brewing Tradition

by William Schottelkotte, music editor of Everybody's News— *Cincinnati's weekly newspaper—and founder of rock group* Love America

Ask any bartender or restaurateur in town and they'll tell you, "People in Cincinnati love their beer." And they very well should, for the art of brewing occupies a special place in the city's history.

Thirsty for the quality drink of their homeland and ready to seek out the American dream, members of the predominantly German population set up brewing operations throughout Cincinnati, mostly in Over-the-Rhine but also across the Ohio River in Covington and Newport. Brewing soon turned out to be a fulfilling and profitable career for a number of Cincinnatians, from the brewmasters to the common laborers, who were offered a comfortable wage and all the beer they could drink. By the mid- to late 1800s, Cincinnati was considered by many to be the undisputed beer capital of the world.

In 1856 the city's 36 breweries brewed more than 8 million gallons of beer, mostly the renowned lager for which the city was famous. Almost two-thirds of all that beer was consumed in Cincinnati itself! By the end of the nineteenth century, there were dozens more breweries, along with even more beer halls. Cincinnati was brewing almost 1.5 million barrels of beer annually, and while most of the lagers, pilsners, and ales were shipped abroad to satisfy the ever-increasing demand, Cincinnatians managed to consume more than 22 million gallons locally. With a population of 500,000, that means approximately 50 gallons for every man, woman, and child.

In all, more than 250 breweries have helped make up an important part of Cincinnati's history. City streets have been named after such former brewer barons as Klotter, Sohn, and Rohs. And while such brands as Wiedemann, Hudepohl, Christian Moerlein, and Oldenberg even today stand as a testament to Cincinnati's age-old tradition, the several microbreweries currently in operation point to an equally promising future.

p.m.–2:30 Sat–Sun; music usually starts around 10. $2 after 10 on Fri and Sat. (Uptown Cincinnati)

BLIND LEMON
936 Hatch St., Mt. Adams
513/241-3885
This popular Mt. Adams basement hangout with an outdoor patio features a bonfire in the cooler months. The decor is Olde English and extremely cozy. There's live music nightly, usually a guitarist singing covers and a few originals. Open 6 p.m.–2:30 a.m. Mon–Fri, 3 p.m.–2:30 a.m. Sat and Sun. No cover charge. (East Cincinnati)

BOBBY MACKEY'S CONCERT AND DANCE HALL
44 Licking Pike, Wilder, KY
606/431-5588
Bobby Mackey's has several noteworthy attractions. First, it's supposedly haunted and has been the subject of several television shows. In fact, the Amazing Kreskin once broadcast a live séance from here. Second, it has a mechanical bull. And third, it features the talents of country band Bobby Mackey and the Big Mac Band. Open 7:30 p.m.–2:30 a.m. Fri and Sat. Cover charge varies. (South of the River)

BREWWORKS RESTAURANT AND PUB
1100 BrewWorks Blvd.
Covington, KY
513/581-2739
Housed in the old Bavarian Brewery, this microbrewery spans three floors with an outdoor patio on the first, a humidor and small bar on the second, and the main bar on the third. Three of its beers were awarded silver medals in the World Beer Championships: Schott Ale, Kut in the Hill Kolsch, and

Mephistopheles Metamorphosis. The cuisine is eclectic, ranging from gourmet pizzas to burgers to Cajun pasta. Also in the building is the Party Source, a gourmand's delight with an incredible selection of wine, beer, and specialty food items. Lunch and dinner daily; no reservations. ♿ (South of the River)

THE COMET
4579 Hamilton Ave., Northside
513/541-8900
This Northside bar has quickly established itself as one of the most popular hangouts in town. Known for its generously portioned burritos and homemade salsa, the bar serves food until 1 a.m. daily. It also has an espresso machine, one of the best jukeboxes in town, and three pool tables, two of them full-sized. On Sundays, 7–9 p.m., The Comet presents live bluegrass. Open 4 p.m.–2:30 a.m. daily. No cover charge. (West Cincinnati)

COVINGTON LANDING AT RIVERCENTER
Foot of Madison Avenue,
Covington, KY
606/291-5410
The nation's largest floating entertainment complex, located west of the John A. Roebling Suspension Bridge at the foot of Madison Avenue, has a great view of the Cincinnati skyline and includes a Yucatan Liquor Stand, a T.G.I.Friday, and an Applebee's. (South of the River)

MADONNA'S CASUAL DINING AND SPIRITS
11 E. 7th St., Cincinnati
513/621-8838
Madonna's serves food until 2:30 a.m., making it one of the few places downtown where you can get a bite

Late-Night Eats In Cincinnati

by Amy McDonald, freelance writer and former music editor of Everybody's News.

Looking for a place to eat late at night in Cincinnati can become an adventure in itself, since most area restaurants close their kitchens around 10 p.m.—and after 11 p.m., you'll have to settle for bar food, chili parlors, and greasy spoons. If you're interested in testing your digestive system, head to **Camp Washington Chili** *(corner of Hopple Street and Colerain Avenue, Camp Washington, 513/541-0061, open 24 hours every day except Sunday), where you can find the usual assortment of Cincinnati-famous chili dishes, as well as salads, soups, and sandwiches, at cheap prices.*

Bar- and club-hoppers love to head down to the kitschy greasy-spoon atmosphere of **Anchor Grill** *(438 Pike Street, Covington, KY, 606/431-9498, open 24 hours a day), where the slogan, "We may doze, but we never close" is proudly displayed. Simple sandwiches, salads, and breakfast items are served around the clock by a sluggish wait-staff, but the highlights are the Johnny Cash and Patsy Cline–filled jukeboxes at the booths. When songs are played, a charming mechanical big-band in a corner display case lights up and plays along. Just a stone's throw away from Covington is another favorite all-night diner, the* **Pepper Pod**

to eat after 10 p.m. It has mirrors on the walls and a pool table, and it's a comfortable spot to go for a drink. Open 11–2:30 p.m. Mon–Fri, 3 p.m.–2:30 a.m. Sat; closed Sun. (Downtown Cincinnati)

MAIN STREET BREWERY
1203 Main St., Over-the-Rhine
513/665-4677

This microbrewery is part of the Main Street Entertainment District. The handcrafted beers are excellent and its Old Scotch Winter Warmer Ale was the winner of a silver medal at Denver's Great American Beer Festival. It has a raw bar serving crab legs, shrimp, and oysters, and its menu is upscale pub grub with an emphasis on gourmet pizzas. Cigars are sold here. The Swing Lounge, on the second floor, has jazz and blues on Fridays and Saturdays, and pool tables. Cover charge varies. Open 11

Restaurant (703 Monmouth, Newport, KY, 606/431-7455, open 24 hours a day), where you can sample from a menu similar to the Anchor Grill's.

*Locals know that the place to get a decent hot meal late at night is at one of the **Perkins Family Restaurants** (20 locations throughout Cincinnati), a national chain that grew out of the Queen City. The original Cincinnati Perkins was famous for its buttermilk pancakes, which are still a popular menu item. Breakfast, lunch, and dinner are served 24 hours a day at most of the restaurants.*

*If you're a vegetarian, the hunt for good food is harder. The late-night hot-spot is the trendy **Carol's Corner Café** (825 Main Street, downtown, 513/651-2667, open until 1 a.m. Tue–Sat), where excellent vegetarian food and even meat-eater delights at good prices are served by an energetic wait-staff. **Rock Bottom Brewery** (1 Fountain Square, downtown, 513/621-1588), one of the latest microbreweries to hit the Queen City, is a good place to dine after a play. A large variety of pizzas, salads, pasta, and grilled entrées are served until midnight on Fridays and Saturdays. Many of the local coffeehouses offer late-night sandwiches, including **Kaldi's Coffeehouse and Bookstore** (1204 Main Street, 513/241-3070, open until 1 a.m. Fri and Sat, midnight Mon–Fri), where the menu includes such items as tofu burritos and red beans and rice.*

a.m.–1 a.m. Mon–Thur, 11 a.m.–2:30 a.m. Fri, 12 p.m.–2:30 a.m. Sat; closed Sun. (Uptown Cincinnati)

MOUNT ADAMS BAR AND GRILL
938 Hatch St., Mt. Adams
513/621-3666

This neighborhood bar has a lot of personality. The walls are decorated with signed celebrity photos, stuffed animal heads, and other trinkets. A sign above the bar reads,

"No sniveling." The highlight of the menu is the jalapeño-stuffed ravioli, 12 p.m.–2:30 a.m. Sat; serves food until 11 Mon–Sat and until 10 Sun. Open 11 a.m.–2:30 a.m. Mon–Sat, 12–12 Sun. (East Cincinnati)

NICHOLSON'S TAVERN AND PUB
625 Walnut
513/564-9111

Just across the street from the Aronoff Center for the Arts,

Mt. Adams Bar and Grill, p. 177

Nicholson's Tavern and Pub is one of downtown's latest additions. The Scottish-themed pub boasts 69 varieties of single-malt scotch and a wide selection of on-tap beers from Great Britain, including Newcastle's Brown Ale, Tennant's of Scotland, and Guiness. The menu hails from the old country too, its highlights being the smoked salmon (served with capers, fresh lemon, cracked black pepper, and buttered whole-wheat bread), fish and chips, shepherd's pie, and, of course, bangers and mash. Black and white marbled floors, plush wood, high ceilings, roomy booths, and the gorgeous bar make this a pleasant place to hang out. Open 11 a.m.–10 p.m. Mon–Thur, 11–11 Fri–Sat, 4–9 Sat. (Downtown Cincinnati)

OGDEN'S PLACE
25 W. Ogden Pl., Cincinnati
513/381-3114
This cozy bar with 11 booths and 12 bar stools serves soup and

sandwiches later than most—until 2:30 a.m. Ogden's stays open on Saturdays only if there's a home baseball game. Open 11 a.m.–2:30 a.m. Mon–Fri. (Downtown Cincinnati)

PLUM STREET CAFÉ
423 Plum St., Cincinnati
513/651-4341
A neighborhood bar close to the Albert B. Sabin Convention Center with a pinball machine and cool jukebox selection, Plum Street serves food— soups and sandwiches—until closing time. If there is a home football game, it opens at 11 a.m. Open 10:30 a.m.–2:30 a.m. Mon–Fri, 12 p.m.–2:30 a.m. Sat, 12 p.m.–2:30 a.m. Sun. (Downtown Cincinnati)

ROCK BOTTOM RESTAURANT AND BREWERY
Fountain Square, Cincinnati
513/621-1588
Microbreweries are mushrooming in Cincinnati, and this is downtown's newest addition. The beer is excellent, especially the medium-bodied Raccoon Red. The menu is upscale pub grub—wood-burned pizzas and enchiladas. The place is hopping at happy hour, and the fun continues well into the night. On Fridays there's live music, mostly blues and funk. Cigars are also available. Lunch and dinner daily. ♿ (Downtown Cincinnati)

COFFEE HOUSES

EMIDIO'S
641 Main St., Covington, KY
606/261-2335
One of the newest nighttime attractions in Covington's Mainstrasse Village, Emidio's is a very relaxing place to spend an evening. The front room has a bar and TV, the middle

room has a pool table, and the back room is for reading. They don't have a full menu but serve croissants, scones, and pies. Open 7 a.m.–2 a.m. Mon–Fri, 10 a.m.–2 a.m. Sat and Sun. (South of the River)

HIGHLAND COFFEE HOUSE
2839 Highland Ave., Corryville
513/861-4151
Highland Coffee House was in business way before the coffee craze swept the nation. Kitty-corner to Mecklenburg Gardens, it has a European feel and serves a wide variety of coffee drinks, along with deli sandwiches, salads, ice-cream malts, and soups. It also has an outdoor patio. Open 2 p.m.–1 a.m. Sun–Thur, 2–2 Fri–Sat. (Uptown Cincinnati)

SITWELL'S COFFEEHOUSE
404 Ludlow Ave., Clifton
513/281-7487
Named after author Edith Sitwell, this basement coffeehouse is a good place to go if you're on your own. Books, magazines, and board games are available for public enjoyment, and on Monday Sitwell's has free access to the Internet. It has a small menu, mostly sandwich items, and hosts poetry and tarot readings. Open 10 a.m.–1 a.m. Sun–Thur, 1 p.m.–2 a.m. Fri–Sat. (Uptown Cincinnati)

COMEDY CLUBS

GO BANANAS
8410 Market Pl., Montgomery
513/984-9288
Go Bananas managed to survive the comedy club glut of the Eighties by bringing in national stand-up acts and cultivating local ones. On Wednesday and Thursday, the show begins at 8 p.m. Friday and Saturday offer two

shows: at 8:30 p.m. and 10:55 p.m. Wednesday night is amateur night. Cover charge varies. (East Cincinnati)

DINNER THEATER

FOREST VIEW GARDENS
4508 North Bend Rd.
Monfort Heights
513/661-6434
Dinner at Forest View Gardens, located 1 mile south of I-74 on North Bend Road, is a Cincinnati tradition. The food is German and the servers sing excerpts from musicals. There's no show at lunch, except on the third Thursday of each month when they present a noon matinee. Open for lunch 11–2 Tue–Fri. Dinner begins at 6 Thur, 7 Fri, 5 and 8 Sat, 5 Sun. (West Cincinnati)

MOVIE HOUSES OF NOTE

THE ESQUIRE
320 Ludlow Ave., Clifton
513/281-8750
Located in the gaslight district of Clifton, The Esquire is a welcome addition to Ludlow Avenue, a lively little strip filled with boutiques and restaurants. The theater houses six screening rooms, and the movies are a mix of family entertainment, foreign movies, and art-house fare. (Uptown Cincinnati)

KENWOOD TOWNE CENTRE CINEMAS
7875 Montgomery Rd., Kenwood
513/791-2248
Located in the food court of Kenwood Towne Centre, this five-screen National Amusements theater carries first-run movies as well as more art movies than the others in the chain.

The seats are comfortable, and the audio system, with its Dolby surround sound, is top of the line. (East Cincinnati)

MARIEMONT THEATRE
6906 Wooster Rd., Mariemont
513/272-2002

Situated on Mariemont Square and run by the same people in charge of Clifton's Esquire, the Mariemont has three screening rooms and, like the Esquire, presents a mix of family entertainment, foreign movies, and art-house fare. There are several very good restaurants within walking distance, including the National Exemplar and Bistro Gigi. (East Cincinnati)

MT. LOOKOUT CINEMA GRILL
3187 Linwood Ave., Mt. Lookout
513/321-3211

Located in the heart of Mt. Lookout Square, the Cinema Grill offers both dinner and a movie. You should get there about 20 minutes before the show. On Friday and Saturday there's a midnight late show; and if you want to see Monday Night Football on a really big screen, this nonsmoking establishment is the place to go. (East Cincinnati)

©Marcia Schonberg

13

DAY TRIPS FROM CINCINNATI

DAY TRIP: Lebanon

Distance from Cincinnati: *33 miles*

Lebanon was founded in 1798 and has retained much of its Old World charm, reflected in its architecture and its wealth of antique and gift shops, which number more than 60. Once on Route 48 you'll see signs erected by local farmers, inviting visitors to come in and pick fresh produce.

Your first stop should be the **Golden Lamb** (2 South Broadway, 513/621-8373), where you can dine in the same room in which Harriet Beecher Stowe wrote the foreword to *Uncle Tom's Cabin*. The historic inn, filled with Shaker furniture, was built in 1803 and has 18 rooms, all named after celebrity occupants. Its roster of illustrious visitors is impressive; it includes Samuel Clemens (Mark Twain) and ten United States presidents. The menu is classic American with an emphasis, of course, on lamb dishes.

To keep in the historical mode, visit the **Warren County Historical Society Museum** (105 South Broadway, 513/932-1817), which has a nineteenth-century village green, a splendid collection of Shaker furniture, and an extensive collection of artifacts dating back to prehistoric times. In late September, the museum holds a flea market and sells fresh bread. **Glendower State Memorial** (105 Cincinnati Avenue, 513/932-1817) is an excellent example of a Greek Revival mansion; its 13 rooms, furnished in period pieces, are open to the public. During summer a Civil War re-enactment takes place on the grounds with a free live encampment.

The **Turtle Creek Valley Railway** (Lebanon Station, 198 South Broadway, 513/398-8584) follows an old stagecoach route through the countryside. The

CINCINNATI REGION

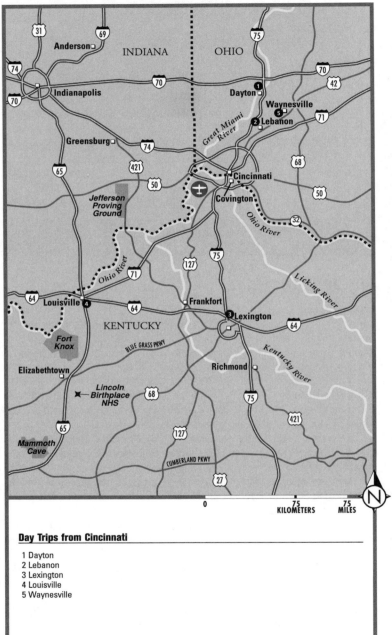

Day Trips from Cincinnati

1 Dayton
2 Lebanon
3 Lexington
4 Louisville
5 Waynesville

tracks were laid in 1880; the locomotive was built in the 1950s for the Chicago, Burlington and Quincey Railroad; and the enclosed passenger railroads were constructed in the 1930s for the Delaware, Lackawanna, and Western Railroad. On sunny days you can enjoy the ride on the open gondola car. If you go on a Sunday between May and October, ask about the Dinner Tours, which combine a meal at the Golden Lamb with a one-hour ride. Occasionally, the Crime Time Theater Players put on a mystery tour. The drama unfolds throughout the evening, starting during the train ride and ending at the Golden Lamb. During the holidays, Santa boards the train, too.

While you're in the area, make sure you visit **Fort Ancient State Memorial** (State Route 350, 513/932-4421), a 100-acre prehistoric earthen enclosure 7 miles south of Lebanon, built by the Hopewell Indians. Sometime during October the site holds an Archaeology Day, when visitors can dig for Indian artifacts. **Cowan Lake State Park** (State Route 350, 937/289-2105) is also nearby and offers a plethora of activities, including hiking, fishing, hunting, swimming, and boating. If you enjoy harness racing, check out **Lebanon Raceway** (State Route 48, 513/932-4936), which has simulcasts throughout the day and live racing at night.

Annual events in the area include March's **Great Midwest Quilt Show and Sale**, June's **Strawberry Festival**, July's **Warren County Fair**, August's **Ice Cream Social Tours**, September's **Ohio Honey Festival** and **Applefest**, October's **Ohio Cider Festival**, and December's **Historic Lebanon's Christmas Festival**. The **Lebanon Antique Show** takes place twice a year, in October and in January.

Getting there from downtown Cincinnati: Take I-71 N for 26 miles. Bear left onto S.R. 48 N for 4 miles.

DAY TRIP: Waynesville

Distance from Cincinnati: *37 miles*

Hailed as the Antiques Capital of the Midwest, Waynesville has more than 100 dealers and antique shops. The **Waynesville Antique Mall** (69 South Main Street, 513/897-6937) alone is home to more than 50 dealers. Annual events in downtown Waynesville include the **Old Main Street Antiques Show** in May and **Christmas in the Village** in December. If you want to stop for lunch, try **Der Dutchman Restaurant** (230 North State Route 42, 513/897-4716), an Amish-style eatery with a children's menu.

One of the year's biggest events is the **Ohio Renaissance Festival** (State Route 73, 513/897-7000), which takes place every weekend from August to October. A sixteenth-century village is re-created on 30 acres of land 5 miles east of Waynesville (in Harveysburg) and includes costumed performers doing everything from jousting to juggling to Maypole dancing. The **Ohio Sauerkraut Festival** (513/897-8855) is held during the second full weekend in October and offers an outrageous assortment of sauerkraut dishes. If you begin to tire of the food, there are more than 400 arts-and-craft booths in which to browse.

Five miles east of Waynesville is **Caesar Creek State Park** (Route 73,

513/897-3055), which has a beautiful lake and offers a variety of outdoor activities, including boating, fishing, horseback riding, hunting, and swimming. The park holds a **Winter Hike** in February, a **Great Fossil Hunt** in May, a **Pioneer Festival** in July, and a **Meteor Shower Campout** in August. **Waynesville Airport** (State Route 42, 513/897-7717), a recreational airport with a grass runway and older model planes, offers biplane rides, glider flights, and flight instruction.

Getting there from downtown Cincinnati: Take U.S. 42 N for 3.5 miles. Turn left onto Paddock Road for 2.5 miles. Bear right onto I-75 N for 29 miles. Bear right onto West Central Avenue for 2 miles.

DAY TRIP: Dayton

Distance from Cincinnati: *50 miles*

Founded in 1796, Dayton is known as the birthplace of flight because of aviation pioneers Orville and Wilbur Wright. The brothers built their first plane, the Wright Flyer, here and took it to Kitty Hawk, North Carolina, to test it. On December 17, 1903, they managed to keep the Flyer airborne for 57 seconds. Not surprisingly, Dayton is replete with aviation-related attractions. The **United States Air Force Museum** at Wright Patterson Air Force Base (937/255-3284) is the largest museum of its kind in the world and features the Apollo 15 command module, hot-air balloons, and a B-1 bomber. The museum also houses an IMAX theater. Annual events include the **United States Air and Trade Show** (800/848-3699), held at Dayton International Airport in July, and August's **Kite Festival**.

The genuine article, the **Wright Cycle Company** (22 South Williams Street, 937/443-0793), was designated a National Historic Landmark in 1990 and is open to the public. It was here that the brothers founded a printing press, started up their bicycle shop, and began to dabble in aviation. The Wright brothers printed work by another Daytonian, the African American poet Paul Laurence Dunbar. The **Paul Laurence Dunbar State Memorial** (219 North Paul Laurence Dunbar Street, 937/224-7061) has been restored to the way it was when Dunbar lived there, down to the desk where he wrote and a bicycle made by his friends Orville and Wilbur.

The **International Women's Air and Space Museum** (26 North Main Street, Centerville, 937/433-6766), housed in the former home of Asahel Wright, the Wright brothers' great-uncle, pays tribute to female aviation pioneers such as Amelia Earhart and Jacqueline Cochran. The museum also commemorates Katherine Wright, Orville and Wilbur's sister, the first female to fly in a plane. The 65-acre **Carillon Park** (2001 South Patterson Boulevard, 937/293-2841) features Dayton's first house, Newcom Tavern, a Concord stagecoach, a pioneer home, a Conestoga wagon, an early locomotive, the Wright Flyer III (a restored version of the brothers' 1905 model), and a replica of their bicycle shop.

The **Dayton Museum of Natural History** (2600 DeWeese Parkway, 937/275-7431) contains artifacts pertaining to the Miami Valley. It also offers computerized planetarium shows, and Wild Ohio, a collection of native Buckeye animals in their natural surroundings. Other area attractions include the **Trap Shooting Hall of Fame and Museum** (601 National Road, 937/898-1945), which holds an annual contest in August; the **Citizens Motorcar Co.**, the **Packard Museum** (420 South Ludlow Street, 937/226-1917); and the **Dayton Art Institute** (456 Belmonte Park North, 937/223-5277).

For those who prefer the outdoors, check out **SunWatch Indian Village** (2301 West River Road, 513/268-8199), a reconstructed prehistoric Native American village; **Cox Arboretum** (6733 Springboro Pike, 937/434-9005), a 160-acre park with nature trails and an edible landscape garden; **Aullwood Audubon Center and Farm** (1000 Aullwood Road, 937/890-7360), a 350-acre wildlife refuge with nature trails and a hands-on nature center; and **Carriage Hill Farm** (7800 Shull Road, 937/879-0461), a restored 1880s farm that offers hiking, horseback riding, fishing, and cross-country skiing. Bicyclists might want to take advantage of the **River Bikeway**, a 24-mile hike/bike trail along the Great Miami and Stillwater Rivers.

For lunch, try **Anticoli's** (3045 Salem Avenue, 937/277-2264), an Italian restaurant that has been run by the same family for 65 years, or **The Barnsider** (5202 North Main Street, 937/277-1332), a popular local surf-and-turf eatery. Both restaurants have children's menus.

Getting there from downtown Cincinnati: Take I-75N for 50 miles to Exit 54B, the OH 48/Downtown Dayton Exit.

DAY TRIP: Louisville, Kentucky

Distance from Cincinnati: *95 miles*
Louisville was founded in 1778 by George Rogers Clark and named after France's Louis XVI. Known primarily for the Kentucky Derby, it also produces

SunWatch Indian Village in Dayton

©Marcia Schonberg

more than half the world's supply of bourbon. Like Cincinnati, Louisville is situated beside the Ohio River; one way to get there from the Queen City is aboard the riverboat *Delta Queen*.

The Kentucky Derby is run on the first Saturday in May at **Churchill Downs** (700 Central Avenue, 502/636-4400). Although the race is only two minutes long, the festivities last for ten days, beginning with an enormous ball, the selection of the Derby Queen, and the drinking of mint juleps—a heady concoction of bourbon, mint leaves, granulated sugar, and crushed ice served in a silver cup. Live racing takes place from late April to June, and in November. The **Kentucky Derby Museum** (704 Central Avenue, 502/637-1111) is next to Churchill Downs' Gate 1 and traces the history of the famous horse race from its 1875 inception to the present.

The **Filson Club** (1310 South 3rd Street, 502/635-5083) was founded in 1884 and contains more than 50,000 Kentucky artifacts, including a 3-foot beech-tree log allegedly carved by Daniel Boone. The **Louisville Science Center** (727 West Main Street, 502/561-6111) contains an Apollo 13 capsule, circus artifacts, an IMAX theater, and Then-Hotep, a 2,000-year old Egyptian mummy that survived the flood of 1937. Literally soaked to the skin, her linen cloth was unraveled, dried at a laundry, and wrapped around her again—this time, we hope, for eternity.

The **J.B. Speed Art Museum** (2035 South 3rd Street, 502/636-2893), near the University of Louisville campus, was founded in 1925 and is Kentucky's oldest and largest art museum. It's hard to miss the **Louisville Slugger Museum** (800 West Main Street, 502/588-7228) since a 120-foot baseball bat guards the entrance. Visitors can view the baseball memorabilia on display and then take a guided tour of the bat production plant. If you're a fan of Kentucky Fried Chicken, check out the **Colonel Harland Sanders Museum** (1441 Gardiner Lane, 502/456-8353), which chronicles the growth of the business and includes a 25-minute taped interview with the Colonel himself.

Other area attractions include the **Louisville Zoo** (1100 Trevilian Way, 502/451-0440); the **Zachary Taylor National Cemetery** (4701 Brownsboro Road, 502/893-3852), where "Old Rough and Ready," the nation's twelfth president, is buried; **Farmington** (561 Blankenbaker Lane), a Federal-style home designed by Thomas Jefferson; and **Locust Grove Historic Home** (561 Blankenbaker Lane, 502/897-9845), a 1790 Georgian mansion where Louisville founder George Rogers Clark spent his final years.

For lunch, try the **Uptown Cafe** (1624 Bardstown Road, 502/458-4212), which serves regional cuisine.

Getting there from downtown Cincinnati: Take I-71S for 91 miles to I-64. Go south for 4 miles.

DAY TRIP: Lexington, Kentucky

Distance from Cincinnati: *73 miles*
Lexington, home to the University of Kentucky, has managed to retain its Old

Louisville skyline, where north meets south

World charm despite the onslaught of the twentieth century. This is horse country, and racing enthusiasts can find plenty to do and see here. You can tour **Kentucky Horse Park** (Iron Works Pike at I-75 junction, 606/233-4303) by foot or on a horse-drawn trolley. A monument to the great thoroughbred race-horse Man o' War is here, as is the International Museum of the Horse. The Parade of Breeds Show takes place every day from April through October. Thoroughbred racing runs at **Keeneland Race Course** (U.S. 60, 606/254-3412) in April and October, and you can watch the horses' morning workouts from March to November. Other horse-related attractions include the **American Saddle Horse Museum** (Iron Works Pike, at I-75 junction, 606/259-2746) and the **Kentucky Horse Center** (3380 Paris Pike, 606/293-1853).

The **Headley-Whitney Museum** (4435 Old Frankfort Pike, 606/255-6653) pays tribute to the decorative arts and contains jewelry by George W. Headley as well as Chinese textiles and porcelains. The **University of Kentucky Art Museum** (606/257-3595) is on the corner of Euclid and Rose Streets in the Singletary Center for the Arts, and the **Lexington Art League** (209 Castlewood Drive, 606/254-7024) has changing exhibits by both national and regional artists. The **Lexington Children's Museum** (401 West Main Street, 606/258-3256) has hands-on exhibits about a variety of subjects, including technology, science, history, and civics.

Lexington also has a wealth of gorgeous houses. **Ashland** (East Main Street, 606/266-8581) is the 18-room estate of Henry Clay, "the Great Compromiser," and is surrounded by beautiful gardens as well as a smoke-house, several icehouses, and a carriage house. The **Hunt-Morgan House** (201 North Mill Road, 606/233-3290), built by John Wesley Hunt, was home to Confederate hero John Hunt Morgan and Nobel Prize–winner Thomas Hunt Morgan. The **Mary Todd Lincoln House** (578 West Main Street, 606/233-9999) was the childhood home of the former First Lady, who is buried in **Lexington Cemetery** (833 West Main Street, 606/255-5522), along with several other local luminaries, including University of Kentucky basketball coach Adolph F. Rupp, Henry Clay, and John Hunt Morgan.

Try the **Coach House Restaurant** (855 South Broadway, 606/252-7777) for fine dining with some regional offerings. The **Mansion at Griffin Gate** (1800 Newtown Pike, 606/288-6142) offers haute cuisine in elegant surroundings. Built in 1853 as an Italian villa, it burned down 20 years later and was rebuilt as an antebellum mansion with Corinthian columns.

Getting there from downtown Cincinnati: *Take I-75 S for 70 miles to Exit 99, the U.S. 25, U.S. 421 Exit. Go right on U.S. 25 for 3 miles.*

IMPORTANT PHONE NUMBERS

EMERGENCY
Police, 911
Fire Department, 911
Ambulance, 911

MAJOR HOSPITALS AND MEDICAL CENTERS
Bethesda North, 513/745-1112
Bethesda Oak, 513/569-6064
Children's Hospital Medical Center, 513/559-4293
Christ Hospital, 513/369-2000
Deaconess Hospital, 513/559-2236
Good Samaritan Hospital, 513/872-1400
The Jewish Hospital Kenwood, 513/745-2204
Providence Hospital, 513/853-5222
St. Elizabeth Medical Center North, 606/292-4353
St. Elizabeth Medical Center South, 606/344-2255
St. Francis-St. George Hospital, 513/389-5942
St. Luke Hospital East, 606/572-3100
St. Luke Hospital West, 606/525-5200
University Hospital, 513/558-4571

VISITOR INFORMATION

Greater Cincinnati Chamber of Commerce
Carew Tower
441 Vine St.
Cincinnati, OH 45202
513/579-3100 or 800/246-2987

Northern Kentucky Chamber of Commerce
50 East River Center Blvd., Ste. 100
Covington, KY 41011
606/291-5000

Greater Cincinnati Convention and Visitors Bureau
300 W. 6th St.
Cincinnati, OH 45202
513/621-6994 or 800/344-3445

Northern Kentucky Convention and Visitors Bureau
605 Philadelphia St.
Covington, KY 41011
606/655-4155 or 800/354-9718

CAR RENTAL

Avis, 800/831-2847
Budget, 800/527-0700
Enterprise Rent-A-Car, 800/325-8007
Hertz, 800/654-3131
National Car Rental Interrent, 800/227-7368
Rent A Wreck, 800/421-7253

CITY MEDIA

DAILIES
The Cincinnati Enquirer, 513/721-1700
The Cincinnati Post, 513/352-2000

WEEKLIES
The American Israelite, 513/621-3145
The Business Record, 513/421-9300
Catholic Telegraph, 513/381-2722
Cincinnati Business Courier, 513/621-6665
Cincinnati City Beat, 513/665-4700
The Cincinnati Herald, 513/961-3331
The Downtowner, 513/241-9906
Everybody's News, 513/381-2606

MAGAZINES

Applause, 513/761-6900
Cincinnati Magazine, 513/421-4300
NIP, 513/281-6416
St. Anthony Messenger,
 513/241-5615

TV STATIONS

Channel 5, WLWT, NBC
Channel 9, WCPO, ABC
Channel 12, WKRC, CBS
Channel 19, WXIX, FOX
Channel 25, WBQZ, independent
Channel 48, WCET, PBS, Cincinnati
Channel 54, WCVN, PBS, Covington
Channel 64, WSTR, independent

AM RADIO STATIONS

550 WCKY, talk, news, sports
700 WLW, news, sports talk, Reds,
 UC and XU basketball
740 WNOP, jazz
1230 WUBE, talk, sports
1320 WCVG, gospel
1360 WAQZ, news, sports, Silverbacks
1480 WCIN, R&B
1530 WSAI, standards, Cyclones,
 UK basketball
1560 WCNW, religious

FM RADIO STATIONS

88.3 WAIF, community radio
88.5 WMUB, big band
88.7 WOBO, country
89.3, WMKV, big band
89.7, WNKU, folk, rock, bluegrass,
 NPR
90.9 WGUC, classical, classic
 comedy, NPR
91.7 WVXU, classical, jazz, new age,
 NPR
92.5 WOFX, classic rock
93.3 WAKW, religious
94.1 WWNK, adult contemporary
94.9 WVAE, smooth jazz
96.5 WYGY, country
97.7 WOXY, alternative rock

98.5 WRRM, adult contemporary
100.9 WIZF, urban contemporary
101.9 WKRQ, rock
102.7 WEBN, rock
105.1 WUBE, country
105.5 WGRR, oldies
106.5 WNKR, country, UK basketball
107.1 WAQZ, alternative rock

BOOKSELLERS

B Dalton Bookseller
7500 Beechmont Ave., 513/232-2970
North Gate Mall, 9577 Colerain Ave.,
 513/385-5608
Tri-County Mall, 11700 Princeton
 Pike Rd., 513/671-3420

Barnes & Noble
895 E. Kemper Rd., Springdale,
 513/671-3822
7800 Montgomery Rd., 513/794-9440
9891 Waterstone Blvd., 513/683-5599
Hyde Park Plaza, 3802 Paxton Ave.,
 513/871-4300

Bee Tree Bookstore
3615 Glenmore Ave., 513/661-3433

Black World
521 Race St., 513/651-0122

Blue Marble Bookstore
3054 Madison Rd., 513/731-2665

Blue Marble Children's Bookstore
1356 S. Fort Thomas Ave., Fort
 Thomas, 606/781-0602

Bookshelf
7754 Camargo Rd., 513/271-9140

Borders
Princeton Plaza Shopping Center,
 11711 Princeton Pike Rd.,
 513/671-5852

Brentanos
Tower Place, 28 W. Fourth St.,
513/723-9656
Tri-County Mall, 11700 Princeton
Pike Rd., 513/671-5441

Crazy Ladies Bookstore
4039 Hamilton Ave., 513/541-4198

DuBois Bookstore
321 Calhoun St., 513/281-4120

Grailville Art & Bookstore
932 O'Bannonville Rd., Loveland,
513/683-0202

Host Marriott Bookstores
Greater Cincinnati International
Airport, 606/767-3265

Joseph-Beth Booksellers
2692 Madison Rd., 513-396-8960

Little Professor Book Center
1018 Forest Fair Dr., 513/671-9797
Brentwood Plaza, 8537 Winton Rd.,
513/931-4433
Clermon Shopping Center, 814 Main
St., Milford, 513/248-2665

Media Play
Surrey Square, 4488 Montgomery
Rd., 513/531-5250
Western Hills Plaza, 6174 Glenway
Ave., 513/481-4775

Montgomery Book Company
9917 Montgomery Rd., 513/891-2227

Mt. Adams Bookstore & Cafe
1101 St. Gregory Pl., 513/241-9009

New World Bookshop
336 Ludlow Ave., 513/861-6100

Pink Pyramid Bookstore
907 Race St., 513/621-7465

University of Cincinnati Bookstore
123 W. University, 513/556-1400

Victory Books
609 Main St., Covington,
606/581-5839

Villager Variety & Books
6932 Madisonville Rd., 513/271-0523

Waldenbooks
Crestview Hill Mall, Crestview Hills,
606/341-0158
Eastgate Mall, 4601 Eastgate Blvd.,
513/752-9591
Kenwood Towne Centre, 7875 Mont-
gomery Rd., 513/791-0011
Northgate Mall, 9483 Colerain Ave.,
513/385-5454
Tri-Country Mall, 11700 Princeton
Pike Rd., 513/671-0777
Western Hills, 6139 Glenway Ave.,
513/662-5837

MAIL SERVICE

U.S. Post Office
Main Office Station
1623 Dalton Ave., Queensgate
513/684-5634

U.S. Post Office
Queen City Station
525 Vine St., Downtown
513/684-5667

United Parcel Service (UPS)
640 W. 3rd St., Downtown
800/742-5877

Red Express (local delivery)
1207 Maryland Ave., Covington, KY
606/431-5000

BANKS

Bank One
525 Vine St., Cincinnati
   513/985-5100
7269 Kenwood Rd., Kenwood
   513/985-5140

Fifth Third Bank
Fifth Third Center at Fountain Square,
   Cincinnati, 513/579-5203
401 East 5th St., Cincinnati
   513/721-7733
201 East 4th St., Cincinnati
   513/369-0700
30 West Corry St., Corryville
   513/861-5100

Provident Bank
7th and Vine Sts., Cincinnati
   513/579-2222
1 East 4th St., Cincinnati
   513/579-2036
2522 Vine St., Corryville
   513/281-1662

Star Bank
5th and Walnut Sts., Cincinnati
   513/632-4234
125 East Court St., Cincinnati
   513/361-8220
4th and Elm, Cincinnati
   513/361-8243
425 Ludlow Ave., Clifton
   513/475-6060

PUBLIC HOLIDAYS

New Year's Day
Martin Luther King Jr. Day
Presidents' Day
Memorial Day
Independence Day
Labor Day
Veterans' Day
Thanksgiving
Christmas Day

OTHER RESOURCES

BABYSITTING/CHILD CARE
Childtime Children's Center
312 Walnut St., Suite 100, Cincinnati
513/721-7181

DISABLED ACCESS INFORMATION
Metro, 513/632-7590
TANK, 513/331-TANK
Cincinnati Riding for Handicapped
   513/575-2194

MULTICULTURAL SOURCES
Traveler's Aid International of
Cincinnati, 513/721-7660

TIME AND TEMPERATURE
Weather, 513/241-1010
Time and Temperature, 513/721-1700

INDEX

Abraham Lincoln Statue, 111–112
accommodations, 32–51; downtown, 34–35; uptown, 36–39; east, 39–44; west, 44–45; south of the river, 46–51
Aggravation De L'espace, 112
airports, 28–30
American Museum of Brewing History and Arts, 106
Americana, 100–101
Anderson Ferry, 90
Art Academy of Cincinnati, 108
Atman, 112
Attic Gallery, 108
Ault Park, 115

Base Art Gallery, 108–109
baseball, 140–141
BB Riverboats, 74–75
Behringer-Crawford Museum of Natural History, 95–96, 104–105
Betts House Research Center, 106
Bicentennial Commons, 75–77, 102, 116
Big Bone Lick State Park, 120
biking, 28, 122, 144
Blue Marble Children's Book Store, 99–100
blues, 168–169
boating, 144–145
bowling, 145
"The Boy and the Book," 112
bridges, 22
bus service, 31
business and economy, 11–14

calendar of events, 15–18
camping/backpacking, 145
canoeing, 146
Capitoline Wolf Sculpture, 112
Carew Tower Complex, 77
Carl Solway and Michael Solway Galleries, 109
Cary Cottage, 88–89
Cathedral Basilica of the Assumption, 90–91
Central Trust Tower, 77
Children's Theatre, The, 98
Cincinnati Art Galleries, 109
Cincinnati Art Museum, 96, 104
Cincinnati Ballet, 98
Cincinnati Carriage Co., 75

Cincinnati City Hall, 77
Cincinnati Fire Museum, 94–95
Cincinnati Gas & Electric Model Train Display, 95
Cincinnati Museum Center at Union Terminal, 96–97, 105
Cincinnati/Northern Kentucky International Airport, 28–29
Cincinnati Playhouse in the Park, 99
Cincinnati Zoo and Botanical Gardens, 93–94
Cincinnatus Building, 77–78
city layout, 19–23
city tours, 74–75
classical music, 160–161
Closson's Gallery, 109
CO-OP Aircraft Service, 75
coffeehouses, 178–179
comedy clubs, 179
concert venues, 164–165
Coney Island/Sunlite Pool, 102
Contemporary Arts Center, 104
Cormorant Fisherman Sculpture, 112
country and western music, 170–171

Dan Carter Beard Home, 91
dance clubs, 171–173
dance performances, 162–163
Dayton, 184–185
Delta Queen, 78
Devou Park, 116
Devou Summer Classics Theater, 116
dinner theater, 179
Dixie Terminal, 78
Dr. Albert B. Sabin Cincinnati Convention Center, 20, 78
Duveneck Home, 91

East Fork State Park, 120
Eden Park, 116–117
Elsinore Tower, 86–87
Embshoff Woods and Nature Preserve, 117–118
Ensemble Theatre of Cincinnati, 99

Fairview Park, 118
festivals, 14, 15–18, 85
Findlay Market, 84
fishing, 116, 119, 147–148
fitness clubs, 148
football, 141

Fountain Square, 79
Freeman Gallery, 109, 111

Galleries, 103–114
Gallery at Wellage and Buxton, The, 111
golf, 119, 122, 141, 148–152
Gorman Heritage Farm, 94
Gray History of Wireless, The, 106

H.H. Richardson Monument, 112–113
Hamilton County Courthouse, 79
Harriet Beecher Stowe House, 84
Harrison, William Henry, 3
Harrison Memorial Park, 89
Hauck Botanic Gardens, 118
Hebrew Union College Museum/Skirball, 105–106
hiking, 121, 122, 123, 146–147
history, 2–4, 8–10, 13, 14, 20
hockey, 141–143
horse racing, 143
hunting, 152

ice skating, 116, 152–153
Indian Mound, 87
Ingalls Building, 79–80

James Abrams Garfield Monument, 113
Jazz, 166–168
Jerry Springer Show, The, 36
Jewish Cemetery, 84, 86
John A. Roebling Suspension Bridge, 80
John Hauck House, 89

Kids Shop at the Museum Center, The, 100
Kids' Stuff, 93–102
Kilgour Fountain, 113
King Arthur's Court, 100
Krohn Conservatory, 94, 118

Lake Isabella, 118–119
Lebanon, 181–183
Lexington, Kentucky, 186–188
Literary Club of Cincinnati, 80
Louisville, Kentucky, 185–186
Lunken Airport Playfield Complex, 102, 119
Lytle Park, 119

Mainstrasse Village, 91

Mariemont Village, 87
Meier's Wine Cellars, 88
Memorial Hall, 86
Memorial Pioneer Cemetery, 87
Miami Whitewater Forest, 120
Miller-Leuser Log House, 87–88
Mimosa Museum, 91–92
Mirror Lake, 88
Mitchell Memorial Forest, 119
movie houses, 179–180
Mt. Airy Forest, 119, 121
Mt. Echo Park, 121
Mt. Storm Park, 121
Museums, 103–114
Music Hall, 86

Only Artists, 111
opera, 160–161

Paramount's King's Island, 101
Personal Touch Tour of Cincinnati, 75
Piatt Park, 121
Plum Street Temple, 80
Public Art, 103–114
Public Library of Cincinnati and Hamilton County, 97
pubs and bars, 173–178
Pugh Building, 80–81

Queen City Club, The, 81
Queen City Riverboat Tours, 75

Railway Exposition Company, 97
recommended reading, 5
restaurants, 52–73; downtown, 54–63; uptown, 63–65; east, 65–68; west, 68–69; south of the river, 69–73
riverboat gambling, 153
rock, 169–170
rollerblading, 153
Rookwood Pottery, 88, 110
Rookwood Pottery Building, 88

Schmidt Aviation, 75
Sharon Woods Park, 121–122
Sharon Woods Village, 89, 95
Shawnee Lookout, 123
shopping, 124–139; City Center, 124–128; Downtown/Over the Rhine, 128–134; Other Noteable Stores, 134–136; Major Department Stores, 136–137; Shopping Malls, 138–139; Outlet Centers, 139
Showboat Majestic, 81

sights, 74–92; down-
town, 75–84; uptown,
84–86; east, 86–88;
west, 88–90; south of
the river, 90–92
skiing, 153–154
soccer, 143
Southgate House, 92
Spring Grove Cemetery
and Arboretum, 90,
122–123
St. Peter-In-Chains
Cathedral, 81
Stephen Foster Statue,
113
Sunlite Pool/Coney
Island, 88
Sunrock Farm, 94
Surf Cincinnati
Waterpark, 101–102
swimming, 118, 154

Taft Museum, 98, 104
taxis, 26
Temple of Love, 86
tennis, 143–144, 154–155
theater, 116, 156–160
tickets, 165
Time-Star Building, 81,
84
transportation, 24–31
Tyler Davidson
Fountain/The Genius of
Water, 113

Union Terminal, 90
United States Playing
Card Museum, 107–108
University of Cincinnati,
11, 12
University of Cincinnati
Observatory, 88

Vent Haven Museum,
108
Vietnam Veterans
Memorial, 114

Water Tower, 88
Waynesville, 183–184
weather, 17–18
Weston Art Gallery, 111
William Henry Harrison
Monument, 114

William Howard Taft
National Historic Site,
86
Winton Woods, 123
World War I Memorial,
114

YWCA Women's Art
Gallery, 111

You'll Feel like a Local When You Travel with Guides from John Muir Publications

CiTY-SMaRT™ GUIDEBOOKS

Pick one for your favorite city: *Albuquerque, Anchorage, Austin, Calgary, Cincinnati, Cleveland, Denver, Indianapolis, Kansas City, Memphis, Milwaukee, Minneapolis/St. Paul, Nashville, Portland, Richmond, San Antonio, St. Louis, Tampa/St. Petersburg*

Guides for kids 6 to 10 years old about what to do, where to go, and how to have fun in: *Atlanta, Austin, Boston, Chicago, Cleveland, Denver, Indianapolis, Kansas City, Miami, Milwaukee, Minneapolis/St. Paul, Nashville, Portland, San Francisco, Seattle, Washington D.C.*

TRAVEL✦SMART®

Trip planners with select recommendations to: *Alaska, American Southwest, Carolinas, Colorado, Deep South, Eastern Canada, Florida Gulf Coast, Hawaii, Kentucky/Tennessee, Michigan, Minnesota/Wisconsin, Montana/Wyoming/Idaho, New England, New York State, Northern California, Ohio, Pacific Northwest, South Florida and the Keys, Southern California, Texas, Western Canada*

Rick Steves' GUIDES

See *Europe Through the Back Door* and take along country guides to: *France, Belgium & the Netherlands; Germany, Austria & Switzerland; Great Britain & Ireland; Italy; Russia & the Baltics; Scandinavia; Spain & Portugal;* or the *Best of Europe*

ADVENTURES IN NATURE

Plan your next adventure in: *Alaska, Belize, Guatemala, Honduras*

JMP travel guides are available at your favorite bookstores. For a FREE catalog or to place a mail order, call: 800-888-7504.

John Muir Publications ✦ P.O. Box 613 ✦ Santa Fe, NM 8750

Cater to Your Interests on Your Next Vacation

Charles Behlow

ABOUT THE AUTHOR

Billie Felix Jeyes began writing at an early age—not on paper, but on the walls of her bedroom in England, where she grew up. She moved to Cincinnati at the age of 16, graduated summa cum laude from Northern Kentucky University, and has lived in the tri-county area ever since. Jeyes was a founding member of a comedy troupe that toured for seven years. She later worked as the literary editor for *Cincinnati CityBeat* and then become the managing editor of Cincinnati's other weekly newspaper, *Everybody's News*. Jeyes lives in Covington, Kentucky, three blocks from the Ohio River. She is currently working on her first novel.

JOHN MUIR PUBLICATIONS
and its City•Smart Guidebook authors
are dedicated to building community
awareness within City•Smart cities.
We are proud to work with the Literacy
Network of Greater Cincinnati as we
publish this guide to Cincinnati.

The Literacy Network of Greater Cincinnati was
founded in 1986 under Project Literacy U.S. (PLUS) to bring
together local forces to combat illiteracy. LNGC focuses on
raising public awareness about the literacy cause and uniting students and tutors with appropriate literacy programs. Today it is a
resource center of vital importance in the community. LNGC boasts
a membership of over 50 literacy providers; sites include public
school systems, churches, community centers, libraries, hospitals,
and the workplace.

For more information, please contact:
Literacy Network of Greater Cincinnati
635 W. 7th St. Suite 103
Cincinnati, OH 45203
Phone: 513-621-READ or 513-621-7323
Fax: 513-381-7440

**LITERACY NETWORK
OF
GREATER CINCINNATI**